Maureen G. Millar   June '8.

SPECIES	JANUARY	FEBRUARY	MARCH	APRIL	MAY	JUNE	JULY	AUGUST	SEPTEMBER	OCTOBER	NOVEMBER	DECEMBER
FROGHOPPER				CUCKOO SPIT								
GRASSHOPPER					NYMPHS			ADULTS	SINGING			
BURNET MOTH	HIBERNATES	HIBERNATES				FLYING					HIBERNATES	HIBERNATES
CINNABAR MOTH					FLYING		CATERPILLARS	CATERPILLARS				
ELEPHANT HAWK MOTH		UNDERGROUND PUPAE			FLYING		CATERPILLARS			UNDERGROUND PUPAE		
EMPEROR MOTH	PUPA IN COCOON	PUPA IN COCOON		FLYING		PUPAE	CATERPILLARS		PUPA IN COCOON		PUPA IN COCOON	
GARDEN TIGER MOTH		HIBERNATES			CATERPILLARS	PUPAE	FLYING		CATERPILLARS		HIBERNATES	
HERALD MOTH		HIBERNATES			FLYING	CATERPILLARS		FLYING			HIBERNATES	
LACKEY MOTH				CATERPILLARS		FLYING						
PEPPERED MOTH			PUPAE		FLYING	PUPAE		CATERPILLARS				
PUSS MOTH		PUPAE			FLYING		CATERPILLARS	CATERPILLARS		PUPAE		
COMMON WASP	QUEEN HIBERNATES	QUEEN HIBERNATES				WORKERS		QUEENS	DRONES		QUEEN HIBERNATES	
DIGGER WASP						FLYING		FLYING				
CRUCIAN CARP				SPAWNING								
MINNOW					SPAWNING							
SALMON				MIGRATE TO SEA					MIGRATE UPRIVER			
THREE-SPINED STICKLEBACK					SPAWNING							
TENCH					SPAWNING							
TROUT	SPAWNING										SPAWNING	
ADDER		HIBERNATES		MATING				YOUNG BORN		HIBERNATES		
COMMON FROG		HIBERNATES	SPAWNING		FROGLETS LEAVE POND				HIBERNATES			
GRASS SNAKE		HIBERNATES	SPAWNING		MATING		EGGS LAID		HIBERNATES			
COMMON LIZARD		HIBERNATES			MATING		YOUNG BORN		HIBERNATES			
SAND LIZARD			HIBERNATES		MATING		EGGS LAID	EGGS HATCH	HIBERNATES			
NEWTS	HIBERNATES	HIBERNATES	RETURN TO POND	BREEDING	MATING		LEAVE POND		HIBERNATES			
SLOW-WORM	HIBERNATES		HIBERNATES		MATING			YOUNG BORN	HIBERNATES			
COMMON TOAD			SPAWNING	BREEDING	MATING	TOADLETS LEAVE POND			HIBERNATES			
BLACKBIRD		SONG		BREEDING	BREEDING							
BUZZARD					BREEDING							
CORMORANT					BREEDING							
CUCKOO			SUMMER VISITOR		CALLING	BREEDING			MIGRATES			
DABCHICK					BREEDING							
DUNLIN	WINTER VISITOR	WINTER VISITOR				BREEDING				WINTER VISITOR		
FIELDFARE	WINTER VISITOR	WINTER VISITOR				BREEDING				WINTER VISITOR		
FULMAR		WINTER VISITOR			BREEDING			WINTER VISITOR				
BARNACLE GOOSE												
CANADA GOOSE					BREEDING							
GREAT CRESTED GREBE				BREEDING								
SPARROWHAWK					BREEDING							
HERON			BREEDING									
KESTREL					BREEDING							
KINGFISHER					BREEDING							
KITTIWAKE					BREEDING							
LAPWING	FLOCKS			BREEDING					FLOCKS			
MALLARD				BREEDING		IN ECLIPSE						

FISHES   AMPHIBIANS AND REPTILES   BIRDS

THE BOOK OF THE YEAR

The illustrations on these pages show the stages in the
development of the red admiral butterfly on nettle from eggs
and caterpillars in silk tents, to pupae and emerging adults. You
will find more information on caterpillars and butterflies on
pages 72, 78 and 104.

THE BOOK OF THE YEAR

A natural history of Britain through the seasons

Photographs by Jane Burton
and Kim Taylor

Text by Robert Burton

Frederick Warne

AUTHORS' ACKNOWLEDGEMENTS

During the preparation of this book, a great many people provided invaluable advice, assistance and guidance, and to all those concerned we offer our grateful thanks. In particular we should like to record the contributions of Jill Burton, who so efficiently sorted all the photographs; Susan Chitty, who equally efficiently typed the manuscript; Janet Brown, who helped with the photograph on page 145; Hazel and Mark Taylor, who kindly allowed the use of photographs from the family album; and Nick Eddison, whose tireless enthusiasm throughout was stimulation for us all.

First published by Frederick Warne Publishers Ltd
in association with Books for Children

Frederick Warne Publishers Ltd
40 Bedford Square
London WC1B 3HE

ISBN 0 7232 2997 X

Edited, designed and produced by
Eddison/Sadd Editions Limited
2 Julian Court, Julian Hill, Harrow-on-the-Hill
Middlesex HA1 3NF

Phototypeset by SX Composing, Rayleigh, Essex
Origination, printing and binding by Royal Smeets Offset
Weert, Holland

Contents

Introduction

This book tells the story of the countryside throughout the year. It is an immense story, covering all aspects of wildlife, and so there is room in one book for only selected parts. THE BOOK OF THE YEAR has been designed to show you many of the animals and plants you are most likely to see in the course of one year. It is not a text book, nor is it a field guide, but it is full of suggestions on what you can look for in the countryside at any time of the year.

Nearly all the animals and plants described here are easy to find. They may turn up in the garden or a town park, or they may be seen while walking in the woods, across fields or along the seashore. A few need more luck, or skill, to find but this makes them all the more exciting to see, perhaps when you are on a special outing.

How to use this book

THE BOOK OF THE YEAR has four main chapters: spring, summer, autumn and winter and each one tells you what to look for in that particular season. Some animals and plants will most likely be present all the year round, but even so there are times when it is best to look for them, for instance when plants are flowering or when birds are singing.

As well as pointing out what to look for, the text explains points of interest about these animals and plants. It shows what they are doing and how and why, so that you can begin to understand the part they play in nature. Hints are given on how to observe this behaviour, and there are suggestions about making notes on what you see. But detailed projects involving collecting specimens and keeping live animals, or using equipment and apparatus, are not given. The aim of THE BOOK OF THE YEAR is to show you how easy it is to enjoy the countryside, and at the same time learn about the wildlife that lives within it. At most, all you need is a pair of binoculars for watching shy and distant animals, a hand lens for examining small animals or plants, and a note book for recording regular as well as odd observations.

Watch out for the cross references which will direct you to other pages on which related topics are discussed. And watch out also for the panels in red which indicate when you should be especially careful not to damage yourself or the animals and plants you are observing.

THE COUNTRY CODE

On your excursions to the countryside please remember all the points of the country code, listed here as a convenient reminder:

Guard against fire Careless action can cause much damage and destroy the wildlife of a large area. Do not throw away matches whilst they are alight. Do not leave bottles or jars where they can catch the sun's rays.

Fasten all gates A farm animal wandering on the road can cause a serious accident. Remember that every cow is very valuable to the farmer.

Keep dogs under proper control Your household pet can be a killer in the open countryside. It may worry sheep to death. Almost 4,000 sheep are killed by dogs each year. Remember that every farmer is allowed by law to shoot dogs found worrying his animals.

Keep to the paths across farmland The law tells all walkers to keep to public footpaths. If there is an obstruction, walk round it, but keep to the edge of the field and cause as little damage as possible. Even grass is a valuable crop. Keep in single file when walking along a narrow track.

Use gates and stiles to cross fences, hedges and walls Fencing and drystone walls are very expensive to maintain. Cross at the proper gates or stiles rather than scrambling over.

Using the book throughout the year

According to the calendar, spring lasts from March to May, summer is June to August, autumn is September to November, and winter is December to February. Yet the season does not automatically change with the date. There is a slow change over the weeks and a spell of good or bad weather can make it feel like spring in winter, or like autumn in summer. There is also a difference between the north and south of the country. In the south the weather is warmer, and leaves burst from their buds a week or more earlier. For these reasons the division of the wildlife year into the four seasons is not exact.

More details of when to look for particular species are given on the calendar chart endpapers, and the index will help you to find them in the book. Each chapter also has topics about things that are especially worth looking at during a particular season, woodland flowers in spring, the inhabitants of the seashore in summer, and fungi in autumn; but you will also find them interesting at other times of year. Spring is the best time to look at old walls, for example, but the ivy-leaved toadflax on walls can be found in flower right through until autumn. By looking ahead in the chapter on a particular season, you can use THE BOOK OF THE YEAR to plan where to go and what to look for whatever the time of year.

Leave no litter Take home any litter after a picnic. It is unsightly and it can kill big farm animals as well as small wild animals. Glass bottles become death traps from which mice and shrews cannot escape.

Help to keep all water clean Most of the water we use comes from country streams. Do not pollute them with empty cans and waste food.

Protect wildlife, plants and trees The countryside is a community of animals and plants. All depend on the others for survival. Do not pick the flowers or break off the branches of trees.

Go carefully on country roads Narrow winding country lanes are attractive but dangerous. The tractor coming around a hidden corner, or a flock of sheep filling up the road, can cause a serious accident. Do not park in narrow lanes. When walking, keep to the right, facing oncoming traffic, if there is no footpath.

Enjoy the countryside and respect its life and work You may be visiting the countryside for pleasure but never forget that for many people it is their home and livelihood. Do not harm animals, farm machinery or property, or make an unnecessary noise. Keep the Country Code.

Spring:
life stirs again

Spring starts officially at the beginning of March, but the weather then may still be wintry. Cold winds, frosts and falls of snow can occur at this time, but there is a definite change in the air. The sunshine starts to bring a little warmth and its stronger rays brighten the scenery and catch the first signs of returning colour. After 21st March, which is called the spring equinox or 'equal-night', when day and night have the same length, the days are longer than the nights and winter is really over.

The changing season is caused by the tilting of the earth as it progresses in its year-long orbit around the sun. During the winter the northern hemisphere is tilted away from the sun and its rays are weakened because they have to pass through a greater distance of the atmosphere. From midwinter onwards, the amount of tilt decreases so that the sun is felt more strongly. The days get longer and the sun rises higher above the horizon.

Around the countryside you should see signs that spring has arrived and life is starting again. A pale green tinge to the hedges shows where the leaves of hawthorn are breaking out of their buds.

With the unfolding of the leaves, growth can begin. Water flows up the plants, being sucked in at the roots and released into the atmosphere through the leaves. Food reserves of starch are made available from roots and bulbs and carried to the points of growth, and new food is manufactured in the leaves by photosynthesis. By this process the energy from sunlight is absorbed in the leaf by chlorophyll, the substance which gives plants their green colour, and it is used to combine carbon dioxide gas from the air with water in the plant's tissues to produce carbohydrates. The carbohydrates are used as fuel for the plant's growth and other activities. Photosynthesis is the essential process of life not only because it gives plants their energy, but also because it indirectly provides energy for all other forms of life.

Watch out for the white flowers of blackthorn brightening the bare hedgerow twigs, and the catkins of hazel, willow, poplar, elm and other trees decorating woods and spinneys. The flowers of colt's-foot shine from bare patches of waste ground, while celandines and wood anemones show in tree-shaded places.

The first insects appear on calm sunny days. A few honeybees leave the hive to visit the early flowers, and queen bumblebees zig-zag a few centimetres above the ground searching for nesting places in mouseholes or under piles of vegetation. Early butterflies are on the wing, after waking from their winter sleep. Life is beginning to stir.

First flowers of spring

See also **The woodland floor** on page 24 and **Flowers of grasslands** on page 38

The first flowers we see in spring are usually those which grow from bulbs in parks and gardens. Snowdrops flower during the winter, from January onwards, and they are usually over by spring. Crocuses follow snowdrops and bring bright colours to the garden. The date at which they flower varies slightly from year to year, depending on the weather; they may even grow up through the snow. We can be sure spring has really arrived when daffodils bloom.

Masses of daffodil flowers appear in gardens and public places in March. You may discover wild daffodils in some damp meadows and woods (see page 39), but they are becoming rare because much of the damp ground they prefer has been drained. Also, if the flowers are picked, there may not be enough seeds produced by the remaining plants to ensure a continuation.

Colt's-foot or dandelion?
Colt's-foot is another yellow flower that brightens roadsides and other patches of uncultivated ground near buildings. It is easy to mistake a colt's-foot for a dandelion because the flowers are very similar, and both in fact belong to the daisy family. If you look closely at the stems you will see an obvious difference. Instead of the smooth hollow stem of a dandelion, the colt's-foot stem has pink scales pressed against it. The flower eventually turns into a 'clock' of seeds each with its tiny parachute, again like a dandelion. But colt's-foot leaves are quite different from dandelion leaves. They appear only after the plant has flowered and are 15 to 23 centimetres across.

Primroses, cowslips and oxlips
Primroses have suffered in the same way as wild daffodils. Many have been picked and, worse still, people have dug them up for their gardens. Watch out for primroses if you travel by train in early spring. Some of the best places to see and admire them today are railway embankments.

Until recently the cowslip was a common flower of pastures (see page 38) but its relative the oxlip has

▼This is the colt's-foot flower. At first glance it might look like a dandelion but if you study the flower closely you will see it is more like an all-yellow daisy.

◄Crocuses are among the first flowers to appear in the spring. On dull days they stay closed, but on sunny mornings their flowers open (see page 42) and attract early bees also brought out by the warmth.

▶You should find winter aconites flowering from January to March. This is a flower which has escaped from gardens and now grows wild in woods. It is a member of the buttercup family.

always grown in only a few places. In those woods where the oxlip does make its home, it is very plentiful. Both cowslips and oxlips look like primroses but their flowers grow from the top of a single stem instead of each having its own stem. The oxlip has larger and paler, primrose-like flowers than the cowslip.

The underground storage story

Some of the best-known spring flowers develop from bulbs. Hyacinths and tulips are grown from bulbs indoors or in the garden. Daffodils and snowdrops are either cultivated or occur as wild 'bulbs'.

A good way to see the structure of a bulb is to take an onion and slice it in half. You will see layers of soft, fleshy scales packed tight around a central bud and covered with one or more brown, papery scales. The fleshy scales are food stores. During the summer the carbohydrates made by photosynthesis in the leaves (see page 9) are stored in the bulb. Next spring, the food is used for the growth of a new stem and leaves from a bud in the middle of the bulb. New bulbs develop and 'bud off' from the old bulb so that eventually a cluster of bulbs forms.

Bulbs are only one kind of storage organ from which new plants can develop. A crocus grows from what looks like a bulb but which is a corm, the swollen base of the stem. The rhizomes of iris and lily-of-the-valley are underground stems which spread horizontally and send up new shoots. Couch grass and nettles also spread by rhizomes.

KEEP A FLOWER DIARY
The appearance of flowers, first in spring, then in great abundance in summer and with a few coming into bloom in autumn, provides the countryside with a continually changing succession of colours. Keep a diary of the dates on which you first notice flowers appearing and you will have a record of this succession. If you keep the diary in sufficient detail, it may show how different conditions of light, soil and shelter cause slight variations in the flowering time of plants of the same species.

Pussy willow and lamb's-tails

See also **Flowers, pollen and insects** on page 40

▲These frosted silver birch branches with catkins at the top of the photograph remind us that trees are among the first plants to flower in the spring. When the winter is over the catkins expand, the male ones release clouds of fine yellow pollen which will drift on the wind to the female catkins and fertilize them.

◄These are the catkins of the goat willow or sallow. The silver fur of the young catkins gives the plant its name pussy willow. It is also called 'palm'. Both male and female catkins produce nectar to attract insects which carry the pollen from flower to flower. The catkins may also be wind pollinated.

►You can see why the male catkins of hazel are sometimes called 'lamb's-tails'. At the time these catkins appear lambs are being born in the neighbouring fields. The single bud with the red tassel is the female flower.

►►The individual flowers of the common or pedunculate oak catkin are not evenly spaced along the stalk as are those of hazel. Watch out for these male oak catkins in April, and also for the bud-shaped female catkins from which acorns will grow.

Even when the trees are still bare of leaves, they begin to show signs that spring is in the air as their catkins unfold. Catkins are clusters of tiny flowers. Trees that bear catkins include willows, poplar, birch, alder, hazel, hornbeam, beech and oak. Each individual tree of willow or poplar has either male or female catkins, but the others bear both sexes on the same branches.

Types of catkin

Hazel catkins are a welcome sight in woods and hedges from January to March. The male catkins are pale yellow and hang in pairs from the tips of twigs. Male catkins of silver birch are similar to hazel but brown in colour and they appear in April and May. The female catkins are green and form small winged seeds later in the year. Those of beech hang in yellow 'pom-poms' at the ends of stalks, whereas oak has several small bunches of flowers spaced along the stalk; both appear in April and May.

Clouds of pollen on the breeze

When the wind blows it sets the male catkins dancing and pollen is shaken out, sometimes in visible clouds. Flowering in early spring is an advantage because there are no leaves open to restrict the pollen grains from floating away. The tiny pollen grains are carried in the air to the female flowers where fertilization takes place (see page 40). Pollination by wind is rather haphazard and wasteful because the pollen reaches the female flower by chance. An enormous amount has to be released to ensure that some reaches its destination.

The pollen grains from catkins, and from the flowers of other wind-pollinated plants such as grasses, are easily carried over vast distances on the slightest breeze. Pollen grains have been picked up thousands of kilometres out to sea, but widely scattered grains like these are wasted so far from home. A dense cloud of grains is needed to ensure that the female flowers can trap a few in their feathery stigmas as they drift past.

Furry catkins

The willows are different from other catkin-bearing plants because they are pollinated by insects rather than by the wind. The catkins of the goat willow or sallow are called 'pussy willow' because they have sleek, silvery fur like a cat. Later, the male catkins are covered with yellow pollen, and the female catkins turn green.

Pussy willow is a very important source of food for insects in the early spring. At a time when there are very few flowers, the catkins offer a good supply of nectar and pollen, and they attract large numbers of bees when mild, sunny days bring them out of hibernation.

Grains of time

Pollen has helped to tell the history of plant life. A plant's pollen grains have a unique shape and they can be identified by examination under a microscope. Over the course of centuries, pollen grains have blown into bogs and lakes and been preserved in the accumulated half-rotten plant remains. When the peat from the bog or lake bed is dug out, the pollen can be extracted from different layers and identified. The grains show that the first trees to arrive after the Ice Age were willows and birches, followed by pines. Then came hazels, elms and oaks.

The world of the pond

See also **Fishes in fresh water** on page 184
and **Life under the ice** on page 182

A pond is a self-contained world. You can peer into a pond or search it carefully with a net and find many different kinds of animal. All these animals live together as a community.

A net is needed to find the animals living in the depths of the pond or among masses of weed. Animals have to be caught to be identified, but whenever possible they should be returned alive and unhurt.

Pond watching

Approach the pond quietly, because the inhabitants can feel the vibrations from heavy footfalls, and find a place where you can look down into the water. Sit patiently and you may be lucky enough to see larger animals visiting the pond. Water voles live in burrows in the banks of ponds, rivers and streams, and they will come out to feed on plants.

Life in the pond changes through the year. Plant growth is most abundant late in the summer and most animals can be seen at this time but there is plenty happening in the spring. This is the time that frogs, toads and newts come to lay their spawn, and smaller animals become active. A spell of fine weather entices minnows and sticklebacks to come into shallows and water beetles and waterboatmen also become active.

The pond habitat

As more animals appear, you will notice that some of them are found only in one part of the pond. There are those which live at the surface, such as the whirligig beetle and pondskater, and others that live in or on the mud at the bottom, like the caddis larvae which make shelters of small twigs or sand grains. Water snails crawl over the bottom or climb among the waterplants, and come to the surface at intervals to breathe.

Searching through waterplants reveals a variety of animal life. It is a good place to look for eggs, such as those of snails which are laid in a mass of stiff jelly glued to broad leaves.

The open water is the home for the more active

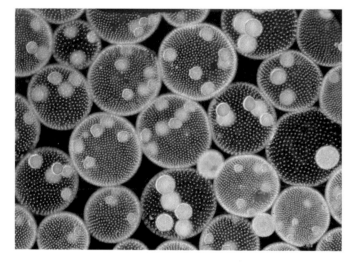

▲ *Volvox* is a pin-head sized plant-like organism made up of a hollow sphere of cells. Each sphere contains daughter *Volvox* growing inside. *Volvox* and minute algae form food for the smallest animals such as water fleas.

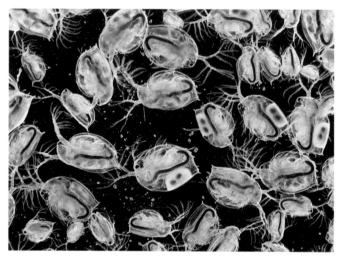

▲ Water fleas or *Daphnia* get their name from their shape and jerky flea-like swimming action. They are not insects like true fleas but crustaceans, related to shrimps and lobsters. These are magnified 8 times.

inhabitants: the fishes, most of the water beetles and waterboatmen. There are two types of waterboatman which are a kind of bug with sucking mouthparts rather than jaws. The greater waterboatman (see page 127) is often called the backswimmer because it swims upside down so that it can catch creatures that fall onto the surface of the pond. The lesser waterboatman feeds on plants and swims the right way up.

The animal life in the pond depends on the plant life, especially on the microscopic algae and bacteria. These are usually too small to be seen with the naked eye, although the algae may be so abundant in late summer that they turn the water green.

DON'T FALL IN!
Take particular care near any area of water, especially if the bank is steep and the water is flowing fast. Never wade in unless you have an adult with you.

▲The plant-eating animals are, in turn, eaten by other animals called carnivores. Here a three-spined stickleback, which preys on *Daphnia*, is itself eaten by a great diving beetle.

A range of the plants and animals you should see both below and above the surface of a pond.

1 Mosquito larvae
2 Pondskater
3 Caddis larva
4 Water-starwort
5 Ramshorn snail
6 Pond snail
7 Lesser waterboatman
8 Three-spined sticklebacks
9 Whirligigs
10 Swan mussel
11 Canadian pondweed
12 Water beetle
13 Bloodworms
14 Broad pondweed

15 Dragonfly
16 Alderfly
17 Reedmace
18 Marsh-marigold
19 Yellow iris or flag

① LAYING THE EGGS

After male frogs emerge from their winter hibernation in the mud at the bottom of the pond, or in some frost-proof nook or cranny, they gather at the breeding pond and set up a croaking chorus to attract the females. The male rides on the back of the female grasping her around the body with a special black, roughened pad on each thumb. As the female lays her eggs, the male fertilizes them.

② SAFE INSIDE THE JELLY

Each egg is a black spot in a blob of jelly. The jelly absorbs water and the mass of eggs, called spawn, rises to float on the surface. Toadspawn is similar, but it is laid in long strings rather than in a mass. The jelly protects the spawn from enemies and helps to keep the eggs warm. Within a few days each black spot develops into a comma-shaped embryo. Not all the eggs will be fertile and some will turn grey and not develop.

KEEP A FROG LOG

Take a handful of spawn and place it in a bowl with enough water for it to float in. Add some weed. Watch the progress of your spawn. Here are some notes to take:

Date spawn collected ....
Date eggs hatched ....
Date gills disappeared ....
Date hind legs appeared ....
Date front legs appeared ....
Date tail disappeared ....
Date released ....

Note the water temperature each time you make an entry in your frog log. If you divide your spawn into two and keep one batch out of doors you can observe the effect of temperature on the tadpoles' rate of development. Once the froglets leave the water let them go where you collected the spawn.

Frogspawn to froglet

It is a sad fact that the common frog is no longer common. Years ago ponds and ditches were filled each spring with masses of frogspawn and wriggling black tadpoles. Today it is almost impossible to find a good frog pond in some parts of the country. The ponds have been filled in, the land has been drained and pesticides have killed the animals that provided the frogs with their food.

Help save the frogs

The main home of frogs now is the garden pond. If there is too much spawn in one pond, many of the tadpoles will die, so it is a good idea to transfer some of the spawn to new ponds. The new home should have plenty of waterplants and mud on the bottom so that there will be food for the tadpoles. There must be no fish to eat them, and stones or bricks, or a natural slope, must be provided around the edge to enable froglets to climb out.

If the froglets cannot climb out they will drown. This is some-

⑦ THE DISAPPEARING TAIL

Once the tadpole's front legs have appeared, the internal gills are replaced by a pair of lungs. The tadpole now has to come to the surface to gulp air. Gradually, the tail is absorbed until, at about ten weeks, the tadpole turns into a froglet. It is now ready to leave the water to begin the second stage of its life, as an adult frog. It will feed at first on tiny insects until it can cope with larger prey.

⑥ ONE PAIR OF LEGS, THEN TWO

All this time the legs have been growing. After about six or seven weeks the hind legs appear from little lumps or buds, one on each side of the base of the tail. They grow quite large before the front legs appear almost suddenly, having previously been hidden by the flap of skin over the gills. Now the head changes shape and the tadpoles begin to resemble miniature frogs. They are also very active and have stopped eating plants altogether.

③ WRIGGLING FREE
Within a few days the tiny black shapes begin to wriggle and the larvae hatch from the eggs. At first they stick to the jelly mass with clinging organs and do not feed because they have no mouths. After about ten days they will have developed a definite head and tail and hang in clusters from plants.

thing you must watch carefully with the tadpoles you have been rearing in bowls. Without any 'land' to clamber on to they will swim round and round until they become exhausted, sink and drown. So, empty out some water from the bowl, and provide some stones or a small log at the edge of the bowl. Also, cover the bowl or the froglets might climb out too soon!

④ FEEDING AND BREATHING
Soon after hatching, feathery gills that extract oxygen from the water grow on each side of the head. The tadpoles' mouths open and they scrape minute algae from every surface in the pond.

⑤ A CHANGE OF MENU
After a few weeks the tadpoles eat less plant material and begin to eat animals. They will feed off the remains of any dead creature in the pond. These tadpoles are about one month old and are feeding on a dead stickleback. At about this time the feathery external gills disappear. A fold of skin grows over them until they are enclosed. The tadpoles are then breathing like fishes with water passing over internal gills.

More animals with two lives

See also **The world of the pond** on page 14
and **Frogspawn to froglet** on page 16

Amphibians are animals that inhabit first the water and then the land. They start as tadpoles living in ponds and grow into adults which live on land. The adults do not have fully waterproof skins, so they gradually dry up unless they live in damp places. You will sometimes find frogs, toads or newts hiding among thick vegetation near water or under stones and logs. They emerge from their shelters to feed at night when the air is cooler and moister. Each spring, frogs, toads and newts come out of hibernation and make their way to ponds and ditches to mate and lay their eggs. Frogs and toads usually return to dry land soon after spawning, but newts stay in the water until the end of July.

Taste a toad?

Toads have dry, warty skins and they crawl rather than hop like frogs. The warts contain a mild poison which helps to protect toads from their enemies. If a dog picks up a toad, it will immediately drop it again and dribble as if it has had a very nasty taste in its mouth.

The toad trail

Toads may travel a kilometre from their winter hideaways to their breeding ponds. They move at night, especially when it is warm and wet, and crawl in procession, slowly and steadily towards the pond. Where the route crosses a road it becomes marked by the flattened bodies of toads that have been hit by cars. The toads will have been using their route for hundreds of years before the road was built and they do not realize their danger.

Common toads gather at the pond about the middle of March, two weeks later than frogs. The males are the first to migrate and they are followed a few days later by the larger females. At the pond the males start to croak, not so loudly as frogs, but loud enough to give away their presence. Amphibians croak by pumping air backwards and forwards between the lungs and mouth. This means that they can call while they are underwater.

Take your partners

The toads gather in the water near the edge of the

THE VANISHING TRICK

Amphibians are carnivorous except when they are young tadpoles. They feed on any animals they can seize and devour but only moving animals are taken; motionless animals are ignored. You can test this by wiggling a stick in the water in front of a newt's nose. It will bite it and only let go when it realizes that the taste or feel is wrong. It will even choke from trying to devour prey too large for it.

Frogs and toads feed on land by catching small animals with their tongues. A toad may sit motionless for many minutes waiting for suitable prey, a beetle larva for example, to walk past. As the larva comes within range, the toad arches its neck and moves its head forward. In this position it is ready to shoot. Suddenly, with a distinctly audible 'plop', the larva vanishes and the toad raises its head and closes its eyes as it swallows. What has happened in a fraction of a second is that the toad's tongue has flicked out and back, picking up the prey with its sticky surface. A high-speed camera is needed to freeze the movement of the tongue and show how it operates. A toad's tongue faces backwards, with its root at the front of the mouth, and it flips over when it is extended. The surface is rough and holds a sticky secretion to pick off the prey.

pond to await the arrival of the females. As soon as a female arrives she is immediately grabbed by a male, whom she carries pick-a-back until they have finished spawning.

There are always more males than females in the pond because the females stay only long enough to mate and lay their spawn. The males stay for as long as a month. This means that the males have to compete for the females. Some manage to find mates on the way to the pond, so they arrive already clinging to their backs.

Toadspawn is laid in strings 2 to 3 metres long. The female swims among the pond plants so that the string becomes wound around them. The development of the eggs and the tadpoles follows the same pattern as in frogs (see page 16).

Gentle dragons

Newts differ from frogs and toads in habits as well as appearance. Male newts become more brightly coloured during the breeding season and they develop a

▼ In an aquarium the courtship and egg-laying sequence of a pair of newts can be followed closely. These are palmate newts and the female (above) is carefully folding a leaf of water-soldier plant on which she has laid an egg.

crest along the back and down the tail. In the great crested, or warty newt, the crest becomes jagged like a saw blade and the newt looks like a gentle dragon. The common newt also develops a fringe on each toe. The male palmate newt grows a filament, like a short length of fine black wire, from the tip of the tail, and the hindfeet become webbed.

Newts, like frogs and toads, will dive into the weeds to hide as soon as they are disturbed. But if you sit quietly, hardly moving, you will see them cautiously emerge again to court in open water.

Dainty dances

Instead of clasping and jostling like frogs and toads, the male newt wins the attention of the female by floating in front of her and flicking his tail so that she is thrown backward by the current. He then folds his tail double and fans it rapidly. This drives scent from his body to stimulate the female.

After mating, the female newt lays her eggs one by one. She can be seen nosing among the weeds and sniffing the leaves. When she has found one that is suitable, she grips it with her hindfeet and lays an egg covered in jelly. The leaf is folded over neatly and stuck down with the jelly.

Birds on the water

See also **Disappearing ducks** on page 129
and **The mute swan's year** on page 186

Birds that live on or near water include not only ducks, swans and geese, moorhen and coot, but also heron, bittern, water rail, kingfisher, dipper, grebes and various long-legged waders. Reed bunting and sedge warbler nest in vegetation growing by the water. Many other birds come to water to drink or to search for food. So ponds, lakes, reservoirs, rivers and canals are good places to go birdwatching. Strange ducks and waders often stop for a rest while on migration and storms will blow seabirds inland.

Waterbirds are easy to study. You always know where you can find them and there is usually no problem about watching them.

▲ A family of Canada geese. The mother always leads the goslings and the father guards them from the rear.

Pairing off for the season

Spring sees the flocks of waterbirds divide up into pairs at the start of the breeding season. Mallards start to court in the autumn but pairing proceeds in earnest in spring. The drakes (males) and ducks (females) swim together and each drake tries to impress his duck with ritual ceremonies. These include swimming with the head and tail raised, hitting the surface of the water with the beak and 'mock-preening', in which the drake lifts one wing and pretends to preen behind it. This action shows off the speculum, the purple patch of feathers on the wing.

When the noise and bustle of courtship is finished, the duck disappears. She finds a quiet place to build her nest. It is usually among thick vegetation or under a bush, hidden from view. She sits on the eggs without moving and her brown, mottled plumage is a very good camouflage. The colourful drake waits nearby for a while, then deserts his family. Male swans and geese, on the other hand, stand guard while their mates incubate the eggs and they remain with the family until the young have dispersed. They usually stay loyal to their mate for life.

Dabblers and divers

A bird's beak is a tool for gathering food and its shape is a good guide to the bird's feeding habits. This can be seen by watching waterbirds. Their various ways of getting food from different places means that they divide up the lake or river so that they are not all competing for the same food.

The mallard's beak is an adaptable all-purpose tool for dealing with both animal and vegetable food. It shovels up all kinds of water animals and tears off pieces of plants. The smallest animals and plants floating in the water are collected by 'dabbling': the duck runs its beak along the surface, and strains out the food by rapidly opening and closing it to pump water in and out.

Mallards feed on the surface, although they 'up-end' to reach food underwater; only young ducklings regularly dive below the surface. The tufted duck, a black and white duck common on lakes and reservoirs, usually dives for its food. It can stay down for over half a minute while searching for snails and insects on the bottom. The mute swan gathers food underwater by reaching down with its long neck. Geese use their sharp beaks to crop grass on land.

Moorhens and coots also feed on animal and plant food, which they get mainly on the surface, but sometimes they dip their heads underwater or pick insects off plants. Moorhens do not dive but coots bring up food which they eat at the surface.

Lakes and gravel pits are inhabited by great crested grebes. They usually stay in the middle of the lake, where they dive for fish and stay underwater for less than 30 seconds. The smaller dabchick or little grebe prefers small ponds. It skulks in the surrounding vegetation where it dives in shallow water for insects, molluscs and fish.

> **WATCHING THE BIRDS**
> Watch the birds on your local lake to see how many different feeding methods you can spot. You should see dabblers, up-enders and divers, large and small. Watch out also for courtship displays in early spring.

Probers and grabbers

The water rail rarely comes into the open and it is difficult to see. Like the sandpipers and other waders, it feeds on small animals it finds on the shore. Long beaks are for probing into the ground, while 'sharp pointed' beaks, such as those of the fish-eating heron and kingfisher, are for seizing prey.

Going, going, gone! This unfortunate eel never even saw the heron. Standing motionless at the water's edge, or stalking quietly along, the heron ambushes its prey in a surprise attack. It also catches other fishes, frogs and voles.

The foliage unfolds

Spring is the season of plant growth. Leaves unfurl, flowers bloom and stems increase in length. The growing points of most plants are sealed in buds which are packages of tiny close-packed leaves folded around a stub of a stem. In some buds there is even a miniature flower formed ready to blossom. When the bud sprouts, the stem lengthens like a telescope and the leaves unfold.

> **WHAT IS INSIDE A BUD?**
> Most buds are small but you can get a good idea of their structure by cutting a cabbage in half. A cabbage is no more than a huge bud with a short stem surrounded by layers of leaves pressed together. The larger, older leaves protect the delicate young leaves in the centre.

The buds of many trees and shrubs are protected by bud scales; the sticky covering of horse chestnut buds is a good example. When growth starts, the bud swells and pushes off the scales, leaving scars which look like a series of narrow rings. Look for these rings at the end of a branch and you can see how much it has grown each year.

Growth has usually finished in a few weeks and the fully spread leaves are carrying out photosynthesis to convert the sun's energy into food (see page 9), some of which is stored for use at a later date. Meanwhile, the plant is constructing new buds for next year's growth. On a tree, the terminal bud, at the tip of each twig, will form the next section of the twig and lateral buds will grow into side branches.

Reaching for the light

When the bud sprouts and the shoot begins to lengthen, it has to grow in the right direction. A young plant grows vertically upwards under the influence of gravity and light. If it is knocked over by the wind it starts to grow in a curve until it is upright again. The influence of gravity will normally produce vertical growth, even in darkness, but if the plant is in a shaded position with light coming from one direction, it will grow towards the light.

You may have noticed that plants are taller on the shaded side of a wall than on the sunny side. Again, the shaded plants have been stimulated to grow faster so that their leaves are spread in more favourable conditions for photosynthesis. Without light they will not develop the chlorophyll which makes them green, and they will be a sickly white colour.

▲The compact, tightly curled fronds of the male fern unfurl in spring.

▼As the sticky bud scales separate, the horse chestnut shoot expands.

GROWING TO CATCH THE SUN

Wood anemones grow from the bare woodland floor between March and May. The stem stretches up and the leaves spread to catch the sun filtering through the leafless branches of the trees. The single flower opens at the tip. It has no petals but it does have pinky-white sepals to attract insects. Wood anemones are perennial which means they live for several years, dying down each summer but reappearing the following spring.

The sequence shows the stages of growth in a wood anemone over 11 days. After three days (**2**) the shoot is nearly upright and after seven days (**3**) it is lengthening, the leaves are spreading and the bud enlarging. At 11 days (**4**) the flower is fully open.

1

2

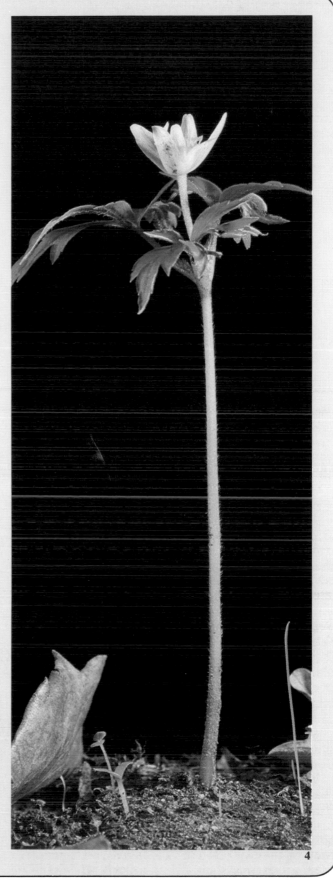

3

4

The woodland floor

See also **The inside story of a wood** on page 26
and **Flowers of grasslands** on page 38

◀Bluebells provide a bright carpet of colour early in spring before the leaves of the trees above them open and shade out the light. Other examples of early flowering woodland herbs are shown opposite.

▶The lesser celandine grows from a tuber each year and produces 'bulbils' on the stem which drop off and grow into new plants.

▶Primroses are a welcome sight in the woods. The name means 'first rose' because they flower early in the year.

▶▼Greater stitchwort is a straggly plant which you will find on the edges of the wood and along the paths where the light is brightest.

Spring is the time to see woodland flowers. The bright colours of bluebells and primroses bring pleasure to a walk through a wood.

Most of the small plants growing on the woodland floor are called herbs by botanists. They are plants which do not have woody stems and which grow and die down every year. Herbs are also found in grassland and on verges and in many other places. Another use of the word 'herb' is to denote plants used to flavour food, such as mint and thyme.

The closing canopy

Woodland herbs flower early in spring because they have to grow and produce flowers and seeds before the trees have unfurled their leaves. Plenty of sunlight shines through the bare twigs and reaches the ground, but after May the growing foliage on the trees turns the wood into a much darker place. Only a few woodland plants, such as enchanter's-nightshade, flower during the summer. Many of the early flowering herbs die down after the spring. The leaves of bluebells and lesser celandine wither and rot as their food material is transferred to the underground bulb or tuber (see page 11).

Some plants are woodland specialists and they are rarely found elsewhere. If you see bluebells growing by a hedge, it is a sure sign that the hedge is all that remains of a wood felled to make fields.

The sunny edges

The most luxurious growth of herbs is found where the ground receives more sun. You will find tall

---

HAVE YOU A NOSE FOR IT!
The next time you walk through a wood, test the power of your nose to identify the plants. Crush a leaf or flower between your finger and thumb and see if you can detect the following smells:

garlic:	ramsons or wild garlic
vanilla:	woodruff
pineapple:	pineapple mayweed
very bad smell:	stinking hellebore
musky smell:	moschatel
tomcats:	early-purple orchid and water mint

growth along the edge of woods and on paths and rides, which easily become overgrown if not kept clear. Sometimes it looks as if the wood is impenetrable because of the dense undergrowth, but this is often only a strip where the light is bright.

Beechwoods may have little or no herb layer. Not only is the foliage very dense but old leaves gather as a thick blanket on the ground. These woods are the home of orchids, such as the helleborines and bird's nest orchid.

Letting in the light

Herbs soon grow up when the canopy of foliage is broken. If a tree falls down or is felled by woodmen it leaves a gap in the foliage and the sun comes streaming in. Herbs spring up almost immediately. They have been waiting either as seeds lying on the ground or as seedlings which have been unable to grow in the shade. Sometimes one plant takes over a large area. Look out for a mass of nettles or the tall spikes of pink-purple rosebay willowherb. As time passes, the kinds of plant in a clearing change as new species arrive and replace the original pioneers. Eventually tree saplings start to rise above the herbs and, after many years, the fallen tree is replaced and the herbs disappear when the canopy closes again.

Overgrown woods with no rides or clearings are not suitable for butterflies. The woodland species need herbs for their caterpillars or larvae to feed on. When woods are turned into nature reserves some trees are cut down to make clearings to encourage flowers and butterflies.

The type of plant found living in the herb layer of the wood is determined by other factors as well as the amount of light available. The plants are also affected by the soil they are growing in. Herb Robert and wood anemone grow well in chalk and limestone country, but foxglove and tormentil do well in acid soils, and wood sorrel likes this soil. Ramsons grows in wet patches in the wood. This is a member of the lily family and closely related to onions and garlic. It has bright green leaves like lily-of-the-valley, a cluster of white flowers and it smells like garlic. It can be used to flavour salads; if cows eat ramsons their milk tastes of garlic.

DON'T PICK!
It is very tempting to pick the first flowers of spring. You may think that it will do no harm to take a bunch home but many plants are now rare because so many people have done this. It is better to admire them in their natural setting. They soon die at home anyway. (See also page 38)

The inside story of a wood

See also **Life in an oak tree** on page 68 and **Leaves and leaf litter** on page 144

At one time the country was almost entirely co-vered by forests. The main trees were oak, lime, pine, birch, field maple, ash and elm, along with beech, black poplar, alder, willow and hornbeam. The shrubs included hazel, crab apple, wild cherry or gean, hawthorn, holly, blackthorn and rowan or mountain ash.

The first farmers started clearing the trees 5,000 years ago, and the forests have been disappearing ever since. Today, there are only a few patches of the old forest left and these remnants have undergone changes because they were an important source of raw material for country people.

Managing the wood

Wood was needed not only as timber for building but also for firewood. Every part of the tree was used including the twigs which were tied in bundles as faggots and the bark which was used for tanning leather. To get the most out of a wood, it had to be managed properly and a common method was by coppicing.

A coppice or copse is a wood which has been cut at regular intervals. The trees, usually hazel, but some-times lime, ash or chestnut, send up a mass of new shoots from the stump or stool and are cut again a few years later. Growth is very rapid and the next crop of wood is soon ready. Coppice wood had many uses, such as firewood, making fencing hurdles and in building. Larger trees, called standards, were left to grow slowly for 50 years or more to provide timber for buildings and ships. Few woods are managed as coppices today but you can spot old coppices. Evidence of coppicing is seen in trees with several trunks

sprouting from a single old stump base.

The disadvantage of coppicing was that the woods had to be fenced to prevent cattle, sheep and deer from eating the young shoots. The alternative, which was practised in parks, was to pollard or lop the trees between 2 and 4 metres above the ground. This left a permanent trunk with shoots growing from the top, like a coppice stool, out of the reach of animals. Watch out for pollarded willows along river banks, and lime trees lining city streets pollarded to keep them neat.

Trees from abroad

Modern timber-producing woods are mainly plantations in which all the trees are the same age. They are usually sitka spruce or other conifers, but poplars are planted for matchwood.

Sitka spruce is a native of North America and is chosen because it grows very quickly. It is only one of several foreign species now growing in Britain.

▲ The horse chestnut is a truly majestic woodland tree. In late spring the conical clusters of white flowers rise from the greenery like fat candles. Each individual flower looks like an orchid.

◄ A wood in spring, showing the three layers: oak and beech trees make up the tree layer; below them, hollies form the shrub layer; the floor, the field layer, is carpeted with bluebells.

► Rowan (top) and crab apple are both small trees that grow in the shrub layer or around the edge of the wood.

Sweet chestnut was introduced by the Romans. The nuts were an important crop in southern Europe but they do not grow well in Britain. Sycamore was first planted in the Middle Ages for its timber and it survives on coasts where salt spray kills other trees. Introduced from central Asia in the last century, rhododendrons form a shrub layer in many woods.

HOW TO TELL A TREE'S AGE

Trees can live for several hundred years but they are usually felled before reaching their first century. The trunk expands each year through the growth of an outer ring of new wood. When the tree is felled these annual rings can be counted. They are 2 to 4 millimetres thick but much broader near the centre. This shows that the tree grew faster when it was young.

LAYERS OF GROWTH

A wood is more than a collection of trees and undergrowth. If you look carefully, you will see that it has three layers. The branches and leaves of the fully grown trees form a canopy which is called the 'tree layer'. Below this are the bushes and young trees of the 'shrub layer', and on the floor of the wood there is the 'field layer' of herbs, ferns and small saplings.

Not every wood has all three layers; the structure depends on a number of conditions. The tree layer itself can affect the layers under the canopy. Beechwoods and plantations of conifers, for example, exclude so much light that they often have little or no shrub and field layers (see page 24). The structure of a wood also depends on the amount of rainfall it receives and the nature of the soil.

tree layer
shrub layer
field layer

Claiming a space

Most animals do not like being too close to each other. Watch a flock of starlings feeding on the lawn or waders roosting on the shore and you will see that they are neatly spaced out. If a bird gets too near its neighbour, one or other will retreat. Keeping distance prevents jostling and arguments but many animals require a much larger living space which they defend against others of their own species. A defended piece of ground is called a territory. Territories are owned by many different kinds of animals. Birds and mammals are the most usual territory holders but butterflies, crickets, dragonflies and sticklebacks also claim a space.

Warning notices
Within its territory, an animal can feed, sleep and rear its family without disturbance. It announces its ownership and discourages trespassers by the equivalent of 'Keep Out' notices. Birds sing from perches around the territory but mammals mark their boundaries with scent. Not all mammals defend a territory. A squirrel, for instance, spends its life in one area but this home range, as it is called, overlaps the home ranges of other squirrels.

Territorial behaviour is most obvious in spring, when males need to set up a place where they can first attract a mate, then rear a family. Some birds defend a territory all the year round. Wrens, robins and blackbirds are examples, but they are more vigorous at the start of the breeding season. Others, such as coots and great tits, are more sociable in the winter and live in flocks. The flocks break up in spring as individuals spend more time in their territories.

Arguing with the neighbours
Actual fighting is rare; animals usually settle their disputes without violence. They usually have no more than an argument because the owner of a territory feels 'superior' when he is on his own property, whereas the intruder feels 'guilty'. The owner may need do no more than appear on the scene to make the intruder retreat.

Disputes are common among garden birds when they are setting up their territories. Singing is a general warning that a place is occupied, but the owner also threatens trespassers with visual displays.

> **DON'T YOU THREATEN ME!**
> A threat display is a signal that an animal is likely to attack – like a man waving a clenched fist. Watch out for threat displays in your garden. A great tit will threaten by tilting back its head to show off the broad black band down the breast, and a robin does the same to show its red breast.

The size of the patch
The territory of an animal may be very small. A goldfinch's territory is only 5 metres square and house sparrows and starlings defend no more than the entrance to the nest. These birds feed outside their territories, but the territory of a fox or a tawny owl is also its hunting ground, so each needs an area large enough to supply it with prey.

The size of the territory will, therefore, depend on how plentiful food is. When food is in short supply, animals need larger territories and the population becomes well spaced out. There are fewer disputes when the animals are widely scattered and it is then more difficult to discover the boundaries of the territories. Sometimes a young animal has to carve out its territory from the corner of an established territory. At first, there are frequent fights and disputes but these eventually die out as the combatants settle down and accept the boundaries. Continuing to argue wastes time during the breeding season.

◄Watch out for squabbles like this on your local lake. Two male coots are battling to decide where the boundary between their territories should be. A female quickly gets out of the way.

►Two male stag beetles contest the right to a rotten stump in which the female will lay her eggs. The stronger has seized his opponent in his large jaws and will toss him to the ground. He will then court the female.

Finding a mate

See also **Claiming a patch in autumn**
on page 154

For many animals, setting up a territory and finding a mate are often part of the same process. The males of many species cannot get a mate unless they have a territory and displays used to drive away rival males also attract females. For example, when the boundary between two blackbird territories runs through your garden, you will often see the males in conflict. They approach each other aggressively with their beaks pointed at the sky or with their tails turned down and the back feathers ruffled. An approaching female will get the same treatment until she shows that she is not a rival male!

Take your partners please
In order for mating to take place, some form of courtship is normally needed to prevent aggression between the sexes. If the pair are then going to stay together to rear the family there will need to be a bond between them. Courtship behaviour helps to form this.

Watch out for sparrow courtship in trees, on the ground or along gutters of houses. The male who becomes more brightly coloured in spring utters a continuous chirping and hops excitedly around his mate with his tail raised and wings drooping. Later the roles are reversed and it is the female who crouches in front of the male with drooping wings and twittering calls.

In town and country alike, male pigeons court by puffing out their neck feathers while bowing and

▼ After entwining their bodies in a courtship 'dance' the male slow-worm grips the female's head as they mate.

▲ It sounds beautiful but the song of the male blackbird is also practical. It announces his ownership of a territory and that he may be interested in meeting a female.

spinning in front of the female, who often continues feeding, pretending not to notice.

When the partnership has been established, many birds strengthen their bond by preening each other's feathers – pigeons and jackdaws do this. The male also feeds the female; this is called courtship feeding and, as well as keeping the partners together, it helps to provide the extra food the female needs to make the eggs. Courtship feeding continues through the incubation period (see page 32), until both parents have to feed the growing chicks.

The courtship of birds is easy to watch but other animals are not so obvious in their behaviour. All they need to do is recognize each other as a male and female of the same species and that they are ready to mate. If the male does not help to rear the young, the pair will soon split up.

The courtship of mammals is brief and usually takes place at night. Only by lucky chance will you

LISTEN TO THE BIRDS

It is always a delight to hear birds singing but practice is needed to identify all the different songs, even of the more common garden birds. Go out in the spring, while the trees are still leafless and the birds are easy to see, and take with you an experienced bird listener. Birdsong is difficult to describe and written descriptions in bird books are not always helpful, unless the song can be translated into words. The 'teacher-teacher' of the great tit and the 'little-bit-of-bread-and-no-che-e-e-se' of the yellowhammer are examples. When the songs have been mastered, you can identify birds without having to track down the bird itself.

The main function of birdsong is as an advertisement. The song says, 'I am a male of a certain species and I own this territory. Other males must keep out but unattached females are welcome.'

The amount of song through the year depends on the habits of the species. Summer visitors, like the cuckoo, will be heard for only a short time. A long breeding season with several broods means a longer song period. Some birds start to sing again at the end of the summer, especially the robin and wren which hold territories throughout the year (see page 154). Keep a daily diary of the birdsongs you hear in your neighbourhood and at the end of the year you can make up a chart like the one shown here.

find a male hedgehog running in circles around his mate, or a dog fox playing with a vixen.

The stickleback father
In fresh water newts and sticklebacks have elaborate courtships. The behaviour of newts is described on page 19. Sticklebacks can be watched in shallow water at the edge of lakes and streams. The male develops a brilliant red throat during the breeding season. The red is both a warning to other males to keep their distance and an advertisement to females. The male makes a nest (see page 34) and signals to females, which he recognizes by their bellies, swollen with eggs. When a female approaches, the male dances in front of her, leading her to his nest where she will lay her eggs, leaving them in his care.

More ways of getting together
Animals use sound, sight or scent to attract the opposite sex. Sound signals include birdsong and the chirruping of grasshoppers and crickets; both are given by males to attract females. The light of glow-worms and the dancing flight of female butterflies are examples of visual signals. Female moths attract males by emitting a strong scent (see page 74).

The clouds of dancing mosquitoes and midges you most often see in the evening, are composed of males waiting for females. The males do not bite, so the swarms, which sometimes gather over people and alarm them, are quite harmless.

▼ A male stickleback sees off a rival on the edge of his territory. Both are in their breeding colours.

	Jan	Feb	Mar	April	May	June	July	Aug	Sept	Oct	Nov	Dec
Cuckoo												
Green woodpecker												
Skylark												
Wren												
Dunnock												
Robin												
Nightingale												
Blackbird												
Song thrush												
Blackcap												
Chiffchaff												
Great tit												
Chaffinch												
Greenfinch												

Birds and their nests

See also **Fledgling fliers**
on page 56

There are two ways in which birds bring up their young. Some birds rear their nestlings in the nest until they are ready to fly. These are called nidicolous birds. Other birds have young called chicks which leave the nest soon after hatching and usually feed themselves. These are called nidifugous birds.

Nestlings hatch blind and naked. Their feathers grow slowly and they must be fed and kept warm until they are independent. They need a solid, safe nest in which to grow up. Most nidicolous birds build the familiar cup-shaped nests that can be seen in hedges and trees. A few, such as the magpie and wren, build a domed nest. Others, like woodpeckers and kingfishers, nest in holes which they excavate themselves, whereas the tits nest in natural holes.

Nidifugous birds, such as ducks, pheasants and waders, build simple nests. Some are no more than shallow hollows scraped in the soil; others are a simple cup of dead plants. The young chicks hatch with their eyes open and have a covering of down. They leave the nest and follow their parents in search of food soon after hatching.

Nest sites for safety
Unless the nest is built in a safe place, like a rook's at the top of a tree, a grebe's on an island, or a sand martin's in a tunnel, it has to be well hidden from predators. Nests are usually built in dense vegetation where they cannot be seen.

The nests of birds on the ground are more vulnerable and these birds rely on camouflage to escape the notice of predators. Female ducks and pheasants have mottled brown plumage which blends in very well with their surroundings. Others, like the moorhen or ringed plover, slip away from the nest when the danger is still remote. Safety then rests on the simple nature of the nest and the camouflage of the eggs.

Keeping the eggs warm
Once the eggs are laid, parent birds lose some of their breast feathers to reveal one or more areas of skin called brood patches. A brood patch is well supplied with blood vessels and acts as a hot-water bottle to keep the eggs warm. If the parent is kept away from its nest the eggs will chill and the developing chicks die. In cold weather, the parent sits tighter and is more reluctant to leave the nest. At intervals, it stands up and turns the eggs with its beak and feet to ensure that the eggs are warmed evenly.

The first sign that an egg is about to hatch is a small star-shaped crack near the broad end. This is made by the chick's beak which is tipped with a white egg-tooth. Eventually it knocks a hole through and the egg is said to be 'pipped'.

Hatching on time
Birds time their breeding so that there will be plenty of food available for the growing nestlings or chicks. Blue tits and great tits are feeding their young in the second half of May when caterpillars are most abun-

▲An oystercatcher's egg is hatching. You can see the tip of the chick's beak, with its special egg-tooth, in the hole it has chipped. The chick will go on chipping as it turns inside the shell until it has cut the egg almost in two and can push itself free.

▶The pheasant's nest is a simple scrape on the ground with a few leaves and stalks around the rim. Notice that the newly hatched chick is well developed. It will soon be able to leave the nest and follow its mother in search of food.

WHEN DID SHE LAY?
The egg-laying dates are more interesting than song dates but they are difficult to establish without keeping a very careful watch on the birds. One way of finding out the laying date is to watch the birds bringing in nest material. They will be very busy flying to and fro. Then the activity ceases; the nest is complete and the hen is laying the eggs. Another way is to watch for adults bringing beakfuls of food, a sign that the eggs have hatched. A bird book will tell you the incubation time of the bird you are watching and you can work out how much earlier the eggs would have been laid. Keep notes of your sightings.

dant in woodland. The caterpillars soon start to change into pupae so the tits do not lay a second clutch. Blackbirds and song thrushes catch worms as well as caterpillars, so they raise two or three clutches in a year, starting earlier than the tits. However, dry weather sends the worms deep into the soil and the blackbirds may then stop nesting, while the song thrush will turn to snails for its food.

The heron and tawny owl are early nesters. They take advantage of good hunting conditions in February and March before the growth of vegetation provides cover for their prey.

For the young birds to hatch at the best time, nest-building and egg-laying must also be started at the appropriate time. The birds cannot know when their food will be abundant; they are stimulated to begin nesting by both the increasing length of the days in spring and the improvement in the weather.

DO NOT DISTURB!
Birds will very quickly desert their nest if they are disturbed, so never approach the site too closely. In autumn old nests are easy to find and you can then examine them more easily (see page 141).

▲ The moorhen's nest is a more complicated structure of plant stems and reeds near or in water. The moorhen bends down tall plants to help hide the nest. There is a picture of a moorhen chick on page 56.

More nesters

See also **Fledgling fliers** on page 56
and **Baby mammals** on page 58

Many animals lay their eggs and simply abandon them. Fishes deposit their eggs in the water, to float freely or to stick to stones, and insects lay their eggs on plants or in the ground. When the eggs hatch, the young animals have to fend for themselves. Only a very small number of animals care for their young.

There is an enormous loss of eggs and young when they are not guarded and so animals which abandon them have to lay vast quantities of eggs. Care by parents helps the young to survive and we find that animals which build nests and look after their young lay fewer eggs. The nest is a cradle which helps to keep the offspring together and enables the parents to guard them.

Insect nesters
Very few cold-blooded animals are nest builders, but bees, wasps and ants make nests which they stock with food for their larvae. Solitary bees and wasps

▲ The female grass snake lays her eggs in a heap of rotting vegetation which keeps them warm.

that live on their own abandon their nests, but the social species have elaborate nests and a community of workers to help rear the young (see pages 98 and 150). Earwigs and some soil-dwelling centipedes dig a small chamber for their eggs and remain with them until they hatch.

Fish nesters
Few fishes make nests. The brown trout, and its relative the salmon, dig holes in the gravelly bed of their spawning streams and lay their eggs in them. The spawn is then covered with gravel and left to develop (see page 184). The bullhead spawns in a nest hollow under a stone. The male remains with the eggs, and drives a current of water over the nest with his fins to prevent the eggs from getting covered with silt.

The best nesters
Birds are the best-known nest builders. The size and shape of birds' nests range from a simple scrape in the soil for a nightjar and a bare ledge for a guillemot, to the great pile of sticks of a heron or rook, and the delicate structure of a long-tailed tit, which may contain over 1,000 feathers as a lining. These birds have to rely on instinct to tell them how to build the nest. There is no time to learn the necessary skill, although they may improve with practice.

Mammal nesters
Small mammals, such as mice, voles and shrews, make nests rather like birds' nests. They are usually placed in underground burrows, at the base of grass tussocks or other well hidden places.

Dormice, harvest mice and squirrels build their

NESTS LARGE AND SMALL
It is easy to spot the large nest or drey of the grey squirrel (**1**). The chaffinch builds the typical bowl-shaped nest (**2**) of a nidicolous bird (see page 32), whereas that of the stickleback (see page 31) is tunnel shaped (**3**). A harvest mouse nest is woven from leaves attached to stalks (**4**), while the potter wasp makes a vase-shaped structure from mud (**5**).

nests above ground. Dormouse nests are found in bramble bushes, about 1 metre up. They are often made of strips of honeysuckle bark, so if honeysuckle is growing near a thicket of brambles or hawthorn, look for signs that the bark has been torn away. Squirrel nests, or dreys, are made of leafy twigs woven into a ball 30 to 60 centimetres across in the fork of a branch. They are usually quite easy to find, unlike the nests of harvest mice. These are made from grass blades slit and woven into a springy ball while still attached to the stalks.

LOOK UNDER THE SHEETS!
A good way of finding the underground nest of a small mammal is to look under sheets of corrugated iron or planks which have been lying on the ground, or by carefully lifting a log or flat stone. Always replace the 'lid' as you found it.

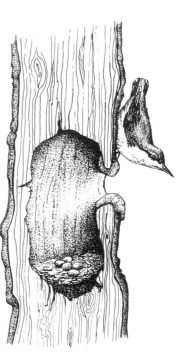

▶The nuthatch is a hole nester and rather than make its own it will often occupy a disused woodpeckers' hole. If the entrance is too large it plasters it with mud to make it exactly nuthatch size.

▼Newly hatched garden spiders crowd into a knot on a stinging nettle. If disturbed they rapidly spread out on fine threads. When danger is past, they regroup in another knot.

▲The kingfisher tunnels about 1 metre into a river or stream bank to make a nesting chamber. The nestlings are soon sitting on a smelly pile of regurgitated fish bones.

▼In the safety of her underground nest, the female rabbit gives birth to blind, deaf and naked young. A rabbit has many enemies and rarely lives for longer than a year.

Wildlife in open country

See also **Heathland and heather** on page 108

The wide, open spaces of moors, heaths and grass-covered hills and downs are among the wildest parts of the country. They are usually remote from towns and factories and they are a refuge for many interesting animals. Because many visitors do not walk far from parked cars and usually keep to well-worn tracks, these animals have the peace and quiet they need to survive. However, the increasing number of people who enjoy visiting wild places to climb, ramble or birdwatch are creating more and more disturbance. Apart from causing danger to animals with young, the trampling by many pairs of heavy boots destroys fragile vegetation, and where the ground is worn bare it may become eroded by rain, wind and frost.

The birds of open country are visible from afar. Skylarks may be abundant and they can be heard everywhere as they sing from high in the air. Pipits call plaintively from tussocks and rocks. Buzzards, grouse, golden plovers, crows and wheatears are seen regularly, but the prize birds such as peregrines and golden eagles require skill, patience – or luck – for a sighting.

For centuries, the open country was used for sheep farming but it has been increasingly turned over to arable farming and forestry so that many animals are becoming rarer.

Nocturnal nightjars

Nightjars are summer migrants which nest on downs, heaths and moors, and in some woodland. Their numbers have been declining for many years. They are active at night and their loud churring song, uttered only in darkness, gives away their presence. A careful approach with a torch may reveal the birds, or you may see them fly past silhouetted against a moonlit sky.

The bird with three names

Lapwings spend the winter in flocks of 100 or more birds. They feed on the bare farmland, moorland and marshes and fly overhead with the slow, flapping flight that has earned them their name. In spring, the flocks split up and pairs of lapwings stake out territories. The male then shows off with exuberant displays of aerobatic skill. He flies well up, then comes tumbling down, twisting and turning, showing off his black-and-white pattern. At the same time, he gives voice to the shrill call that has given the species its alternative name of peewit.

Lapwings are usually wary birds and difficult to approach, but if a close look can be taken in bright light, the tall pointed crest can be seen and the feathers of the back appear a shining green, not black: the lapwing's third name is green plover.

▲A male lapwing calls on the edge of its moorland territory. The cry 'pee-wit' gives the bird one of its names.

▼At rest on the ground, the nightjar is so superbly camouflaged that you might nearly step on it. It keeps its eyes half shut so as not to spoil the camouflage.

▼The brown hare lives in open country where it can see predators a long way off and can escape from them by running.

Although lapwings give themselves away by their bold plumage and loud calls, it is difficult to find their nest. This is no more than a depression in the ground, scantily lined with grasses, and the four eggs are perfectly camouflaged. If a lapwing dives at your head, you are near its nest and should move away quickly so that it can return to incubate the eggs.

MAD MARCH HARES

There is a saying 'As mad as a March hare'. At this time of year hares are preparing for the breeding season and they can be seen more regularly during the day. During their courtship the hares seem crazy. They chase each other around the fields, sometimes leaping high into the air and occasionally coming to blows. Two hares rear up face to face, on their hindfeet, and box with their forepaws.

A baby hare or leveret is born in a nest, called a form, hidden among low vegetation. A leveret has a coat of thick fur, its eyes and ears are open and it can run soon after birth.

Flowers of grasslands

See also **The woodland floor**
on page 24

▲ A field turned golden by meadow buttercups: a lovely sight but of little use to the farmer because the plants are poisonous.

DON'T PICK!
There was a time when people collected masses of wild plants to decorate their own homes and to dry and preserve or to sell. Fields, hedgerows and woods were stripped of bluebells, primroses and daffodils, so that they disappeared from some places. Picking the flowers was bad enough but sometimes the whole plant was dug up. Entire colonies of rare orchids have vanished in this way. The rarer the plant, the keener were unscrupulous collectors to find specimens.

Many of our rarer plants are being threatened by farming, building or other changes to the countryside. People still try to collect rare varieties at the few places where they still grow and so these often have to be kept secret and guarded.

It is now illegal to pick or dig up any of 62 very rare plants. Many of these are orchids or mountain plants. It is illegal to uproot any other wild plant without permission of the landowner or occupier.

This does not mean that you may not go blackberry picking or gathering buttercups and daisies, but please remember that picking large numbers of flowers is selfish. Finally, never pick any flowers in nature reserves or on nature trails.

Five thousand years ago most of the country was covered by forests. Here and there were glades and stretches of open country where the soil was too wet or too thin for trees to grow. Since then, the forests have been gradually cut down and the land used for farming. The trees have been replaced by grasses for cattle and sheep to eat, or by crops, some of which are also grasses (such as wheat and barley).

Pastures and meadows

A variety of herbs grow in grasslands. Some thrive where the grass is kept short; others live where the grass grows to its full height. Grass that is grazed by animals is called pasture. A field where the grass is allowed to grow and eventually mown to make hay, is called a meadow. Some of the herbs are important because they are a valuable food for grazing animals in addition to the grass. These include clovers, yarrow, ribwort plantain and dandelions.

The kinds of flowers and grasses to be found on a pasture depend on the soil. Chalk and limestone soils carry rock-rose, salad burnet, meadow saxifrage and several orchids. Tormentil, common mouse-ear and milkwort are examples of spring flowers on acid grassland.

Wet meadows have some of the most showy flowers. Marsh-marigold and fritillary were more abundant when it was usual to grow grass for hay in water meadows. These are fields that are flooded each winter and are fertilized with silt.

Vanishing grasslands

Today many of the grasslands have been either ploughed and drained to grow crops or they have been treated with fertilizers and weedkillers, which get rid of many of the herbs. Grassland flowers are now often seen only on roadside verges or beside footpaths, except where the old meadows and pastures remain.

▲Watch out for 'cuckoo-spit' in spring. It is froth made by a froghopper nymph who lives inside it. This cuckoo-spit is on creeping buttercup (see also page 126).

▲Compared to those in your garden wild daffodils are smaller and more dainty. They appear in damp meadows and beside rivers. A primrose is growing with this clump.

▲The pale lilac flowers of cuckooflower or lady's-smock stand above dandelions in a damp meadow.

▼This is a real 'find' among the meadow grasses – a bee orchid. You can see how it gets its name.

▲This is ragged-robin, an untidy looking flower which you should find in damp meadows and on roadsides.

▼Meadow saxifrage is a low herb with dainty flowers. Look for it on well-drained drier grasslands.

Flowers, pollen and insects

See also **Pussy willow and lamb's-tails** on page 12
and **Spreading the seed** on page 166

The function of a flower is to produce seeds that will eventually grow into the next generation of plants. The seeds form in the carpel from ovules similar to an animal's eggs. The ovules develop into seed when they are fertilized by pollen grains transferred from the stamens, in most cases of another flower. When pollen settles on a stigma, it sends a pollen-tube down the style and into the ovule.

Transferring the pollen
Pollen has to be carried from one flower to another by some means. Pollen from the anthers of one flower has to be deposited on the stigma of another flower. The pollen of some plants, such as those producing catkins (see page 13), is carried by the wind. Most flowers are pollinated by insects when the pollen is carried directly from one flower to another. The arrangement of the flower ensures that the insect brushes past the anthers and stigma to get at the nectar. Nectar is a sugary fluid that is an important source of energy for many flying insects.

Getting at the nectar
Some plants have nectar that is easy to find. Members of the carrot and parsley family have tiny flowers arranged in flat-topped clusters called umbels. Their nectar can be sipped by insects with short tongues. When you see cow parsley and similar plants in spring and early summer look closely at the umbels and watch the flies and beetles crawling easily from flower to flower as they feed.

Other plants have hidden nectaries. The tubular flowers of dead-nettles, honeysuckle and daffodils are examples. Bees, butterflies and moths have long tongues which they thrust deep into trumpet-shaped flowers. Short-tongued insects are kept out but some get round this by cutting a hole in the side of the flower. You may find such holes in the flowers of comfrey, bluebells, daffodils and dead-nettles. Bees may use the holes as a short cut to the nectar.

Attracting the insects
The flowers attract insects by their bright colours and by scent. Many flowers have patterns of lines and dots on the petals which act as 'guide marks' for leading insects towards the nectar. Forget-me-nots have a yellow centre surrounded by blue, whereas pansies, eyebrights and violets have dark lines leading to the centre of the flower.

A 'rotten' trick
The anthers and stigma of a flower usually ripen at different times so that it is not pollinated by its own pollen. Foxglove flowers produce pollen first, then the anthers wither and the stigmas ripen. Visiting

▲A cuckoo-pint or lords-and-ladies flower cut away to show its structure. The text explains how flies are trapped inside to ensure that they carry pollen with them when they finally escape.

bees pick up pollen from newly opened flowers then deposit it on the stigmas of older flowers. Other plants have separate male and female flowers with either stamens or stigmas only, and one kind ripens before the other.

Cuckoo-pint or lords-and-ladies has a special mechanism to ensure that it is cross-pollinated. The central stalk or spadix is warm to the touch and has a rotten-smelling scent that attracts flies. They fall into the bottom of the flower and a ring of hairs prevents them from getting out. The female flowers are ripe and they are fertilized by pollen which the flies have brought from other cuckoo-pint plants. Next day, the hairs wither and the flies escape by flying past the male flowers. These have now ripened and they shed pollen on to the flies to carry to the next plant.

FLOWER COMPARISONS
Compare the flowers of potato, tomato and bittersweet plants. You will find that they look very similar although the plants themselves look very different. This means that these plants are closely related. Botanists group plants according to the structure of their flowers rather than by the shape of their leaves or other parts.

▲ Even a tiny green aphid can pollinate a wild daffodil. Notice the stigma in the centre of the flower and the pollen grains both on the aphid and on the lip of the trumpet.

THE PARTS OF A FLOWER
The female part of a flower has one or more carpels which contain the ovules. On top of the carpel there is the style and stigma. Pollen is produced in the male part: the anthers at the top of the stamens. The ring of petals (the corolla) and the ring of sepals (the calyx) protect the stamens and stigma.

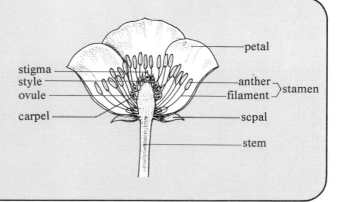

Closing for the night

See also **Plants that eat animals** on page 114 and **Leaves of death** on page 116

Plant movements are not obvious unless you keep watch over a period of time. During the day, daisies on the lawn are wide open. Their white rays make a flat dish around the yellow centre. Go back into the garden as night falls and you will find that they have closed up. The process can also be seen in cloudy weather when the white rays also begin to close. This habit was well known to our ancestors who gave the plant the name 'day's-eye', hence daisy. Wood anemones, lesser celandines and crocuses are other plants that 'go to sleep' at night.

Sleep movements

Closing the petals is called a sleep movement, but not all sleeping plants close only at night. Goat's-beard, a yellow dandelion-like relative of the daisy, had the country name 'Jack-go-to-bed-at-noon'. It is fully open on sunny mornings, then closes around midday. The scarlet pimpernel, which is a weed of corn fields, gardens and waste places, closes its red, sometimes blue, flowers as rain approaches. It used to be called 'the poor-man's-weather-glass'.

The reason for flowers opening and closing and the mechanism of how the petals move is not fully understood. Crocuses, however, are known to react to temperature. As they warm up in the morning sun, growth increases on the upper surface of the petals so that these bend outwards. In the evening, the cooling air leads to increased growth on the underside and the flowers close again.

Some flowers close at times to prevent certain insects from taking their nectar, or to protect the inner parts of the flower from adverse conditions. Closing at night probably protects the flowers when pollinating insects are inactive.

Flowering at night

Nottingham catchfly, night-flowering catchfly and white campion are related plants whose flowers open at night to attract night-flying insects. White campion and night-flowering catchfly are common roadside and farm plants, while Nottingham catchfly is seen less frequently. (The name catchfly is earned by the sticky hairy stems which trap flies or other insects, dead leaves and so on.) The flowers are sweet-scented and the white petals show up well in dim light and attract moths. The petals of flowers that attract moths are often long and narrow, or are divided into narrow strips, as in the Nottingham catchfly. Presumably this makes the flowers easier for the moths to find.

Honeysuckle flowers are a particular favourite with moths and attract the spectacular hawk moths. The long, slender corolla tube (see page 67) is typical of flowers that are visited by long-tongued moths. Although bumblebees visit them by day, their tongues are not long enough to reach the nectar. Honeysuckle flowers open in the evening, before it is dark, and give off an extremely strong scent.

Sleeping leaves

Leaves also show sleep movements. The three-lobed leaves of wood-sorrel collapse at night, like an umbrella folding, and open in the morning. The soft tissues of a plant are kept rigid by the pressure of water in them. When water is removed, the plant wilts and the movement of the wood-sorrel leaf is caused by a sudden wilting at its base. The closing is also stimulated by raindrops hitting the leaves, and you can achieve the same result if you repeatedly flick them with your finger.

◀Plants are capable of limited movement of their leaves and flowers. The daisies on this lawn are wide open during a sunny day but close up with the approach of night.

▶The strange, white flowers of the Nottingham catchfly show up well at night and attract moths and other night-flying insects.

Now you see me, now you don't

See also **Moths by moonlight** on page 74
and **Eight-legged hunters** on page 160

You have probably noticed that as you walk through long grass or push through bushes, butterflies and moths often come fluttering out. Even if you had looked carefully, you probably would not have spotted them before they moved; and when they settle again they are difficult to find. This is because these insects are camouflaged. Their colours, and sometimes their shape, match their background.

Camouflage is used by hunters and by the hunted. A hunting animal needs camouflage so that it can approach its prey without being seen while the prey needs camouflage to avoid being eaten.

Blending with the background

The simplest form of camouflage is to have a colour that matches the background; the green hairstreak shown here is a good example. However, you can still see that this is a butterfly by the shape of its wings. Many moths improve their camouflage with markings. As they rest on the bark of a tree the mottled patterns match and blend with the rough texture of the bark. The pattern of markings may also break up the outline of the body so that the animal is not so easily noticed. This is called disruptive coloration. Military aircraft and tanks are often 'disruptively' painted with green and brown.

Moths press themselves against the tree trunk so that there is no shadow to give them away. Many animals reduce the effect of the shadow by 'countershading'. The sun illuminates the upper parts of a deer for instance and the underparts are in shadow. This would make the deer look solid but its underparts are in fact pale in colour so the body has a uniform shade and it does not stand out.

Camouflage colours and disruptive patterns only work if the animal is seen against the right background. The animals are aware of this and it is difficult to get them to settle in the wrong place.

Colour changes

A few animals can actually change their own colour to match their background; the chameleon is a well-known example. Adult butterflies and moths cannot do this but the colour of their pupae often matches that of their background. When the caterpillar of a cabbage white butterfly is about to pupate it instinctively notes the colour of its background and colours the pupal skin accordingly.

One moth, two ways to hide

The peppered moth exists in two forms: a speckled form which resembles lichens, and a black form. During the Industrial Revolution factory chimneys belched out black smoke polluting and killing the

lichens growing in neighbouring woods. The speckled moths were no longer camouflaged and they were picked off by the birds, while the black moths went unnoticed in the sooty environment and multiplied. Today the black form is common in industrial areas and the speckled form common in unpolluted country areas where lichens still flourish.

Hidden death

You have to examine flowers carefully to find crab spiders because their colours blend perfectly to give them an excellent camouflage. This is the spider's plan: instead of spinning a web, it lies in wait for an

◄The peppered moth, both adult and larva, is a master of camouflage. Look how closely its caterpillar matches the colour and shape of the sallow twig.

►The crab spider blends so well with the bramble flower that all it has to do is sit and wait for unsuspecting prey to alight. Here it has pounced on a bumblebee. You sometimes find the spider by noticing its prey first, apparently just sitting in a strange position on a flower.

◄Here are the two forms of the adult peppered moth on the bark of a silver birch tree. The black form is obvious, but how quickly can you spot the two normal or peppered forms?

▼When it settles on the young leaves of honeysuckle, the colour of the green hairstreak butterfly matches them perfectly, and makes it difficult for a bird to spot.

HOW MANY ANIMALS?
Take a quick glance at the pictures on these pages and try to guess how many animals are shown. You should be able to count seven: a moth larva, three moths, a butterfly, a spider, and a bumblebee.

unsuspecting insect to land on the flower. The insect is immediately seized and paralysed with a venomous bite from the spider's fangs.

There are many kinds of crab spiders, so-called because they scuttle sideways like real crabs. White, pink and pale yellow crab spiders live in matching flowers and catch flies and butterflies as they come to collect nectar. Others are green in colour to match leaves. Some species of crab spider can even surprise and overpower bumblebees which are many times their own size.

Life on the wall

See also **Wild nightlife**
on page 50

An old wall is a good place to look for animals and plants. There are two basic kinds of walls: brick and mortar walls, and drystone walls in which slabs of stone are carefully fitted together without mortar. Drystone walls are used instead of hedges and fences in hilly country.

The wall dwellers

A wall of the house or a wall in the garden will support a lot of animal and plant life. All sorts of small creatures such as slugs and snails, woodlice and spiders crawl over the bricks. They are easy to watch because there is no cover; the early mornings and evenings are the best times to seach for them (see page 50).

During the day butterflies and other insects settle on sunny walls to bask (see page 49). They are chased by the tiny zebra spider, whose black-and-white striped body is hard to spot until it rushes over the bricks. This is one of the jumping spiders, that run after their prey instead of spinning a web.

Scattered holes in the mortar between bricks are the nests of mason bees and mason wasps. Mason bees look like small honeybees but they have orange red hairs on the abdomen and they nest alone rather than in hives. Each bee builds cells of mud in its hole and stocks them with pollen and nectar before laying an egg in each. The mason wasp, which has more

▲ Stonecrop is a rock plant very much at home on an old churchyard wall. This is biting stonecrop, which has a peppery taste.

▶ The depression in the centre of each leaf gives navelwort its name. It grows on shaded walls and turns red under drought conditions.

◄A mossy old wall with crumbling mortar provides safe homes for dozens of spiders. Each one makes a silken tunnel leading back into the brickwork, well spaced from its neighbours. During the day not one spider is to be seen, but after dark they come out to prey on woodlice, earwigs and beetles.

▲The wall butterfly appreciates the vertical surface of a wall on which to bask when the sun is low. The small ferns are wall rue.

◄Lichens are simple plants with no roots. They absorb rainwater and gases through their upper surfaces, so are very sensitive to air pollution and cannot survive near towns (see page 198).

black and less yellow than common wasps, stocks its nest with living but paralysed caterpillars.

Roots in nooks and crannies

A well-weathered wall can support a flourishing growth of plants which send their roots into crannies where soil has accumulated. Some walls even have small trees growing out of them. The types of plant growing on walls are often those that live on rock faces and sea cliffs and they are well adapted to the spartan conditions of the wall. They do not need much soil and they can survive with very little moisture. The stonecrops are well named for their habit of growing on rocks and walls; they store water in their fleshy leaves.

Ivy-leaved toadflax has a special adaptation for ensuring that its seeds fall in suitable places. After the flowers have been pollinated, the stems grow away from the light to deposit the seeds in dark crevices.

Where the wall remains damp, it becomes the home of ferns and mosses (see page 118). These are plants which cannot stand drying out. Mosses grip almost perfectly smooth surfaces with their tiny roots, then dust and debris gathers around them to hold the moisture and allow other plants to root.

▲Red valerian is an introduced plant which needs lime so favours limestone cliffs or the mortar of old walls. It is popular with butterflies and here you should spot a comma feeding on its nectar.

Soaking up the sun

Everyone likes to sunbathe. Basking in the sun is enjoyable because we like the feel of the sun warming our skin. Many animals sunbathe and look as if they also are enjoying themselves.

Birds sunbathe by fluffing out their feathers and spreading their wings and tail, so that the greatest area of feathers is exposed to the sun. Even nocturnal creatures such as owls and badgers come out during the day to bask.

Why sunbathing is good for you
In the days when all houses were warmed only by coal fires and factories used coal-fired boilers, the sun was often obscured by clouds of smoke. City children developed a disease called rickets, in which their bones became very weak. Rickets is caused by a lack of vitamin D, which is formed naturally by the action of sunlight on substances in our skin. When birds and mammals sunbathe, the natural oils on their feathers and fur are converted into vitamin D, which is then licked up and swallowed during preening and grooming.

WATCH A RABBIT WASH
The next time you see a pet rabbit washing note how it pays particular attention to its ears. It first licks a forepaw then runs it over an ear. Then it licks the paw again and repeats the operation. Minute quantities of natural oil containing vitamin D are wiped off the ears and licked from the paws. Experiments showed that if a rabbit's ears were cleaned to remove the oil, the rabbit developed rickets. When the cleaning was stopped and the rabbit allowed to sunbathe, the rickets were cured.

Warming up in the morning
Birds and mammals also like to sit in the sun to warm themselves. You can see them doing this when it is not really 'sunbathing weather', for instance when the sun is shining after a cold night. Town pigeons gather on ledges where a wall faces the rising sun and acts as a sun trap.

Warm-blooded birds and mammals generate heat in their bodies and their temperature is kept very even. Our body temperature is 37 degrees Centigrade when we are healthy but it may change and this is why doctors take a patient's temperature. Cold-blooded animals cannot generate heat in their bodies, so their temperature stays the same as their

▼A common lizard must warm up in the morning sunshine before it can become fully active. Sunny banks are good places to look for lizards.

surroundings unless they can use another method of keeping warm. That is why warming up in the sun is important for cold-blooded animals which frequently bask to warm their bodies. Their muscles and other bodily functions work better at higher temperatures. When a snake or lizard comes out of its hiding place in the morning it can move only slowly. It finds a sunny spot and warms its body before it sets out to hunt for food.

As well as enabling an animal to move more rapidly, a warm body also allows it to grow faster and for eggs and young to develop quickly. Tadpoles and fishes come into sun-warmed shallow water to bask for these reasons.

Warming up for take-off

Insects have to warm up before they can fly properly. Some kinds need to be as warm as a warm-blooded animal. Watch out for bumblebees clinging to plants in the early morning. If they are prodded gently, they can hardly move and just buzz angrily. As the sun climbs in the sky, the bumblebee's black, furry body absorbs its rays and off it flies.

Butterflies also like to bask on walls or flowers. They sit with their wings spread and they turn so that their wings face the sun.

Night-flying moths cannot, of course, bask in the sun. These insects warm up by vibrating their wings. Exercising muscles generates heat and the quivering of the insects' wings has the same warming effect as our shivering when we get cold.

▼A male orangetip butterfly spreads his wings to the sun from a cow parsley flower. If disturbed it will turn to face the sun again.

Wild nightlife

See also **Life on the wall** on page 46
and **Snail trails** on page 53

◀This is a cockchafer beetle about to take off from among oak leaves at night. In May and June evenings listen for cockchafers clattering by in flight or look for them bumping into street lights and lighted windows.

▼The dormouse sleeps all day in a nest woven from shredded honeysuckle bark. At night it climbs nimbly to feed on the honeysuckle buds and flowers or, at other times of the year, on its leaves or berries.

We tend to go indoors when darkness falls and stay inside until it is light again next morning. This means that we miss most of the activity in the garden and countryside. The majority of animals come out of their hiding places when humans are safely out of the way.

There is no need to stay up late to search for the animals of the night. The greatest activity is around dusk and dawn. The animals come out at twilight, just after the sun has set, and they can still be seen when the sun has risen. This is just as well because it is not so easy to watch animals in the dark. Scientists studying nocturnal animals have to use special night-viewing equipment, but there is plenty for you to see without special equipment. A torch or the light from windows is sufficient to reveal the activities of many smaller animals.

Moths at the window

The easiest night animals to watch are the moths that settle on the outside of lighted windows. Some moths fly by day but most rest on walls and trees, or hide in vegetation. They are protected by their good camouflage (see page 44) and move only when disturbed.

The moths on your window have been distracted by the light (see page 74) from their search for nectar. They visit the same flowers that attract butterflies by day but they prefer white flowers which show up better in the dim light (see page 42). Valerian, honeysuckle and pussy willow catkins are favourites. Moths can also be attracted by painting a tree or fence at a convenient height with a streak of black treacle. Entomologists call this 'sugaring' and it quickly attracts a variety of moths.

Night-flying beetles

Some of the most spectacular beetles are nocturnal. Warm May and June nights bring out cockchafers, sometimes called Maybugs although they are not true bugs (see page 126). These are heavy-bodied beetles which are not very agile fliers. They bump into windowpanes with a loud crack, as do round-bodied dung beetles. Stag beetles fly in the evening but they are more likely to be found on the woodland floor. The devil's coach-horse wanders over garden paths and flower beds in search of live or dead animals to eat. If you prod it with a stick it will give an angry display by raising its abdomen and opening its jaws, but this is harmless bluff.

Tree trunks and walls (see page 46) are good places for finding many forms of life at night. Slugs and snails, spiders, woodlice and other 'creepy-crawlies' are on the move. Bright lights or heavy footfalls and knocks will disturb them, but care and patience are usually rewarded.

▲ One of the most rewarding sights for the night watcher – two badger cubs snuffling near their woodland sett.

MAKE A NIGHT LIGHT
You can convert your torch for watching animals at night by painting the lens with red nail varnish or covering it with red tissue paper. The red light it casts will be bright enough to show you the animals but it will not disturb them because their eyes do not respond to it.

Sights of the night

Using a night light you can watch hedgehogs coming to feed on saucers of bread and milk, or mice lured to baits of grain or rolled oats. In time these animals will become used to ordinary white light if it is not too bright. By using a red light and treading very softly you can also spot earthworms on your lawn. They stretch over the surface but leave the tail in the burrow so they can retreat in an instant. Stamp your foot and they will vanish before your eyes. The worms are searching for dead leaves to eat and they pull them back into their burrows to be nibbled in safety (see page 144).

Eyes that glow

If you hold your torch near your own eyes you will see the eyes of some moths and spiders glow like cats' eyes in the dark. To improve the sensitivity of the eye in dim light, there is a mirror-like layer, the tapetum, at the back of the eye. This reflects light that has already entered the eye back through the retina which is thus stimulated a second time. Some of this reflected light is returned through the lens so that it glows like the rear reflector of a bicycle.

A warm, damp night

Nocturnal animals are most active in warm, moist weather, and particularly after it has stopped raining. The main advantage to these animals of coming out at night is that the damp night air is more favourable for them. This is especially true for soft-bodied animals like worms and slugs whose skins are not fully waterproof and who would soon dry up. Snails can retreat into their shells but they require damp conditions to become fully active. Woodlice have a fairly hard skin but they, too, easily suffer from loss of water, as do amphibians.

Insects and mammals are fully waterproof and do not need damp air. They come out at night because darkness helps to protect them from their predators, especially from the birds which are mostly active by day. This protection is not complete because other predators such as owls, nightjars, bats, foxes, weasels and hedgehogs hunt by night. Moreover, the nocturnal hunting mammals seek their prey mainly by scent so they are unaffected by darkness.

Continued on page 52

BE PREPARED AT NIGHT!
Wrap up well (it can be cold at night, even in summer) and start your night-time watching in the garden. If you want to go further afield ask your parents and, if they agree, make sure you have first made at least one daylight visit to the area in order to get your bearings.

Bats: insect-hunters of the night

Bats are insect-eating mammals that chase their prey through the air. They do not compete with insect-eating birds because they fly at night when few birds are active. To hunt flying insects at night bats use ultrasonic squeaks, too high-pitched for us to hear. These squeaks bounce off the insects, or other objects, back to the bat's ears. The time between the squeak and the echo tells the bat how far away from the object it is. So even in total darkness, bats can find their prey and avoid crashing into trees and houses.

Bats seek out concentrations of flying insects. Good places to look for bats at night are rubbish dumps, street lights and country lanes where insects are attracted by the warmth of the tarmac or are concentrated by wind eddies over a hedge.

Even when a bat is flying to and fro in the early evening and there is enough light to see it well, identification is difficult. A small bat flying around houses is likely to be a pipistrelle, which is easily the most common species. It occasionally comes out during the day, even in winter, but the bat to emerge earliest in the evening is usually the noctule, which has slender wings and may fly in groups.

Feeding on the wing

While there is still some light, watch closely to see the bats' hunting technique. They fly in a roughly straight line or a wide circle, then suddenly dart to one side or other, up or down, to catch an insect. This is caught in the mouth or is scooped up in the membrane between the hindlegs and then picked out with the mouth. Some naturalists use a detector to study bats. This is an instrument that converts the ultrasonic squeaks and chirrups into sounds we can hear. These are different for each species and so the detector helps to identify bats. Using the detector you can hear a bat emitting a steady stream of 'clicks' which speeds up to a 'buzz' as it closes in on an insect.

> **FOOL A BAT!**
> It is easy to lure down a bat by throwing up a small pebble. The bat will dive after it, but usually realizes its mistake when it gets within 30 centimetres of the pebble.

Bat tracking

Bats spend the day in their roosts: in hollow trees, caves or the roofs of houses and churches. If you see a stream of bats flying over in the evening, you can track them back over the next few evenings to their roost. The position of the roost is marked by small, dry droppings under the entrance, often with the wings of moths and the wing-cases of beetles. The roost should be left strictly alone. In winter hibernating bats are very vulnerable to disturbance.

▼ It is a pity that many bats are now rare and that some people are afraid of them. They are fascinating animals that eat many insect pests. This is a serotine bat eating an eyed hawk moth.

Snail trails

See also **Life on the shore**
on page 84

Snails and slugs are molluscs, a group of animals to which cockles, mussels, winkles and whelks, squids and octopuses also belong. Broadly speaking, slugs are shell-less snails, although this is not strictly true because some species do have a very small shell.

At first sight slugs and snails can appear dull, if not unpleasant, and they are unpopular with gardeners because they eat prized plants. They have some interesting habits however. During the day their soft bodies are in danger of drying up, and so slugs and snails emerge mainly at night; they will remain active by day if it has rained or when there has been a heavy dew.

Long-distance gliders

The scientific name for slugs and snails is gastropods, which means 'stomach foot'. This describes the way that the body is one long foot on which the animal creeps slowly but surely. How fast do you think a snail can crawl? A medium-sized snail should cover 10 centimetres in a minute (you can easily check this), which would work out to one kilometre in a week, if it kept going!

At this speed, you can study the workings of the foot. The snail glides across the roughest ground, over stones and up the stems of plants, without difficulty. It can even climb safely over the sharp edge of a razor blade. Propulsion comes from the waves of muscle contraction which pass along the

Continued on page 54

▲ The silvery trails of common, or garden, snails reveal their nocturnal wanderings on a house wall. See if you can spot one still heading for home!

▼ A snail will not rush off when you get close so take the opportunity of having a good look at how it moves. You will see waves of contractions flowing down its muscular foot as it glides along. This is a Roman snail.

length of the foot. You can watch this by placing a slug or snail on a window pane or inside a jam jar. Viewed through the glass, movement can be seen passing from tail to head along the foot, where the sole is being lifted up and shifted forwards before being replaced.

The movements are controlled by a very delicate sense of touch which enables the snail to position its foot very carefully, especially when it is climbing over a razor blade. Movement is assisted by slimy mucus from glands under the head that lay a slippery carpet on which the snail glides. This hardens into the silvery trail that shows where a slug or snail has travelled.

When they are not active, slugs and snails retreat under cover. Favourite places in the garden are in piles of flower pots, bricks or old sacks where they can crawl into a cool and moist shelter. In periods of dry weather slugs avoid drying up by contracting into a compact shape and coating themselves with mucus. Snails retire into their shells and seal the entrance with several layers of mucus which sets hard and waterproof.

▲ The shell of the white-lipped snail is very variable in colour and pattern. This picture shows six varieties.

▼ This is the large black slug which also occurs in red or orange varieties. The opening in its side is the breathing hole or spiracle. Slugs are molluscs in which the shell is very reduced or even absent.

WATCH YOUR TONGUE!

You can watch a snail feeding if you dab the inside of a jar with a thin layer of flour and water paste and allow it to dry. The mouth of a slug or snail is equipped with a horny tongue called a radula. It is set with hundreds of tiny teeth like a file and you can see it rasping away at the paste as the animal moves forward. Water snails can be seen feeding in a similar fashion as they crawl over the film of green slime that grows on the sides of an aquarium.

Damp weather will bring them out again and they set out in search of food. Most slugs and snails are vegetarians, preferring fungi and rotting leaves to the fresh leaves of lettuces and dahlias, but some are carnivores and attack earthworms or other slow-moving animals.

HOMING SNAILS

Mark a cluster of garden snails on the shell with nail varnish or typewriter correcting fluid, release them in the garden and you can make a daily check to see if they return to the same hiding place. Some slugs and snails are known to find their way home either by following trails back or by picking up the scent of their shelter. Not all species have a fixed home, however, and you may find that some settle in any convenient place.

Song thrush anvils

Snails which have not found a safe place during the day run the risk of being found by a song thrush. This bird will smash open their shells by hammering them against a stone or concrete path. In the country, where there is often a shortage of suitable stones, any that are available may be surrounded by piles of broken shells where the thrushes regularly have to take their catch.

The piles of shells have been used by scientists to study the efficiency of snail camouflage and the way species have evolved to fit their surroundings. Inspection of these 'anvils' shows that the shells which are most conspicuous against a particular background are those likely to be found as casualties.

Snails are an easy group of animals to study because species are identified by their shells, which are convenient to handle and preserve.

▶ A strong smell of garlic distinguishes the garlic glass snail. It has a glossy clear shell through which you can see its body.

◀ No colour on the lip of the shell usually identifies the white-lipped banded snail. It lives in shady damp places.

▼ The tree snail lives in crevices of trees, hardly ever on the ground. The shell has a pear-shaped, toothed opening.

▲ The grove, or dark-lipped, banded snail has a black-lipped shell. You can find it in yellow or pink varieties, with various patterns of bands.

▶ The biggest of our snails is the Roman snail, so called because it is often found near ancient Roman camps.

▲ That very common small grey slug that does so much damage in the garden is the netted slug.

▶ The great grey slug performs a mating 'dance' at night, shown by slime trails next morning.

Fledgling fliers

See also **Birds and their nests**
on page 32

Towards the end of spring you will notice the first broods of baby birds making their appearances. When a young bird can fly it is called a juvenile or fledgling. It still has a short tail and wing feathers, and traces of fluffy down among the body feathers. In most birds, the juvenile plumage is different from that of the adult.

Flying first time

Birds do not have to learn to fly; they know how to stay airborne by instinct. Those that are brought up in cramped nests, like house martins, do not even get a chance to exercise their wings, yet they can stay up and balance correctly as soon as they launch themselves into the air. Nevertheless, the flight of most juvenile birds is inexpert and wobbly at first, as you may be when you first ride a bicycle. They are not very good at steering or landing, and they need time to learn the fine control of flight.

Following the family

When the juveniles leave their nest they are still dependent on their parents to bring them food and protect them from enemies. For a while young tits and finches may live in the bushes and trees near the old nest, but they never return to it. They spend most of their time perching quietly among the foliage, or following their parents and uttering shrill calls.

Watch out for juvenile blackbirds, thrushes and starlings appearing on the lawn with their parents. The starlings are very active, following their parents and prodding the ground with their sharp bills to learn how to find worms and leatherjackets. Blackbirds and thrushes are restrained in their behaviour. They wait patiently under a bush or in a hedge for the parent to bring them food.

Going it alone

Families of tits stay together for two to three weeks, occasionally for longer. They do not move far from the nest for the first few days, but as the juveniles finish growing their wing and tail feathers and become more skilful fliers, they wander farther away and leave the old territory. The family eventually breaks up and the juveniles become independent. Families of long-tailed tits, however, stay together for the winter.

Compared with a short period of a week or two for young garden birds to mature, the adolescence of tawny owls is long, the young staying with their parents for as much as three months. Tawny owls nest early (see page 33) and the juveniles are on the

▼ This fluffy moorhen chick is not long out of the egg because it still has its egg-tooth (see page 32). Note the claws on its tiny wings, which it uses when scrambling among waterside plants or even underwater.

◄This appealing character is a fledgling mistle thrush perched on a stump beside red campion flowers. It has only just left the nest high up in a nearby tree. Its wings are short, its tail is not yet grown and it still has some baby down.

▼Both the fledgling jackdaw here and mistle thrush are calling for food. The bright colours inside the gape of the beak stimulate the parent bird to push food in.

wing in late May. Listen on summer nights for their wheezing calls from trees around the nesting place. The owls need a long period with their parents to learn and practise the skills of hunting.

HANDS OFF!
Every year, baby birds are 'rescued' unnecessarily. Thrushes and blackbirds are most often discovered. Someone finds one and notices that it does not fly away, so it is picked up and taken home in the mistaken belief that it has been abandoned by its parents. In fact the baby bird is simply waiting for its parents to bring it food and it does not fly away because it is relying on its camouflage for safety.

In theory it is easy to hand-rear baby birds, but in practice, they often die. If there is any doubt about the safety of a young bird you have found, retreat as far as you can and wait. In time you should see the parent bird return to feed its youngster.

Baby mammals

See also **Animals small and furry** on page 168
and **Seals at sea** on page 174

Like birds, baby mammals are born either quite helpless or almost ready for adult life. Those that are helpless remain in a nest until they have developed sufficiently to follow their parents. Examples are the young of many rodents: rats, mice, voles and squirrels; and carnivores: cats, foxes, weasels and badgers. The babies of hares, guinea pigs and hoofed animals are able to see, hear and walk as soon as they are born.

Rats, rats, rats
The eyes and ears of a baby rat are shut and its skin has only a sparse covering of hair. Like a human baby, all it does at this stage is sleep and feed, and of course call to its mother. But unlike the wail of the human baby, many baby rodents emit powerful ultrasonic squeaks. These calls are too high-pitched for our ears to detect, but the mother rodent responds as soon as she hears them.

A litter of rats – usually of between 4 and 12 in number – grows up very quickly. From the time they are newborn and helpless, it is less than three weeks before they are making short trips from the nest burrow with their mother. Soon afterwards the family breaks up and the young rats go their separate ways. At three months old they are adult and ready to breed. Meanwhile their parents are continuing to produce more litters, and so in theory the population could rise alarmingly. A single pair of rats could produce 2,000 offspring in one year. In practice plagues on this scale rarely happen because the majority of young rats do not get the chance to breed. Being inexperienced, they are easy prey for cats, stoats, foxes and owls. Young rats also have to compete with their elders for living space and for food. As the population expands, competition increases, and the young rats are driven away by older ones.

Alone but not abandoned
Roe deer kids are born from mid-May to mid-June. The doe retires to a thicket where she can give birth

▶This young grey squirrel is now well developed and has left the nest, but at birth it was blind and naked and quite helpless. A squirrel on the ground will rarely be far from a tree, up which it will scamper as soon as danger threatens.

◀Soon after birth the pony foal is able to stagger to its feet and will soon follow its mother to begin learning the skills of life.

▶It may look abandoned but this roe kid is just lying perfectly still until its mother returns. When she comes back and calls it, it will get up and run to her to feed, then lie down again while she browses.

without being disturbed. In contrast to the baby rat or squirrel, the kids, usually twins, are able to walk when only a few hours old but they are left in the thicket while their mother feeds. They lie among thick vegetation where their dappled coats make them difficult to see. If you find a roe kid it is easy to assume it has been abandoned by its parents and you may be tempted to take it home. You must resist the temptation, however, because hand-rearing a young deer is a very difficult task.

Learning from mother
The time spent with its mother is all-important for a baby mammal, less so for a baby bird. A bird's behaviour is mostly instinctive: it is born with the knowledge of how to behave properly. Mammals, on the other hand, have to learn most of the information they need for life. They do this mainly by trial and error and by constantly practising their skills.

▼Rats are always associated with man and his rubbish. Here a young common or brown rat peers out from inside his latest meal – a loaf of bread. Rats breed rapidly but many are killed by predators while still young, or die from the effects of overcrowding. A rat rarely lives longer than 18 months.

The ups and downs of the rabbit

Today rabbits are widespread, familiar animals. Their original home was Spain, Portugal and North Africa and they were introduced to Britain as domesticated animals for their meat and fur. Some rabbits escaped from the warrens in which they were kept and set up wild colonies but they did not spread far.

Fewer predators and more food

For several hundred years the rabbit remained a rare animal but a change came in the eighteenth century when the countryside altered for two reasons. Landowners became interested in rearing pheasants, partridges and other gamebirds and declared war on vermin: foxes, stoats, weasels, polecats, owls and hawks and any other predator that attacked game. The result was that the rabbits had fewer enemies to prune their numbers. At about the same time farmers started to grow fodder crops on which to feed their animals in winter. The crops also fed the rabbits, and many more were able to survive the winter and increase the numbers breeding in the following spring.

The changes in the countryside enabled the rabbits to increase at a very rapid rate. From being rather rare, they became the most abundant mammals. The original man-made warrens went out of use and many people made a living by trapping wild rabbits. Farmers also found that they had to kill rabbits to protect their crops.

Changing the countryside

The enormous numbers of rabbits had an effect on the countryside greater than that produced by any other wild animal. Over the centuries they have completely changed the appearance of some places, especially on poor, dry soils. Where rabbits infested a wood, they joined the mice and voles in destroying tree seedlings and preventing the replacement of dead trees. Where sheep and cattle were also browsing some woods were completely destroyed. Today, modern plantations have rabbit-proof fencing to protect newly planted trees until they are established. However, even well-grown trees can be killed in winter when rabbits gnaw the bark.

Rabbits are choosy in what they eat and they alter the composition of the vegetation as they feed. They avoid thorny, poisonous and tough plants, so that thistles, nettles and ragwort spring up where rabbits have eaten out other plants. When rabbits are extremely abundant they can completely destroy the grass and other perennial plants around their burrows both by grazing and by scattering earth. This enables annual plants to colonize the area. Heather cannot withstand grazing by rabbits and is gradually replaced by grass.

The myxomatosis factor

The effect of grazing by rabbits has been demonstrated in the years following 1953, when myxomatosis, a virus disease, almost destroyed the rabbit

---

GNAWING AND NIBBLING

The rabbit is a gnawing animal. It has chisel-shaped incisor teeth for neatly and cleanly snipping off all sorts of succulent plants. A feeding rabbit often bites a stem off close to the ground and sits back with it sticking out of its mouth. It then munches the stem in, chewing it with its ridged cheek teeth before swallowing it. Its chief food is grass and tender shoots, especially of gorse. Where rabbits are plentiful they will keep the grass trimmed like a lawn and prune gorse and heather into hedge-like shapes. When tender plants are all eaten down or have died back for the winter, the rabbit uses its incisors to strip bark off tree saplings or fallen twigs.

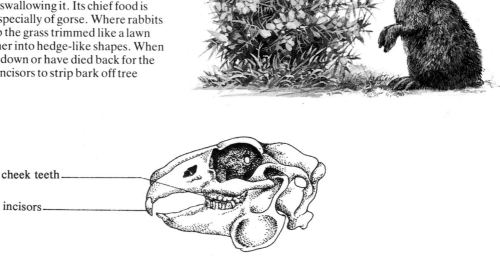

cheek teeth

incisors

HOW RABBITS CHANGE PLANT GROWTH

Where rabbits are still abundant, the vegetation demonstrates the effects of their intensive grazing. These photographs were taken on an island where normally a grass called red fescue grows freely. In the first picture grazing by rabbits has suppressed the grass and allowed the pink seaside flower, thrift, to flourish. In the second picture the grass has been protected inside a rabbit-proof enclosure and is now dominant.

population. Before this date there were an estimated 100 million rabbits in Britain; myxomatosis killed about 99 million. Rabbits disappeared entirely from some areas, and they became rare elsewhere. The huge burrow systems, called warrens after the original rabbit farms, were deserted. Farm output soared because crops were not destroyed and there was more grass for cattle and sheep.

The close-cropped, springy grass sward with its abundance of summer flowers disappeared under an invasion of taller, coarser herbs, previously kept out by the rabbits. This was followed by birch, hawthorn and other scrubby vegetation and, where left unchecked, woodland has eventually returned.

Long-term effects

More changes also took place in the animal community. When the rabbits disappeared, many predators starved or sought other food. Stoats and buzzards especially suffered. Voles may have suffered increased attentions from the predators but the longer vegetation gave them more food and shelter. As scrub vegetation developed, the bird life changed. Blackbirds, thrushes, wood pigeons and finches all benefited from the rabbits' decline by taking advantage of the new nesting sites and food supplies offered. The rabbit population has now recovered from the myxomatosis epidemic but outbreaks continue to keep the numbers in check.

▼Three rabbits bask in the spring sunshine outside their burrow on a cliff edge, high above the sea. Note the close cropped grass and the deadheads of last summer's thrift.

The quick brown fox

Foxes have been hunted for hundreds of years, yet they are still very common wild mammals. Some even live boldly in towns and cities, where they steal food from dustbins and bird tables, sunbathe on roofs and rear their cubs under garden sheds.

A litter is born

The fox's year starts in spring with the birth of the cubs, mainly in March. The litter of four or five cubs is born on the bare floor of an 'earth'. This may be a burrow dug by the female, the vixen, or taken over from badgers or rabbits, or it may be a drain, a hollow under a rock or in a tree, or any other sheltered place.

The cubs are blind and deaf at birth; their eyes open at eleven to fourteen days and their ears become erect at four weeks. At first the fur is short and almost black, but it turns to a chocolate colour in two weeks. For the first three weeks the vixen remains in the earth with the cubs but later she lies up nearby and visits to feed them. Sometimes she is helped by

'nannies' who bring food, guard and play with the cubs while she is away, or even take some of the cubs to another earth. The nannies are her sisters or daughters from a previous year. The father may join in bringing food and playing with the cubs at this time.

Growing, playing and learning

At four weeks old the cubs start to take pieces of solid meat brought by the vixen. The position of the earth now becomes obvious because the cubs are coming above ground and flattening the vegetation with their games and littering the area with fragments of fur, birds' wings and bones. These make excellent playthings and the cubs use this carefree stage of their lives to practise the skills they will need when they have grown up.

The day of the young cubs is divided between sleeping and enthusiastically investigating everything around them. Although they do not wander more than a few metres from the earth, they find plenty to satisfy their curiosity. Every object is examined closely with eyes, ears and nose, and finally tested to see if it is edible. These explorations are interrupted by boisterous rough and tumble games.

As a cub grows it loses its appealing puppy look. The woolly brown coat is gradually covered by longer reddish hair and the snub nose grows into a long snout. The vixen now leads her cubs on hunting expeditions, but she does not teach them how to hunt. The cubs know instinctively how to catch prey, although practice, at first when playing, is necessary for refining their skills.

By the end of the summer, at four months of age, the young foxes are ready to become independent.

DASHING AND JUMPING

Foxes use different techniques to catch rabbits and voles. Rabbits feed together in groups and many pairs of eyes keeping watch makes it difficult for the fox to approach unseen. The fox stalks as close as possible and then sprints into the group, hoping to cause alarm and confusion so that it can grab one individual before it reaches safety. Young and inexperienced or old and sick rabbits are most likely to be caught in this way.

Mice and voles are caught by the 'mouse jump'. The fox rises up in a rearing leap and bangs its nose and forepaws down on the victim at the same time.

◀ This vixen has had a litter of three cubs whose fur still shows the early dark colour.

▼ This older cub is snapping at insects as it plays in the long grass and is thus developing a hunting skill.

The males generally move away from the mother's home but the females often remain with her.

Food and the fox

One reason why foxes have survived so well in the countryside and in built-up areas is because they are very adaptable and will eat almost anything. The main prey is small mammals, such as rabbits, mice and voles. Foxes eat more field voles than bank voles and wood mice, probably because field voles live in pastures where they are easier to find and catch; bank voles live in undergrowth and wood mice live in underground burrows. The fox does not actually know which kind of small mammal it is hunting. It sees or hears something moving and pounces automatically.

Birds, worms and blackberries

Birds feature in a fox's diet in spring and summer when it needs extra food for its cubs. The birds are caught on their nests. Insects are a summer food when caterpillars are abundant, and beetles and grasshoppers are about in the pastures. Earthworms are another favourite. The step of a fox is light enough for it to sneak up on them as they lie on the surface (see page 51), especially on damp, still nights. In late summer and autumn, fruit and berries are appreciated. Foxes even go blackberrying; they reach up on their hindlegs and daintily pluck the berries from among the prickles.

Foxes have always been unpopular with farmers and landowners for killing lambs, poultry and game-birds. When helpless animals are crowded together, like hens in a hen house, they are easy prey for a predator and a fox may kill more than it can eat. Normally, however, a predator kills only enough to satisfy its hunger. Surplus food, like eggs from a pheasant's nest, is hidden.

Fox watch

A fox is most likely to be seen caught in the head-lights of a car at night. The light makes its eyes glow (see page 51) and it is easy to mistake it for a large cat until it bounds away and shows its bushy tail or brush. At other times foxes are elusive creatures, except for those in towns which can become tame enough to approach people for food. If they are not disturbed, foxes will sometimes come out to hunt during the day, when their pupils contract to slits, like those of a cat.

Foxes are more likely to give away their presence by signs. In winter snow, look out for fresh tracks of foxes to follow. These will often reveal the activity of the fox the previous night. A successful hunt will end with the scattered remains of the prey and the trail may eventually lead you to the earth. At intervals there will be a characteristic smell of 'fox' where it has marked its territory like a dog.

Summer: drowsy sounds in the sun

The weather can be very warm in May but summer does not truly start until June. After the changeable weather of spring, when snap frosts in May catch out gardeners by nipping tender new growth, the early summer is more settled. There are warm dry spells, and June is the sunniest month of the year and has fewest gales. July and August are high summer and have the very hottest days, but they can also be extremely wet.

In high summer there is sometimes a 'heat wave' which is followed by thunderstorms. The hot, dry weather is caused by air masses which come from North Africa. At the end of a heat wave the atmosphere feels 'heavy' because cooler moist air has flowed in from the Atlantic Ocean and mixed with the dry air. At first this makes the air very humid, then tall thunder clouds form and the weather breaks.

Midsummer's day is 21st June, the summer solstice, and the longest day of the year. The sun rises very early and reaches it highest point in the sky at midday. It seems strange that midsummer's day is at the beginning of summer and falls before the peak holiday season has started. But it takes time for the warm summer sun to heat the earth and give us high summer.

By the start of summer, plants have finished growing their leaves and the pale green of the fresh spring foliage has darkened. The plants are taking advantage of the long hours of sunlight to make food by photosynthesis and are storing it for later use. Some plants have finished flowering by now, but there are still plenty of flowers around to colour the countryside. When the petals have fallen, the plant gathers carbohydrates and other food materials in the remains of the flowers to make the seeds. This stored food will nurture the first growth of the next generation of plants.

Warm days and the masses of plant life bring out swarms of insects. Woodland clearings and the hedgerows are full of the drowsy buzzing of flies, which join the bees and butterflies at the flowers. From the undergrowth comes the scratchy, chirping songs of grasshoppers and crickets. These and other small animals, as well as plants, provide food for larger animals. Parent birds are busy collecting caterpillars and other insects for nest-bound young and, later, the fledglings will learn how to find their own food.

In lakes, ponds and streams the water warms up more slowly than the air but, underwater, life goes on, too. In late summer, water plants grow in profusion and there is much activity beneath the surface.

Climbing and scrambling

See also **Home in the hedgerow**
on page 140

Nearly all plants must have sunlight to survive. On page 24 you saw how plants find it difficult to live in the gloom of the woodland floor under the dense canopy of trees. Trees dominate the wood by growing solid wooden trunks to support their foliage high above the ground.

A trunk takes time and energy to grow, but certain plants have found an alternative to growing their own trunk. The climbing plants make use of the trunks of trees to hoist themselves towards the light. In this way the climbers are cheating because they are using the tree trunks for support and do not need to grow strong stems of their own. They can use their energy to grow very rapidly, and their slender stems soon reach the open where their leaves can spread and absorb the sunlight. The flowers of climbing plants are raised to a conspicuous position, too, for easier pollination and the seeds are well placed for dispersal (see page 166).

The most spectacular climbing plants grow in tropical forests. There the forest floor is bare of plants because the giant trees have cut out all the sunlight but there is a tangle of lianas and other climbers threading their way towards the sky, just right for Tarzan to swing from!

Twisting and twining

You don't need to go to a jungle to find all sorts of climbers; they are growing in the garden and countryside. Honeysuckle is a vigorous climber which can smother the tops of tall trees. It may have woody stems as thick as ropes.

Honeysuckle climbs by twining around neighbouring plants, or even around its own stems to make a sort of rope to bridge a gap. It always curls in a clockwise direction. The growing tip of the stem hangs over and turns in a wide circle until it finds something to coil around. Then the tiny leaves near the tip grow to their full size. If the plant does not find a support, it will probably die.

WHICH WAY DOES IT TWIST?
Look carefully at climbers in the hedgerow and note which way they spiral as they climb. Black bryony and bindweed are common twining climbers. Black bryony grows clockwise but bindweed twists in an anticlockwise direction. Woody nightshade, or bittersweet, twines in either direction.

Grappling and grasping
There are other plants which scramble rather than climb. As young plants, they grow upwards until they cannot support their own weight and flop over. Then the shoot turns upwards and grows up again. The process may be repeated several times until a support is found.

Scrambling plants do not grow spirally like honeysuckle or black bryony, but they are armed with spines or thorns for holding on rather like the way a mountaineer uses an ice-axe and crampons. You have probably already found out the painful way how well the prickly thorns of brambles and dog roses, or briars, can grasp and cling.

Dog roses have strong enough stems to grow upright by themselves but they quickly take advantage of support when they grow up through hedges. Brambles also grow by themselves and form a prickly knee-high carpet over the woodland floor. Long shoots grow out and scramble over other shrubs, grappling with their thorns, or sink down under their own weight to take root and spread the carpet.

A less obvious scrambler on the woodland floor and in the hedgebottom is goosegrass, or cleavers. Its leaves and stems feel sticky because of the small, hooked prickles which cover them.

◄Brambles may use their thorns like grappling irons to scramble over other plants and themselves. The flowers are pollinated by bees and other insects which feed on nectar.

►Honeysuckle twines in a clockwise spiral around any woody stem it can reach. As it climbs, it may even bind one of its own flower heads as it grows towards the light.

CLIMBING BY TENDRILS

Specialized climbers, such as white bryony, have tendrils which are slender stalks for securing the plant. In this photograph you can see a tendril uncoiling like a watch spring. It will then whip about with a circular motion, in the same way as a honeysuckle stem, until it meets a support around which it will hook. As the plant sways in the breeze, the tendril is rubbed against the support. This stimulates the tendril to grow faster on its other side so that it curls and grips firmly. The rest of the tendril then shortens by coiling up like a telephone receiver cable. In this way the tendril is less likely to be dragged away from its support in a strong wind while it is still soft and pliable. Once in place, the tendril grows thicker and rigid to make a permanent anchor. The plant may scramble many metres up a hedgerow, held by the tendrils.

Life in an oak tree

See also **The inside story of a wood** on page 26

▲A magnificent pedunculate oak standing on its own may be all that is now left to remind us that the country was once covered with vast areas of oak forest teeming with wildlife.

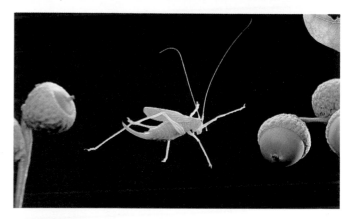

Huge stretches of oak forest once covered the land but now only a few patches of oak woodland are left. The trees have been cut or burnt to make way for farmland or to provide charcoal for iron foundries. Oak timber was extremely valuable for building houses and ships. It took 3,000 large oaks to build a man o' war in Nelson's navy. The bark yielded tannic acid for tanning leather and the acorns were fed to pigs.

Oakwoods must be preserved to conserve wildlife. Many plants can grow under oaks because their leaf canopy is not dense, so oakwoods provide food and shelter for a variety of animals.

Caterpillar plagues feed the birds

More species of insects feed on oaks than on any other kinds of tree. More than 100 species of moth have caterpillars that feed on oak leaves. Some become so numerous that they strip the trees of all their leaves. Look at the rings on an oak stump (see page 27). You will see that some rings are narrow. This wood was formed when caterpillars stripped the tree so that there was little growth that year. The caterpillars hatch just before the leaves appear so that they are ready to eat them as they are growing. It is mainly the caterpillars of three kinds of moth that plague oak trees. These are the oak tortrix, the mottled umber and the winter moth. Oak tortrix adults appear in July but the two others are adult in autumn and winter. Their females are wingless and

selves by camouflage, by living in a rolled-up leaf, or by dropping off the leaf on the end of a silken thread if disturbed.

Leaves, acorns and galls

Beetles are also abundant in oak trees. The grubs of Europe's largest beetle, the stag beetle, live in old stumps. Adult cockchafers, which fly on fine summer evenings, feed on oak leaves. Weevils are beetles with long, slender snouts. The acorn weevil lays a single egg in an acorn; the larva eats the flesh inside and burrows out when the acorn falls. It then buries itself in the soil. Another type of weevil rolls up part of an oak leaf into a tube and lays an egg inside. The leaf is cut through, except for the midrib. When the larva hatches out it eats away inside the hanging, rolled part of the leaf. The tube eventually withers and falls off, the weevil larva crawls out and pupates under the leaf litter.

Look closely at oak leaves and you will find caterpillars and weevil grubs rolled up in them. You can also find galls (see page 136) which may be the 'homes' of other insects, or perhaps have been caused by a fungus.

climb the trunks of trees to lay their eggs on the leaves.

Many woodland birds nest so that their young are being fed when there are plenty of caterpillars available, but this seems to have little effect on the number of caterpillars. The caterpillars protect them-

▲ ◀ A lesser-spotted woodpecker fledgling in an oak. Oak trees provide nest sites for many sorts of birds, while many more feed among the foliage on caterpillars and other insects in summer, and on the acorns in autumn.

◀ An oak bush cricket leaps from acorn to acorn. These bush crickets are active at night and spend the day well camouflaged beneath oak leaves.

◀ A gall wasp on an oak marble gall which was its home and food supply throughout its early life. It has just emerged through the neat, round hole.

▶ A female purple hairstreak butterfly basks in the sunshine on an oak shoot. Its caterpillars feed on oak leaves; the adults fly around the tops of oak trees in July and August.

Dead but not lifeless

See also **Bark to cover and protect**
on page 196

An oak tree usually lives for at least 250 years. If it is coppiced or pollarded (see page 27), it may survive for twice as long. Branches are blown off by storms, fungi (see page 164) get into the stumps so that the wood rots and hollows form. Eventually, the central, dead timber of the trunk rots away and the tree becomes hollow. So long as the bark remains intact, the tree will live and sprout new leaves each spring. Eventually the oak falls and decays. The nutrients which the tree's roots took from the soil are returned to nourish other plants.

Homes in hollows and holes
During the oak tree's slow death it becomes home for nearly as many animals as lived in it while it was growing. Small holes, which mark where a branch has come off, are nesting places for tits, redstarts, tree sparrows and nuthatches. Nuthatches make the entrance hole smaller by plastering its rim with mud. Tits may reveal their presence by hissing when they are disturbed, but the best way of finding nests in holes is to watch for birds carrying food in their beaks, and follow them as they fly back to feed their

young. Do not disturb the nest as you watch the birds come and go. Be very careful if you peer into a large hole. It could hold an owl's nest and an angry owl is very dangerous.

The hollow could also hold the nest of bees or wasps (see pages 96 and 150) or a colony of bats (see page 52). Bats can be seen flying out at dusk. They emerge at about the same time each evening and you may hear them squeaking before they emerge.

The boring life of a beetle grub
Pull off a section of bark from a dead oak and underneath you will find patterns of tunnels made by the grubs or larvae of beetles. You might see the yellowish, flattened grubs of the cardinal beetle that spends its larval life boring into rotten wood. The stag beetle, Europe's largest beetle, also lays its eggs in old stumps, usually of oak. The grubs spend several years feeding on the rotten wood (see page 29).

Woodpeckers find dead oaks particularly attractive. The loud hammering sound tells you a woodpecker is chiselling out beetle grubs from their tunnels in the old and rotten timber.

▲ A treecreeper's nest behind loose bark curling from a dead oak trunk. The young birds are nearly ready to fly and have scrambled out of the nest to meet their parent bringing food.

LIFE IN A LOG
The fallen trunk or branch of a tree supports its own group of plants and animals. The species you will find on a log depend on how long it has been in place. Many of the animals are the same as those living on a wall (see page 46); they hide in crevices by day and come out at night.

Use a torch to look for them after dark or lift the bark to expose them, but remember, this will destroy their hiding places unless you are careful. Woodlice will be the most common animals but there will also be centipedes and millipedes, slugs and worms, spiders, beetles and earwigs.

If a log is small enough, you can move it carefully and look underneath. There will be more centipedes and slugs nestling on the bare earth, as well as small earthworm tunnels. Moles often tunnel under logs (or planks or sheets of corrugated iron left on the ground) so they can catch the small animals living there. If you are very lucky you might find a toad or a grass snake sheltering in a cavity in the soil, or a vole in its nest of grass. The vole will rush to safety so you have to lift the log sharply to catch a glimpse of it.

►The great spotted woodpecker hops up tree trunks searching for insects and their larvae which it drills out of the wood with chisel-like bill.

▲Only active in bright sunshine the parasitic ruby-tailed wasp lays its eggs in other wasps' nests.

►The tiny pipistrelle bat squeezes into a crack beneath loose bark and hangs up there to roost.

▲▼Both the poisonous-clawed centipede (*above*) and the harmless silk-producing millipede (*below*) hide under dead bark or logs by day and emerge to feed at night.

▼By day the common earwig hides away in any crevice under loose bark. At night it feeds on other insects and fruit.

▲Larvae of the eyed longhorn beetle mine galleries under the bark of dead trees.

▼Female cardinal beetles lay their eggs in cracks in dead oak bark. They hatch into flattened yellowish larvae.

▼Woodlice dry out easily, so congregate in damp places by day. Hundreds may be found together under loose barks.

◄The keeled slug has a tough shell-less body which contracts to a blob when it is disturbed.

Butterfly watching

See also **A butterfly year** on page 104

▲ A female large white butterfly sucking nectar from a field scabious flower. The male is similar but has no black spots on the forewings.

We all enjoy seeing brightly coloured butterflies flying past on some secret errand, or busily feeding on flowers. Do you ever wonder what these beautiful insects might be doing? With a little practice, you will soon be able to identify the different species and discover that butterfly watching can be as fascinating as birdwatching.

An adult butterfly usually lives for only two or three weeks unless it spends the winter in hibernation. During their active lifetime, butterflies visit flowers to sip nectar as fuel to power their flight. Then the male butterfly must find a mate either by actively patrolling to look for her or by waiting on a perch for her to fly by.

Patrollers and perchers
The patrollers fly long distances, hoping to find a female. The male orange tip or brimstone, for instance, flies more than a kilometre checking every other pale-coloured butterfly he finds to see if it is a female of his species. The male grayling is a patroller too. It is difficult to follow the behaviour of patrolling males because they move quite fast, especially if a breeze is blowing them along.

The perchers are easier to watch because they simply wait in one place for the females to pass by.

Peacocks and small tortoiseshells are perchers. The male spends the morning feeding and basking and sets up his territory in the afternoon. He prefers a sunny area with a hedge, a wall or a row of trees behind it. The peacock also likes to have stinging nettles growing nearby, where the female can lay her eggs. Female butterflies tend to fly along a wall or line of plants so the males will be ideally placed to fly up and intercept them. After mating the female tortoiseshell leaves her mate to find some nettles.

The speckled wood male holds a territory in a patch of sunlight on the woodland floor. Like the other perchers, he defends his patch against males of his own kind. As soon as an intruder approaches, the resident flies up and the two circle each other, getting higher and higher as each tries to fly above the other. Eventually the intruder beats a retreat and the owner returns to his perch.

The male wears the scent
You will easily be able to distinguish males and females of several butterfly species. A male butterfly

▼A pair of mating dark green fritillaries hangs from a thistle flower revealing the greenish undersides from which they get their name.

probably also recognizes a mate by her appearance. He will woo her, however, with scent from special scales on his wings. The pattern of courtship varies from species to species. It may be accomplished quickly or it may be prolonged with the male fluttering around the female.

After mating, the female searches for the right kind of plant on which to lay her eggs. The eggs are usually glued in place. Common blue and meadow brown butterflies place them singly, whereas the small tortoiseshell and large white lay clusters.

MAKE A BUTTERFLY CHART

Not all butterflies can be seen at the same time of the year. Brimstones, small tortoiseshells and commas appear in spring, but meadow browns are not on the wing until June, and graylings and ringlets may not be seen until well into July.

Make up a chart and mark in the butterflies you see each day. This will show you the flight time of each species. The early butterflies will have spent the winter hibernating as adults. After laying their eggs, they disappear but from the eggs, comes a second generation of butterflies later in the year. Keep a record of the weather, too; cold, damp spells will usually explain gaps in the chart, although some species fly even on dull or rainy days.

If you want to learn more about butterfly habits, take a regular 'butterfly walk'. Find a suitable woodland ride, lane, park or garden, and on the walk note the butterflies you see once a week. Count the butterflies for 5 metres on each side and ahead of you. (The exact distance does not matter but it must be the same each time.) If you make counts more often, you will see the effects of the weather, too. Counts in different places will reveal the kinds of habitat each species prefers. Late morning and early afternoon are the best times, but try some hourly counts to show the pattern of daily activity. If you follow a butterfly in the late afternoon you may trace it to its roost under a leaf or on a grass stem.

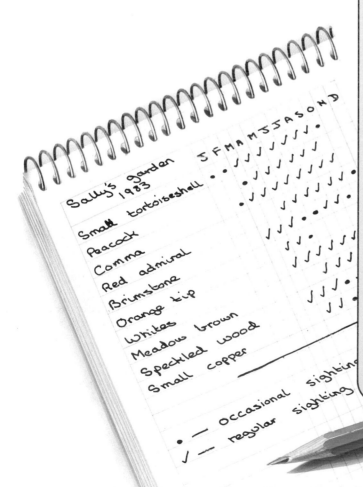

Moths by moonlight

Moths and butterflies belong to the group of insects called the Lepidoptera. This name means 'scale winged', and the wings of these insects are covered with tiny scales that overlap like the tiles on a roof. Most moths are small and dull but a few are large and spectacular.

Butterfly or moth?
It is nearly always easy to tell if an insect is a moth or a butterfly, but there is no single character that distinguishes between them. Butterflies fly by day and most moths fly by night, but you might see a day-flying moth. Most butterflies sit with their wings pressed together vertically over their backs, and moths sit with their wings fanned horizontally. There are exceptions, however, and to be sure you must look at the antennae. Butterfly antennae are like slender wires with a knob at the tip, whereas most moths have feathery antennae. Only burnet moths have knobbed antennae. They fly by day, too, and are brightly coloured but they are easily identified by their narrow crimson-spotted wings and lazy, buzzing flight. Similarly, it is possible to mistake skipper butterflies for moths, because they are dull coloured, have slender-knobbed antennae and sit with their wings held in a rather moth-like way.

Following the scent
The males of many types of moth have more elaborate, feathery antennae than the females. When ready to mate, the female moth gives off a scent, called a pheromone, which will stimulate the male to search for her and then guide him towards her. When the male moth first detects the female's scent with his antennae, he takes off and flies upwind. Eventually he flies close enough to her to be able to steer towards her.

Some female moths have no wings. The female winter moth, for example, looks rather like a spider with six legs instead of eight. These females do not need to fly because the males come looking for them. They climb the trunks of oak trees to lay their eggs on the leaves (see page 68).

WHY DO MOTHS FLY INTO LIGHTS?
Moths navigate using the light from the moon. The moon is almost 385,000 kilometres from earth so that its rays of reflected light are near parallel. The moths steer by flying at a constant angle to the light rays, in much the same way as a sailor steers by the sun or moon.

You have probably noticed that on summer nights moths gather around outside light bulbs. The moths fly in spirals around the light until they crash into it (or perish in the flame of a candle). Why is this? The rays of light from an artificial source spread out like the spokes of a wheel so a moth flying at a constant angle to them is continually turning inwards. Moths fly into lights because their behaviour evolved millions of years before light bulbs were invented.

▶ Unlike most moths the six-spot burnet flies by day. It buzzes round downland flowers such as this creeping thistle. Its bright colours warn birds that it is bitter-tasting and poisonous.

LEAVE ME ALONE!
During the day, the night-flying moths are difficult to find because they are so well camouflaged (see page 44). Some, if they are discovered by accident, may try to defend themselves by suddenly spreading their wings and displaying brightly coloured underwings which had been hidden under the camouflaged forewings. The flashing bright colours of the garden tiger moth shown here are a warning to a bird that the moth is poisonous.

The ragged-leaved ragwort

You must have noticed ragwort. It is one of the most conspicuous plants growing on grassland. It is common on chalk downs, on sea coasts where sand dunes have become grass covered, by roadsides and in pastures. It grows up to 1 metre high and, from June to November, the long stems are topped with clusters of yellow, daisy-like flowers. The name comes from the ragged appearance of its leaves.

Bright but poisonous

Ragwort is very conspicuous partly because the plants growing around it are often very short. Ragwort is poisonous and is not usually eaten by grazing animals such as horses and rabbits, although sheep eat it without apparent harm. It is a nuisance to farmers, not only because it is a danger to animals but also because it prevents edible plants from growing. The poison it contains is a substance called an alkaloid. It helps blood to clot, and ragwort has been used in herbal medicines. You must never eat it because it can have dangerous effects.

Some fields are almost choked with ragwort although it is illegal to allow it to grow. There are five injurious weeds which by law should not be allowed to spread. These are two species of dock, two species of thistle, and ragwort.

Although ragwort may not be popular with farmers and their animals, ragwort flowers are attractive to insects which come to feed on the pollen and nectar. Butterflies, flies and beetles gather in large numbers so that you can watch them closely.

HAS IT REACHED YOU YET?

The Oxford ragwort, despite its name, is a native plant of southern Italy. It has spread over a remarkably wide area of Britain because of its wind-blown seeds.

More than 200 years ago a specimen plant was taken from Sicily and grown in the Botanic Garden in Oxford. In 1794 it was recorded on walls outside the Botanic Garden and it reached London 70 years later, by spreading along the railway line. Less than 30 years ago Oxford ragwort started to appear all over Britain.

No one knows why Oxford ragwort began to spread rapidly after such a long time. Next time you see some ragwort, have a close look at the plants. Oxford ragwort has pointed lobes on each leaf, whereas those of common ragwort are rounded.

Parachute seeds on the wind

After pollination, ragwort flowers develop into seed heads. The petals fall off, the green base of the flower opens and a 'powder puff' of fine grey hairs unfolds. The hairs make up the parachutes which will transport the seeds when they are ripe. Each seed has about 50 hairs attached to its tip and, when the seed is released, the hairs spread to make a flat parachute that will carry it away on the wind.

The parachutes of ragwort, like those of dandelions, the willowherbs and colt's-foot, help to disperse the seeds over wide areas. On dry, windy days the hairs spread out, the air is filled with clouds of 'down', and the seeds are carried considerable distances. Rain or moist air cause the parachutes to close so that the seeds drop to the ground and are washed into cracks in the soil.

It is difficult for farmers to keep their fields free from ragwort because the seeds are carried on the wind from plants on uncultivated ground nearby.

▼ Rabbits eat most plants to the ground but they will not touch ragwort because its poisonous juices make it taste nasty.

CINNABARS PASS THE POISON

Ragwort has one serious enemy. It is the cinnabar moth caterpillar whose chief food plant is ragwort although it will also eat groundsel and colt's-foot. When the caterpillars are abundant, ragwort leaves are stripped down to the veins.

Whereas other animals avoid eating ragwort because of the poisonous alkaloid, cinnabar caterpillars turn the poison to their advantage. They store it in their bodies to make them distasteful to birds. The bold black and yellow stripes, which make cinnabar caterpillars so easy to find are, therefore, not a disadvantage. Instead of relying on camouflage for safety, the caterpillars are conspicuously coloured as a warning to birds that they have a nasty taste. Once a bird has bitten a cinnabar caterpillar, it will never touch another. Warning coloration is also used by the adult cinnabar moth, which shows off its shining scarlet wings as a signal that it, too, has ragwort alkaloids in its body.

Caterpillars: machines for eating

See also **A butterfly year** on page 104

From the time it hatches from an egg, perfectly formed, to the time it turns into a pupa, a caterpillar spends almost all its time eating. The food is digested and stored in the body until the energy is needed to convert the caterpillar into a butterfly or moth within the pupa. As the food accumulates, the caterpillar becomes too big for its skin. At intervals the old skin splits and the caterpillar climbs out. A soft new larger skin has already grown under the hard old one so that the caterpillar can grow.

Watch a caterpillar as it works its way along the edge of a leaf. Like a combine harvester, it moves forward fast enough to ensure that there is always food within reach of the constantly working jaws.

Legs for crawling and looping

The head is the only rigid part of the caterpillar's body. It needs a 'skull' on which to anchor the jaw muscles. The body is a soft tube composed of 13 segments. It is supported by three pairs of true legs at the front end which are equivalent to the legs of the adult insect, and a variable number of prolegs. Most caterpillars have five pairs of prolegs but some have only two pairs. Caterpillars with two pairs are called 'loopers' because they walk by bending the body into a vertical loop, anchoring the prolegs, releasing the true legs and straightening out again.

What's on the caterpillar's menu?

Each adult insect lays its eggs only on the correct food plant for its own caterpillars. So, if you are planning to conserve butterflies and moths, growing flowers to provide nectar is not the only thing to do for them. You must also provide the right food plants for their caterpillars.

Stinging nettles are useful food plants. They are eaten by the caterpillars of small tortoiseshells, peacocks, commas and red admirals. Those of the large tortoiseshell prefer elm but they also feed on sallows, apples, pears and cherries. Some of the fritillaries choose violets, and the blues favour clovers and vetches. The elephant hawk moth is to be found mainly on willowherb, but also on fuchsias, evening primrose and Virginia creeper.

Hiding and bluffing

Caterpillars are not always easy to find; many are well camouflaged. Their colours match the background of their food plants. Some, like the caterpillar of the peppered moth (see page 44), disguise

▲ This puss moth caterpillar has just crawled out of its old skin which had become too small for it. You can see the whip-like 'tails' which are standing up to make the larva seem fierce.

▼ On meeting a toad, this elephant hawk moth caterpillar jerks in its head and displays its bold eyespots. The toad reacts as if confronted by a snake and puffs up its body (see page 80).

▼ Caterpillars of the large white butterfly rest conspicuously on nasturtium leaves between feeds. They are protected by their warning coloration and evil smell.

▶ Lackey moth caterpillars protect themselves by clustering tightly together and twitching in unison. They build silk tents which festoon hedgerows looking like pieces of polythene.

themselves as twigs by posing with rigid bodies stretched at an angle to the twig on which they are resting. Camouflage is needed so that some individuals will escape the attentions of tits, robins and other birds which feed their young on caterpillars.

There are other ways that caterpillars may defend themselves. Some, such as those of the silver-washed fritillary, fall off the leaf and lie curled up if they are disturbed. Others, like the cinnabar caterpillar (see page 77), display warning colours. The caterpillar of the large white or 'cabbage white' butterfly is unusual because, when it is disturbed, it gives off a bright green fluid with an evil smell.

The caterpillar of the elephant hawk moth frightens away its enemies. When disturbed, the caterpillar draws in the front part of its body so that two large spots on its flanks look like huge staring eyes.

Some caterpillars live under a silken web for protection. The painted lady and red admiral larvae spin individual webs, but a brood of small tortoiseshells lives under a communal tent on nettle leaves.

SHAKE THEM DOWN!
Place a white sheet under a branch of a bush or tree and give it a good shake. You will be surprised at how many caterpillars will fall on to the sheet, although you previously couldn't see any. Please replace them.

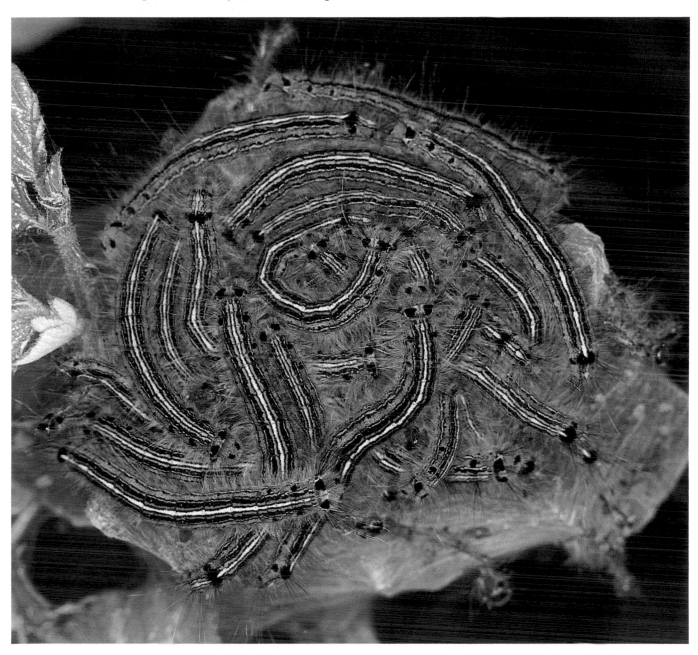

Tricks to stay alive

▲ The slow-crawling toad has little chance of evading a hungry grass snake by running away. With this inflated, stiff-legged posture it attempts to make itself too large for the snake to swallow. There is another example of this on page 78.

S nakes are among a toad's main enemies. The poison glands of a toad deter many animals from trying to eat it (see page 18), but it is still attacked by grass snakes and adders.

The toad has little chance of escape by crawling and its defence is to make it as difficult as it can for the snake to deal with it. It inflates its body and straightens its legs so that the snake, which can only swallow its prey whole, cannot get its mouth around the toad.

Confuse a toad

The toad is stimulated to take up its defence posture by the sight of the snake and the feel of the snake's jaws attempting to seize it. Sometimes it makes a mistake though. If it is confronted by a mass of writhing earthworms, it inflates itself but, as individual worms crawl away, the toad realizes its mistake, deflates and devours them. On the other hand, a baby grass snake may be mistaken for a worm and

► When all else fails, a threatened grass snake will pretend to be dead, rolling over with open mouth and lolling tongue. As you can see, it is a very convincing, if puzzling display.

See also **Now you see me, now you don't** on page 44

attacked, only to be dropped as the toad tastes it and quickly inflates itself.

No deterrent is totally effective, however. The hedgehog's coat of spines is sometimes not sufficient to prevent it from being eaten by foxes and badgers, and many toads are eaten by herons and crows.

Pretending to be dead
The grass snake has several lines of defence. If it cannot escape, it will strike as if it were venomous, but with its mouth shut. At the same time, it inflates its body and hisses, so that it appears very fierce. This is mainly bluff because although the snake will bite, its teeth are very small and hardly ever draw blood. Its next defence is to emit a foul stench. Finally, the grass snake feigns death. It coils on to its back with its mouth open and tongue hanging out.

A young edible crab may try to defend itself with its claws but it may also roll on to its back and pull in its claws and legs to look dead. Similarly, spiders fall off their webs and lie with their legs drawn in.

A leg for a life
Like other crabs, the edible crab can save itself by sacrificing one of its legs. When the leg is seized, it snaps near the base where there is a special breaking place. Muscles pull on each side in opposite directions to break the hard shell. The stump heals very quickly so that little blood is lost. At the next moult the lost leg will be replaced, perhaps smaller, but it will regain its full size after a second moult. Lizards throw off their tails in the same way. The predator's attention is held by the tail which continues to wriggle while the lizard runs away to shelter. The lizard will gradually regrow its tail but it is never as long as the original.

Animals such as adders, bees, wasps and ants are able to defend themselves by counter-attacking and harming their attackers. Yet for these venomous animals, as well as for those with the tricks of defence described here, the best form of defence is always to retreat. The defence may not work, and even the victim of an adder's bite might have time to kill the biter before the poison takes effect.

Beware the adder
The only poisonous snake living in Britain and much of northern Europe is the adder although in southern Europe you may come across some poisonous relatives of the adder. The adder's bite is rarely serious, unless the victim is very young, very old or ill. If disturbed, the snake will be more frightened than you and will try to get away. It will only try to bite if it is teased or trodden on.

From February onwards, depending on the

▲ An adder and a hedgehog are wary of one another when they meet. The hedgehog could attack and eat the adder in spite of its venom. It is not immune to the poison, but its dense coat of prickles prevents the fangs from piercing the skin.

weather, adders emerge from their underground winter quarters and lie on banks and logs to bask in the sun. It is then quite easy to creep up to them for a closer look. There is no need to whisper because, although snakes have ears, they cannot hear sounds. They do hear vibrations in the ground, however, so tread lightly and you will get close enough to see the characteristic diamond pattern down the back, and the V or X mark on the head.

A tongue to taste the air
You should also see the snake's forked tongue flicking in and out. An adder picks up particles of scent on its tongue and transfers them into sense organs of smell in the roof of the mouth. It uses its sense of smell to find prey by following its trail. Adders eat small animals such as slugs, worms, insects, frogs, lizards and voles.

DON'T PANIC!
If someone does get bitten by an adder, the victim should lie down and keep calm. Exercise and worry only help to spread the poison. Never attempt to suck the wound but wash it to remove any poison on the surface. Obtain medical aid as soon as possible.

Beside the seaside

See also **Where fresh water meets salty** on page 172 and **Beachcombing** on page 176

The shore is the strip of land between high and low tide marks which is covered and uncovered by the sea twice each day. The variety of animal life you will find depends on the type of shore which may be a sandy beach, a jumble of rocks or, usually near an estuary, a flat expanse of mud.

Not too wet and not too dry
Some inhabitants of the shore are able to live underwater as well as survive drying out, but there are others which cannot afford to be left stranded. On the other hand there are land animals which find food on the shore but which cannot withstand total immersion.

The sandhopper provides a good example of the double life that seashore animals live. It is a crustacean, belonging to the same group of animals as woodlice, shrimps and crabs. It has a sideways flattened body and different kinds of legs for walking

▲ Sandhoppers can swim well in the sea but are easy prey for fish, so when the tides comes in they march in procession ahead of the water.

and for swimming. If a sandhopper wanders too far up the beach, it will dry out or lose too much salt from its body and die. Alternatively, if it is submerged too long it will drown.

Sandhoppers feed on rotten seaweed, or any other dead plant or animal cast up on the shore, so they perform a useful service in cleaning the beaches. To find sandhoppers, all you have to do is lift a piece of seaweed and swarms will leap in all directions. They are nocturnal, spending the day under cover and coming to the surface at night. If you walk along the beach in the evening you will see clouds of sandhoppers leaping along the water's edge.

The seaweed fly
Sandhoppers may escape notice but seaweed flies can be a nuisance when they settle on your body or on your food. They are only 4 millimetres long but they gather in enormous swarms to feed and lay their eggs on rotten seaweed. Watch out for them migrating along the shore, flying in thick streams downwind, about 30 or 40 centimetres above the ground. Unlike most insects, seaweed flies do not get trapped in water. They have greasy, water-repellent bodies and bob to the surface if they are caught by a wave.

Sandhoppers and seaweed flies attract a number of animals that feed on them. Rock pipits, house martins and sanderlings are among the birds that take advantage of the masses of tiny prey. Sanderlings are grey-brown and white wading birds that scamper along the water's edge.

Other waders, such as dunlins and knots, probe for animals living under the surface of the sand or mud. Gulls and crows forage for anything, living or dead, which they can eat. If you see a gull 'dancing' in shallow puddles on the beach, watch it carefully. It takes several rapid steps on one spot, then jumps back and seizes any small animals which have been disturbed by its 'dance'.

Food on the tide
From the seaward side of the shore, sandhoppers, flies and other tiny forms of life attract other animals which swim in as the tide advances up the beach. For most of the month the piles of rotting seaweed at the top of the beach are beyond the reach of the waves even at high tide. But, once a month, at the highest spring tides, the waves reach the seaweed and wash out the fly maggots.

▶ A seaweed fly (*inset*) has settled on a mass of its larvae, exposed when rotting seaweed was turned over.

▶ The pale upper lips of grey mullet can be seen here as the big fishes swim in on the high tide and suck floating seaweed fly maggots off the surface.

WHAT IS A TIDE?

All objects are attracted towards one another by gravitational forces. The moon is quite close to the earth and pulls the waters on the near side of the earth towards itself to cause a 'bulge'. But the moon pulls the earth, too, leaving behind another bulge of ocean on the far side of the earth. There are two tides a day because the earth spins on its axis once a day. Each cycle of high and low tides lasts about 12½ hours, so high and low water are an hour later each day.

The sun is very far from the earth but because it is very big it also has a gravitational pull. When the sun and moon are in line, their combined pull causes the extra high and extra low spring tides. But when, a week later, the sun and moon are at right angles, their forces do not work together and the result is neap tides with the smallest range.

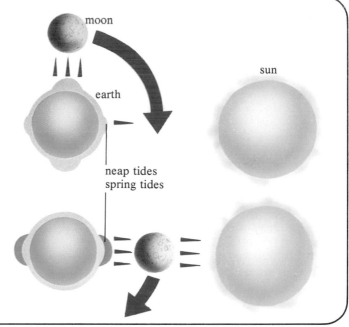

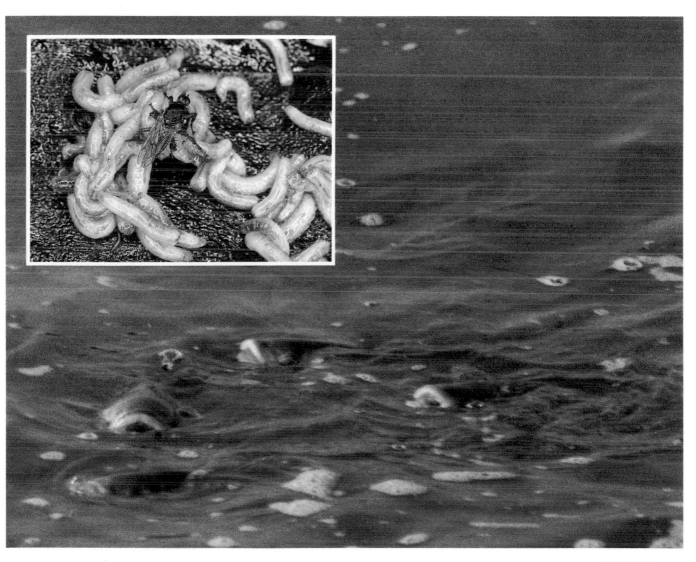

Life on the shore

As you walk down any rocky shore at low tide you will notice that different kinds of seaweeds and animals occur in definite bands or zones from the top of the shore to the bottom. Furthermore, the pattern of zones is roughly the same on every shore that you visit. Each species of plant or animal can live only in a particular zone. This is determined by its ability to survive out of water and so withstand drying up.

There are three main zones and they show most clearly on steep shores with a flat rocky surface. At the top of the shore there is the rather barren splash or supralittoral zone, which is only wetted by spray in stormy weather and is otherwise dry. Here there may be a thin covering of black and orange lichens. A few animals, such as the sea slater, which looks like a very large woodlouse, may live in this zone.

Lower down, over the main part of the shore, the littoral zone is covered and uncovered by each tide. This is the most interesting part of the shore. Finally, at the bottom of the shore there is the sublittoral zone which is never uncovered.

▼ Small periwinkles live in crevices among rocks in the splash zone at the top of the shore. They feed on lichens which they scrape from the rocks. Their dry shells are pale, but when damped by spray turn brown or blue-black.

PATTERNS OF PERIWINKLES

Periwinkles and seaweeds show very clearly how the amount of exposure to the air they receive affects where they are found on the shore. The small periwinkle (1) lives in the splash zone and can survive out of water for weeks by closing the entrance to its shell with a lid, or operculum. Other periwinkles can close their shells, too, but they need to breathe more often and they lose water each time they open up. The rough periwinkle (2) lives just below the splash zone. It copes with drying out better than the flat periwinkle (3) and the common or edible periwinkle (4) which live farther down the shore. The flat periwinkle keeps moist by hiding under clumps of seaweeds.

The brown seaweeds or wracks are anchored to the rocks by tough 'holdfasts'. Channel wrack (1) survives almost in the splash zone, becoming

splash zone (1)   upper shore (2)   middle shore (3)

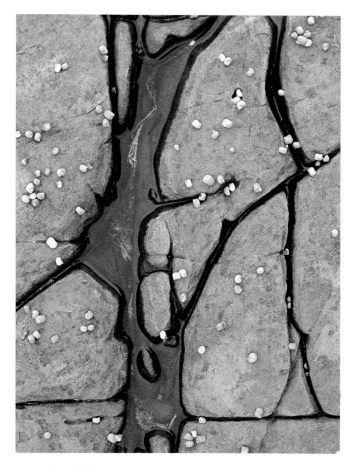

▲ The rough periwinkle has a ribbed shell which gives it its name. Here it is feeding on channel wrack attached to a rock encrusted with black lichen at the top of the shore.

black and crisp when dry and recovering when wetted again. Spiral wrack, too, lives at the top of the shore. These two are replaced in the middle of the shore by bladder wrack (**3**) and knotted wrack. Farther down grows saw wrack (**4**) which cannot withstand as much drying as the others. The larger brown seaweeds, oarweed (**5**) and thongweed, are exposed only at low spring tides.

No two shores have exactly the same zonation because the force of the waves differs from shore to shore. Knotted wrack cannot withstand wave action and is only found in sheltered places, whereas bladder wrack is abundant on exposed shores. On very exposed shores you will not find any wracks but you should see purple laver weed, limpets and barnacles instead. Barnacles are prevented from settling on rocks on sheltered shores because of the movement of the wracks in the waves.

▲ The edible or common periwinkle is the largest periwinkle and is often found in clusters. It lives lower down the shore than the other species of periwinkle.

| lower shore (4) | shallow water zone (5) |

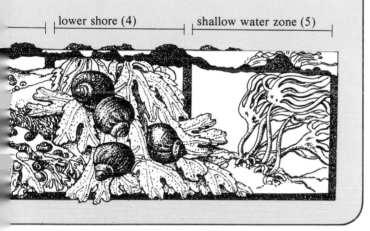

▼ Flat periwinkles may be yellow, brown, orange or striped. The name 'flat' seems misleading because, as you can see, the shell looks round; but its spire is flat. These colourful periwinkles live among seaweed on the middle shore; here they glide on saw wrack.

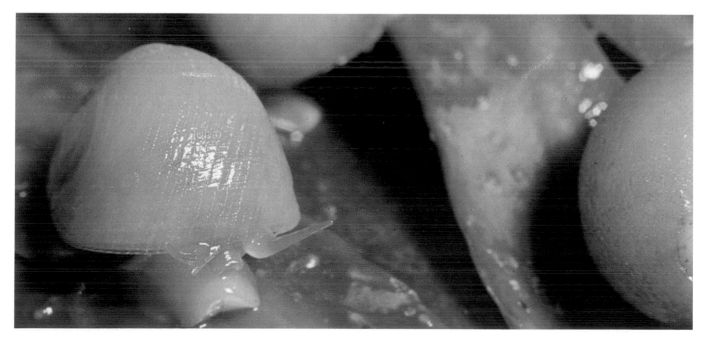

Life in the sand

When the tide goes out, a sandy beach may seem fit only for sunbathing and building sandcastles. Nothing seems to be living there. However, the birds at the tide's edge are feeding and, if you look closely, you will find other signs of life. There are small tunnels disappearing into the sand and empty shells are scattered over the beach. The animals are hiding under the sand which protects them against the force of the waves at high tide and from drying out at low tide.

Sand eaters

Animals on a sandy beach are hidden below the surface and they are difficult to find, unless they have left signs on the surface. The lugworm, for instance, lives in a U-shaped burrow and one end fills with sand at each high tide. The worm eats the sand and a depression forms at the entrance to the burrow as the sand slips down. The grains are passed out at the rear end of the worm's body to form a cast at the other end of the burrow.

Animals living in sand get their food from the particles of decaying animal and plant remains mixed with the sand. They consume large quantities of sand, extracting the edible particles and rejecting the sand grains. Even though they live under the

◀The whitened test or skeleton of a sea potato left by the tide among lugworm casts. The living sea potato is covered with a coat of prickles with which it digs itself into the sand.

◀◀▼The flounder (*inset left*) is a flatfish that changes its colour to match the sand on which it rests.

◀▼Only its shadow gives away the tiny sand-coloured shore crab (*inset right*) scampering sideways across the sand. If alarmed, down it clamps, motionless and instantly invisible.

sand, these animals are not safe from predation. Waders probe for them with their long beaks and they are also eaten by ragworms, starfish and the sea mouse, a slug-like worm with brilliant, shining bristles. Neat, round holes, 1 millimetre across, in bivalve (two-shelled) seashells show that their owners were attacked by a predatory snail called the necklace shell, which drilled the holes with its file-like radula, or tongue (see page 55), and scooped out the contents.

Strainers and pumpers

The edible particles brought in on the incoming tide are a second source of food for sand dwellers. The finest particles are caught by the filter feeders which strain them from the water. Peacock worms and sand mason worms live in tubes of cemented sand grains which can be seen protruding at low tide. When the tide is in, these animals unfold a fan of tentacles which catches tiny floating particles.

Bivalved animals, such as cockles, razorshells and tellins, filter out edible particles from the water or off the surface of the sand by pumping water through the body. They do this by means of two tubes, or siphons; water is drawn in through one and pumped out through the other.

Larger pieces of seaweed and animal remains as well as whole small animals are eaten by shore crabs, masked crabs and shrimps which lie buried while the tide is out. At high tide they are joined by small flatfishes, sandeels and gobies that come inshore.

Flatfishes change colour to match their background and are very difficult to see as they rest camouflaged on the sand; but you can see them darting out of the way as you wade through clear water, or feel them trying to wriggle free as you tread on them with bare feet. They search for the tentacles and siphons of buried animals and bite them off.

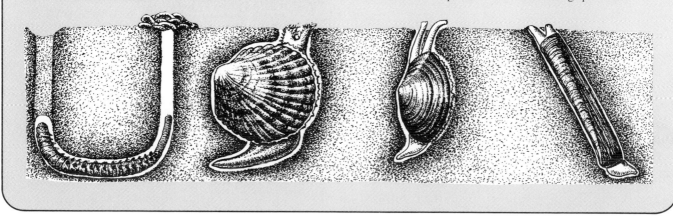

As the lugworm feeds in its burrow it makes a cast on the surface of the sand and a little pit nearby.

The edible cockle lives just below the surface of the sand, its two short siphons extended when the tide is in.

Cockles filter particles from the water, but tellins feed by vacuum-cleaning bits off the sand with mobile siphons.

Razor shells can burrow deep into the sand faster than you can dig. This is the large pod razor.

▲The underside of a rock encrusted with animals: a colony of golden-stars sea squirts, snail-like white worm tubes, and a brittle star scrambling away from the light.

▲Two beadlet anemones in a tug-of-war with a prawn, stunned and held by the tiny stinging cells that arm their tentacles.

►▲The fierce-mouthed fatherlasher is much too big a prey for a snakelocks anemone. Though stunned, it soon recovered and wrenched free from the writhing tentacles.

►►▲Like tiny green volcanic cones, a breadcrumb sponge encrusts a sheltered rock on the middle shore.

►At low tide, animals survive under damp rocks and weed. The beadlet anemone contracts to a blob of red jelly; two common starfish cling close to the rock. When the tide returns, the anemone will open out and the starfishes will move about on their tube feet.

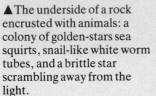

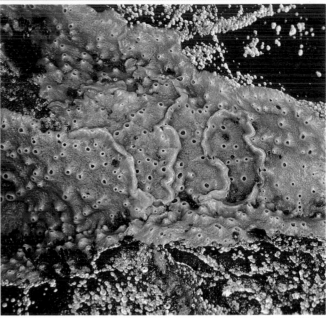

The rock pool world

The rock pools that are left behind when the tide goes out are among the best places to search for wildlife. Elsewhere, seashore animals have to hide or close up their shells but, in a rock pool, they can continue to move and feed and they may be joined by fishes, lobsters, spider crabs, and even octopuses which normally live in deep water below the shore. Indeed any animal from the shore or shallow sea is likely to turn up in a rock pool, especially one that is well down the shore.

HOW TO EXPLORE A ROCK POOL

Try searching a rock pool with a net; turn over stones and sift through the weed to find animals that are hiding, but remember to replace everything as you found it. Or, better still, sit quietly by a pool and wait for the animals to emerge and carry on their normal lives. You can get a good view into the rock pool world if you wear a swimming mask or goggles. Lie on a rock close to the surface, hold your breath and put your face to the water. Anemones and limpets will be open and active. Blennies and prawns dart from stone to stone; crabs crawl among the weeds; and periwinkles crawl over seaweed. Look carefully at periwinkles: empty shells could well have become the mobile homes of small hermit crabs.

At home in the rock pool

The sides of a rock pool will be covered with a variety of plants and animals. There is the delicately branched coral weed and a seaweed which forms a pink crust over the rock. Looking more like plants than animals, there are colonies of sea mats and sea squirts. Soft, greenish growths with scattered holes like tiny volcanoes are breadcrumb sponges. The purse sponge lives on the underside of rock overhangs. If you are lucky you will find a cowrie or a sea slug feeding on the sponges.

Sea anemones are the most spectacular of the sedentary animals. Beadlet anemones can be red or olive-green with a necklace of blue dots. Strawberry anemones are red with yellow spots. When they are high and dry these anemones retract the tentacles into the body and store water in the stomach to keep themselves moist until the tide comes back. Bright green or grey snakelocks anemones cannot retract their tentacles, so live mainly in rock pools. The tentacles of all sea anemones are armed with tiny stinging hairs that paralyse and cling to small animals swimming into them. Then the tentacles bend over and drag the prey into the anemone's mouth.

Off with the old skin

Shrimps and prawns may be found in rock pools. The prawn has a saw-edged beak on its head. Both animals look like miniature lobsters and have almost transparent bodies. If you sweep carefully through the pool with a fine-meshed net you may pick up their ghostly cast skins. Every couple of weeks, shrimps and prawns shed their skins so that they can grow. Crabs also have to change their solid armour as they increase in size. They retreat into crevices until the new shell hardens. Crabs are very vulnerable while the shell is soft. You can recognize shore crabs by the ten sharp 'teeth' on the front edge of the shell. These crabs are quick to defend themselves and rear up with their claws waving. Other crabs likely to be found in rock pools include velvet fiddlers, which also defend themselves vigorously, and small edible crabs, which lie on their backs and pretend to be dead (see page 81). Clinging to the undersides of rocks you may find small flattened porcelain crabs with rough hairy brown backs but shiny whitish undersides. And if you are lucky you may glimpse a small dark green squat lobster before it shoots away backwards.

◄Take care to avoid the pincers of a shore crab when it is in this mood. They can give you a nasty nip. If left in peace it will hide beneath the bladderwrack again, its dark green back camouflaging it well.

►A sea slug, like a land slug, is a mollusc without a shell. It has two paired tentacles on the head and its back is covered with tentacle-like gills. When disturbed, it thrashes its gills in an alarming manner.

►►The slender body of the shanny or common blenny enables it to hide in crevices in the rock pool. Watch for it darting away as you turn over stones.

ROCK POOL RESIDENTS

Rock pools are the home of shore plants and animals that cannot withstand drying at low tide. Tough bladder wrack (**1**) tolerates drying, but delicate green seaweeds (**2**) and pink encrusting algae (**3**) die if exposed. Beadlet anemones (**4**) remain expanded in the pool; snakelocks anemones (**5**) cannot contract their tentacles so live only in pools. Mussels (**6**) and limpets (**7**) can live above or below the water, but acorn barnacles (**8**) live only above; they are never found in pools. The rock goby (**9**), along with various crabs and prawns, lives in pools. A periwinkle shell could be the home of a hermit crab (**10**).

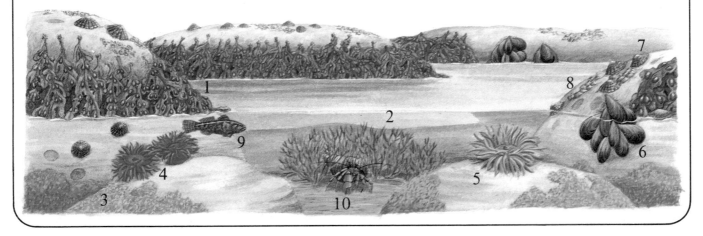

The rock pool nursery

During the summer, female shrimps, prawns and crabs carry their eggs under their bodies. They are then said to be 'in berry'. You can tell the sex of adult shore crabs by looking at their tails which are tucked under the body: that of the female is broad with seven joints, that of the male narrow and five-jointed. The orange eggs are carried by the female under her tail but sometimes, instead of eggs, there is a smooth, yellowish lump which is a parasite called *Sacculina*. The parasite lives on the crab's blood until it spawns and dies. Then the crab returns to a normal life.

If you look carefully, you will see signs that other animals are breeding at this time of year, too. A sea anemone may be surrounded by tiny replicas which have budded from its body. Shore fishes such as shannies and fatherlashers lay their eggs on rocks and these are guarded by the males until they hatch. The male pipefish, a relative of the seahorse, goes one step further and carries the eggs with him, stuck in a double row along his belly.

Birds at the coast

See also **Birds on the water** on page 20 and **Visitors for the winter** on page 208

There are birds to watch at the coast throughout the year, but in summer many seabirds gather in special breeding colonies. As well as seabirds, such as gulls, other birds, like crows and herons, come to the shore to feed. Flocks of waders gather on the shores in winter, while in spring and autumn, migrating birds arrive and depart. There are some places especially good for seeing rare birds. These are usually headlands which the birds spot while they are still far out to sea. Gannets are a delight to watch as they dive for fishes. They hurtle downwards, fold back their wings at the last moment and disappear beneath the surface in a spurt of spray.

Stabbers and probers

Small seashore animals form a rich harvest for birds (see pages 82-91). The black-and-white oystercatcher, a familiar bird on rocky shores, attacks mussels, cockles and similar shellfish. If the shellfish is underwater and its shells are open, the oystercatcher quickly stabs between them to cut the powerful muscles that close the shells. If the shellfish has closed its shells, the bird gets at the muscles by smashing open the shells. Limpets are knocked off rocks with a single blow and crabs are flipped on to their backs and killed with a stab through the brain.

The waders that feed along the edge of the high tide (see pages 82-3) spread out over the beach at low tide. As they probe in the sand with their beaks, they may leave behind a line of tiny holes or a larger hole and the remains of a crab which has been dug out and eaten.

Seabird cities

The huge colonies of seabirds on high cliffs are a breathtaking spectacle. The birds spend most of their lives at sea and come ashore only to nest, in late spring and summer.

Guillemots, razorbills and puffins are auks. Their legs are set well back on their bodies and they stand upright, like penguins. They dive for fishes and swim with their wings. Puffins nest in burrows at the tops of cliffs, but guillemots and razorbills use ledges on the faces of vertical cliffs. The chicks leave the ledges

SEABIRD SIGHTINGS

If you watch birds regularly you will soon recognize the different types by their individual ways of flying. Terns have long, pointed wings and an easy 'bouncing' flight. They are very agile and also excellent long-distance fliers. This is an Arctic tern bringing a sand eel to its chick.

Each flying seabird has a distinctive silhouette. How many can you identify? Check your answers on page 220.

◄Part of a vast colony of nesting seabirds, these guillemots and kittiwakes share a small ledge on a spectacular vertical cliff face.

▲Common gulls and black-headed gulls are in keen competition. As soon as one bird finds food others dive shrieking to grab a share.

before they can fly properly and flutter down to the water, where their parents escort them out to sea.

The kittiwake, a kind of gull named after its screaming call, nests on the smallest ledges but builds a solid mud nest to keep its eggs and chicks safe. Cormorants and shags nest near the bottom of the cliff. They fish near the shore and perch with their wings spread, 'hanging out to dry'. Fulmars have become very common in recent years and have started to nest inland, on rock faces, walls and old buildings.

Gulls, oystercatchers, ringed plovers and colonies of terns nest behind sand and shingle shores. The nests are usually no more than depressions in the ground and the eggs and chicks are extremely well camouflaged.

WATCH YOUR STEP!

Camouflaged eggs and chicks are easily trodden on, so walk very carefully if you hear the alarm calls of the parents. If possible, move away quickly so they can go back to their families. Conservationists are worried about shore-nesting birds because they live where people like to go for holidays. Their nesting grounds are destroyed by buildings and roads, and visitors often prevent them from nesting successfully.

Wild flowers by the sea

See also **Where fresh water meets salty**
on page 172

At high tide when the rock pools are covered and the sea is sweeping over the beach, take a walk along the coast behind the shore and you will find lots of fascinating and colourful plants. Farmers cannot drive ploughs to the edge of the cliff or shore and here you will find an uncultivated strip full of wild flowers. Close to the sea there are plants which are adapted to tolerate soaking with salt spray.

On the cliffs and among boulders at the bottom, grow scattered tufts of pink thrift, lilac-coloured sea lavender, white sea campion and sea plantain. Many of these plants, like the wild carrot, are close relatives of inland species. Sea cabbage, for example, is an ancestor of all our garden cabbages, brussels sprouts and cauliflowers.

Among pebbles and dunes

Shingle beaches and banks may seem lifeless as well as painful on the feet, but a few plants manage to take root among the stones. Here you may find sea-blite, sea pea, yellow horned-poppy and, where the pebbles are compacted and stable, ragwort and docks grow in masses.

Where storms blow sand inland, sand dunes pile up to form a barrier as much as 30 metres high. The dunes are stabilized by tough marram grass which spreads, with a network of rooting stems, across the sand to bind it in place. The tops of the dunes are very dry and the leaves of marram grass roll up to prevent them drying out. Sea rocket and orache store water in their soft swollen leaves and stems. Saltwort has prickly leaves, too, although the prickles are not so sharp as those of sea holly. The roots of sea holly grow deep into the sand.

Between the dunes there are hollows, or slacks, which are damp and covered with a sward of plants which includes lady's bedstraw and wintergreen, with clumps of low willows and rushes.

The saltmarsh scene

Sand dunes are good places to picnic, especially when they can give protection from the wind. Saltmarshes or saltings, which are found in estuaries and behind shingle banks, however, may seem to be among the bleakest places anywhere. They are flat, windswept and appear utterly desolate. From autumn to spring though, they are the homes of flocks of geese and waders and, in summer, plenty of interesting plants grow there. Whereas dune plants have to withstand drought, saltmarsh plants have to survive frequent covering with sea water.

The marshes form where mud has accumulated and has been stabilized by plants. Narrow winding channels drain the flood water from the marsh at each tide. Late summer is the best time to visit saltmarshes. Then the drier parts of the marsh are covered with flowering sea-lavender, with thrift and with sea-purslane. Near the sea, the bare mud is colonized by the fleshy stems of glasswort and by eelgrass, which is an important food for wild geese.

Seaside cliffs are the habitat of a few tough plants that tolerate salt spray. The plants that are at home on cliffs may also be found growing among rocks on mountains.

A shingle bank is constantly battered and rolled about by waves between the tides. But at the top of the ridge above the high tide a few specialized plants can flourish.

▼Sea campion has sepal-tubes inflated to form pinkish-green bladders beneath its white flowers.

◄The green flower spikes of sea plantain can be found on sea cliffs throughout the summer.

◄◄Thrift, or sea pink, is securely anchored by a long, tough root that goes deep into rock crevices.

▼The sea pea creeps on shingle or dunes. Its flowers are purple when new, then fade to blue.

▼Annual sea-blite belongs to the goosefoot family. It has fleshy cylindrical leaves and very small greenish flowers.

◄The horned-poppy is the most striking plant growing on shingle. It has large blue-green leaves, and big golden-yellow flowers. Its 'horns' are the long thin seed pods.

◄Sea kale grows in large clumps above the high tide line on sandy shores and shingle. Its masses of white flowers are often visited by insects, particularly by migrant hoverflies after their sea crossing.

Sand dunes are harsh places. Sand dries out quickly. It is blown about by the wind. Only tough, deep-rooted plants survive the drought, salt spray and shifting sands on dunes.

Saltmarsh is covered by the tide twice a day and a rich, fertile mud is deposited each time. But only salt-loving plants with smooth mud-shedding leaves can survive there.

▼Low-growing saltwort has smooth succulent leaves that quickly shed any sand grains blown onto them.

▼The tough, holly-like leaves of sea-holly resist evaporation and its very long roots probe deep for moisture.

▲Common sea-lavender carpets the margins of the marsh where the mud has settled into banks.

►Also above the level of the marsh shrubby, grey-green sea-purslane flourishes on ridges where the mud is less salty.

◄Even when buried under metres of shifting sand, marram grass grows straight up to the surface again. It has a vast network of roots and underground stems throughout the dune.

Bees and flowers

See also **Wasps and wasp look-alikes**
on page 150

Before our ancestors grew crops of sugar beet and sugar cane, honey was their only sweetener. At first, people gathered it by robbing the nests of wild bees but they soon learned to domesticate the bees by encouraging them to live in man-made hives. The hives are often put in orchards so that the bees can pollinate the blossom for, as well as making honey, bees are also important for pollinating flowers.

The hive is the home of a honeybee colony made up of a queen, drones and worker bees. The main task of the queen is to lay eggs, but she also gives off special chemicals or pheromones from her body as signals to the workers to control their activities. The drones are males which live only to mate with a queen. Most of the bees in a colony are workers which look after the hive, care for the growing grubs and fly in search of flowers. They bring back nectar and pollen for food. Some of the nectar is turned into honey and stored.

Collecting nectar and pollen

Honeybees and some kinds of wild flowers cannot live without each other. The bees depend on flowers for food and the flowers depend on bees to pollinate them.

For a flower to be fertilized so that the seeds will develop, pollen must be transferred from the stamen of one bloom to the stigma of another. Bees are attracted to flowers by the rich supplies of nectar which the plants produce. As a bee flies from flower to flower in search of nectar, it carries pollen with it, picking it up from one and depositing it on the next.

▶A honeybee worker collecting nectar and pollen from the flowers of white bryony. Note the full pollen sac.

▼Worker honeybees tending the comb. Some of the cells may contain pollen but most are full of honey; a few contain a larva. When the larva turns into a pupa, it is sealed into its cell with wax by an attendant worker.

blue-green, blue and ultraviolet. Humans cannot detect ultraviolet light. Scientists have photographed flowers using ultraviolet light and lines have shown up on some flowers which cannot be seen in ordinary white light. The bee can see these lines and they help to guide it to the flower's store of nectar.

Once a bee has found a flower with a supply of nectar, it starts to search for similar flowers which it recognizes by their colours. If you follow a bee, you will see that it concentrates on one sort of flower and ignores others of different colours. The bee will land on pieces of paper of the same hue.

When the bee has gathered a full load, it returns to the nest and signals to the other bees the whereabouts of its discovery. It does this by dancing on the comb to show the direction and distance from the hive of the flowers it has found. The other bees also smell the scent of the flower on the first bee's body to discover the type of flower to look for. Soon there is a stream of bees visiting the flowers.

Today most honeybees live in hives but some still live in the wild.

TAKE A CLOSER LOOK
The next time you see a bee busy feeding at a flower, coax it onto a stick coated with honey so that you can examine it closely. Don't worry, it will be far too engrossed in feeding to sting you! Watch out for its long, tubular tongue uncurling and dipping into the honey.

Hair covering the bee's body sweeps up pollen from the flower's stamens when the insect probes into it. At intervals the bee scrapes the pollen from the hairs with its legs and stuffs it into baskets formed from curved bristles. As the pollen accumulates it shows as a yellow lump on each hind leg.

A bee's eye-view
A honeybee has good colour vision, but its eyes see a different set of colours from those that we see. A bee's eye-view of a flower bed would look strange to us. It cannot see red but it can distinguish yellow,

There are three 'casts' of honeybees in a hive: the queen who lays the eggs, workers that run the hive, and drones that mate with the young queens.

worker   queen   drone

MOVING HOME
Wild bee colonies often come from hives. During the summer the hive becomes crowded and eventually a group of workers flies away with the old queen. This is called swarming. The swarm soon settles on a branch and sends out scouts to look for a suitable nesting place. Beekeepers try to find these swarms, capture them and put them into hives, but many still escape and settle down in nests of their own choosing. If you find a swarm, do not approach too close.

Bees and more bees

Not every bee visiting flowers is a honeybee from a hive. There are about 250 species of bees in Britain alone and only the honeybee and the bumblebee live in colonies with workers caring for the queen and her grubs. The rest live solitary lives.

Miners and potters
Mining bees, which look rather like honeybees, visit pussy willow catkins and the blossom of fruit trees in spring and other flowers in early summer. They nest in burrows in the ground which they excavate themselves. One species, called the lawn bee, nests in lawns and paths. It leaves a little mound of fine soil with a hole in the centre which looks like a tiny volcano.

After laying her eggs on a store of food, the female lawn bee closes the entrance of the nest and leaves it, never to return. After they have hatched out, the grubs feed on the supply of food.

The flower bee or potter bee looks like a small bumblebee but flies much faster. The male and female are very different, and it is easy to follow their courtship. The female, which is black with conspicuous orange pollen baskets on her hind legs,

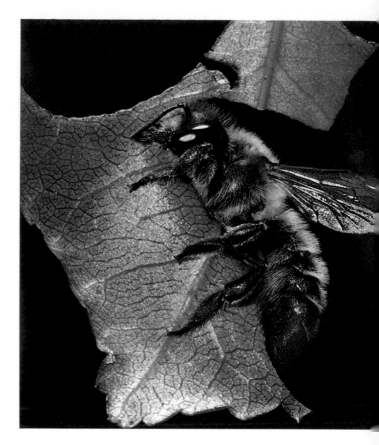

flies from flower to flower and hovers in front of one before advancing to suck up the nectar. The brown male flies up behind her, hovers for a few seconds and then pounces on her. They tumble to the ground and mating takes place. The female digs a nest in loose soil and eggs are laid in small 'pots' of clay filled with food.

Cutters and masons
Many insects make holes in leaves, but the neat semicircular hole in the edges of rose and bramble leaves, or sometimes willow and lilac, are the work of the leafcutter bee. The bee grasps the leaf between its legs and then quickly cuts away a segment with its jaws. The bee then flies off with the piece of leaf tucked under its body. The leafcutter bee makes its nest in a hollow plant stem, in rotten wood or loose soil, or in a crevice in a wall (see page 46). The pieces of leaf are used to make cells, each of which contains one egg and a store of food for the larva.

The red osmia or mason bee is another solitary bee which nests in hollow stems, crevices in brickwork and fences, or even in unused flower pots. It also digs into rotten wooden posts and soft soil. The individual compartments of its nest are made of mud.

Home hunting
The large bumblebees that appear on fine days in spring are queens which have spent the winter in

---

WARMING UP FOR TAKE OFF
Bumblebees look as if they are too heavy for the size of their wings. They are strong fliers, however, and can carry half their own weight of pollen at a speed of 15 kph.

Before it can fly, a bumblebee has to warm up. Unless it can raise its temperature to 30 degrees centigrade, its wings will not beat fast enough (see page 49) to lift it into the air. To raise its temperature, it either basks in the sun or breaks down sugars in its flight muscles to release energy.

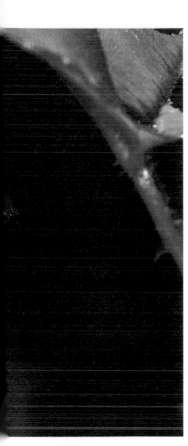

◀A leafcutter bee, using its jaws like scissors, snips out a circular piece of rose leaf while rolling it up with its legs. When free, the piece is carried to the bee's nest to form the wall of a cell.

▼Like honeybees, worker bumblebees collect pollen and nectar, from plants like the teasel, on which future generations are nourished.

hibernation. After feeding on the nectar from early flowering plants, they start to search for a nest site. You can see them flying slowly, a few centimetres above the ground, and disappearing into crevices and mouseholes. Some bumblebees make their nests in tussocks of grass or under piles of dead leaves, but they prefer to find abandoned nests of mice and voles.

Soon, the queen bumblebee gathers a store of nectar and pollen in a cluster of little pots and lays her first eggs. When these have developed into worker bees, she will stay in the nest and concentrate on egg laying. Eventually, there will be between twenty and 300 bees in the nest. Like honeybees, bumblebees patrol from flower to flower but because of their size and strength they can enter flowers which are closed to honeybees. They are large enough to force their way into snapdragons, peas and louseworts.

From midsummer onwards some eggs develop into new queens and males. Male bumblebees, unlike the honeybee drones, lead independent lives. To find a young queen they fly in wide circles and land at intervals on leaves which they mark with a scent by running their jaws around the edge. Females are attracted to the scent and the males meet them as they patrol past.

Safety in disguise

See also **Bees and flowers** on page 96
and **Wasps and wasp look-alikes** on page 150

If a wasp comes into the room we treat it with extreme caution. We try to remove it without angering it, because we know that an enraged wasp will sting. Even the friendly bumblebee will sting if it is provoked too much. We will usually let these insects go without them stinging us because we already know that they are harmful and we leave them alone. Birds that eat insects have also learned to avoid those that sting. The black and yellow stripes of a wasp are a particular warning, as they are on a cinnabar moth caterpillar (see page 77).

Warning stripes

Generally, we will keep away from any wasp-like, black-and-yellow striped insect without bothering to check if it really is a wasp that is likely to harm us. A number of insects make use of this reaction and have copied the wasp's striped body. These insects are called mimics and they are not attacked by enemies that have learned to leave wasps alone.

WHEN IS A WASP NOT A WASP?

Answer: When it is a hoverfly. You can tell that hoverflies are flies and not wasps or bees because they have one pair of wings instead of two and their antennae are very short. Hoverflies can be found in many places, and from spring to autumn, but they are particularly common on the flowers of bramble and hogweed. You can also see them in gardens and woodland glades where the sun catches their wings as they hover for a few seconds, then dart a metre or two and hover again. They are always ready to drive off other males. If you disturb one by walking past, it flies away and comes back when its space is clear again.

Even Samson was fooled

The dronefly is a hoverfly that mimics honeybees. It can be recognized by its heavy bee-like body as it hovers for a minute or so or basks on a stone. The adult fly feeds, as other hoverflies do, on nectar and pollen but its larva feeds on decaying material and putrefying flesh of dead animals. It was the dronefly that gave Samson the idea for his riddle, 'Out of the strong came forth sweetness'. He had seen the adult flies buzzing around the carcass of the lion he had killed and believed, like everyone else in those days, that these were honeybees that had come to life spontaneously in the rotting flesh of a dead animal.

▲Not a wasp after all! Large eyes, short antennae and a single pair of wings give the game away that this is a harmless wasp hoverfly.

◄You (and birds) might think this is a bumblebee and leave it alone in case it should sting; but it is a harmless bee hoverfly which mimics a bumblebee for its own protection. The best clues to its real identity are the wings (folded over its back) and the eyes (very large).

▼The wasp beetle wears the wasp's warning black and yellow stripes but rather than stinging it will squeak if caught. Here it is resting on hogweed.

For mimicry to be effective, the harmful insect must be more common than the harmless mimic, otherwise birds are more likely to learn that the mimics are good to eat because they are only rarely stung when attacking a less common honeybee. The dronefly, however, is very abundant but it seems that droneflies are distasteful anyway, so that the fly and the bee are each benefiting from mimicking one another – the birds are twice as likely to learn to avoid a nasty mouthful.

More wasp and bee copycats
Hoverflies are not the only wasp and bee mimics. The beefly is a different sort of fly, although it can hover. Its wings make a highpitched whine as it flies a few centimetres from the ground. The beefly has a furry body and a long, needle-shaped proboscis.

There are two kinds of moth and a beetle which mimic bees and wasps. Both fly by day so that the mimicry can be effective. The bee hawkmoths are like silent bumblebees. They have black-and-brown furry bodies and, when they first emerge from the pupa, their wings are covered with scales like those of other moths. The scales drop off on the first flight so the wings then resemble the transparent wings of bees. Hornet clearwing moths also have transparent wings and their bodies are striped black and yellow. The wasp beetle, black with narrow yellow stripes, walks with a jerking gait in imitation of some wasps.

Spare the nettle!

Stinging nettles must be the most unpopular plants, especially for anyone walking in the country with bare legs! To most people they are also unattractive to look at, so gardeners usually pull them up wherever they appear and farmers mow them down or spray them with poisons. Yet nettles are very interesting for their own sakes and for the animals that live on them.

USES OF THE NETTLE
Nettles were once thought of as useful plants. The young leaves were boiled and eaten like spinach, dried and used to make tea or brewed as nettle beer. You can still buy the dried leaves to make tea. Cooking destroys the stinging poisons. Nettles used to be used for treating skin complaints and rheumatism and, before the introduction of cotton, nettles were used in weaving cloth. The stems were allowed to rot, leaving the long fibres which were spun into thread. The roots gave a yellow dye.

The nettle family
There are two kinds of stinging nettle. The common stinging nettle grows to 160 centimetres tall. The male flowers are greenish-yellow catkins and pollen is blown by the wind to the small female flowers which are carried on separate plants. The stems grow from yellow roots and horizontal stems which run underground and link the whole of a nettle clump together as one plant. The annual or small nettle is smaller, growing only 60 centimetres tall, and has shorter, more rounded leaves. It grows from seeds each spring and then dies in the autumn.

Clues from nettles
Nettles grow in soil which has been enriched with chemicals called phosphates. They need plenty of phosphate but their roots are not very good at absorbing it from the soil. Phosphate is available in large quantities from animal waste products, so nettles thrive around ruined farms, abandoned pigsties and rubbish tips, as well as under pigeon roosts and around badger setts. A clump of nettles on poor soil in woods or open spaces is often a sign of human activities, perhaps centuries ago. If you investigate such an area carefully, you may well find the remains of buildings and interesting relics.

▶Clumps of stinging nettles are in flower throughout the summer from June onwards.

HOW DOES A STINGING NETTLE STING?

The photograph shows the stinging hair of a nettle. It is a hollow tube of glassy silica, connected to a reservoir of poison at the base. When the tip rubs against your skin, it snaps off leaving a sharp edge which sticks in while the poison is squeezed into your flesh.

If you get stung, rub dock leaves on your sore skin. They contain a substance which relieves the tingling. 'To grasp the nettle' is an expression which means to make a bold decision. If you grasp a nettle firmly, the hairs bend over and do not penetrate the skin.

LIFE ON THE NETTLE

Stinging nettles are important in the life of the countryside. Cattle eat them and several butterflies and moths lay their eggs on nettles and their caterpillars eat the leaves.

Peacock and small tortoiseshell butterflies lay their eggs in batches on the undersides of leaves and the caterpillars group together protecting themselves by spinning a silken tent over the leaves. Red admiral caterpillars live alone and each one lives inside a nettle leaf which it rolls up and secures with silk.

Aphids suck the sap of nettles. They attract predators, such as this ladybird larva.

When is a nettle not a stinging nettle?

Answer: When it is a dead-nettle. Dead-nettles have very similar leaves to stinging nettles and they are covered with fine hairs, but these are not poisonous. They can be recognized by the square stems and the flowers. There are three well-known kinds of dead-nettle: the white and red dead-nettles and henbit dead-nettle with pink flowers. The flowers of dead-nettles have a tubular corolla with two lips, one forming a platform and the other a hood. Dead-nettles are favourite flowers for bumblebees to visit. Their small fruits have an oily secretion which attracts ants and the insects carry the fruits away. White dead-nettle tends to grow in hedgerows and waste places but the red-flowered plant is a common weed of cultivated land (see page 211).

Yellow archangel and hemp-nettles are very similar to dead-nettles. They are all members of the thyme family, non-woody plants with a strong smell. Some of them, such as the mints, basil, marjoram, sage and thyme, are used for flavouring in cooking. There are at least four different kinds of hemp-nettles. Yellow archangel grows in woods, the hemp-nettles are usually found on cultivated land and hedge woundwort is common in hedgerows.

1 PATTERNED EGGS

The female comma lays her eggs singly on the leaves of stinging nettles. To find them, examine the tips and the upper surface with a magnifying glass and using gloved hands or tweezers to hold the leaf steady. Compare the eggs of different species. Each will have its own pattern and you should find many different shapes and sizes. Many butterfly eggs are almost clear, and change colour as the larva develops inside. This is a sign they are going to hatch.

2 FEEDING AND FATTENING

Inside the egg the caterpillar makes a small hole in the top or the side through which it emerges. As soon as it has hatched it eats the remains of the eggshell, without which it will often die, and then spends all its time eating leaves and growing. The comma caterpillar sheds its skin five times as it increases in size. This is the final stage still feeding on nettle leaves.

YOUR BUTTERFLY FILE

Once you have found some butterfly eggs, start a butterfly file to record the stages shown here. Here are some suggestions:

Species of butterfly:
Description.............................

Date eggs laid or seen:
Description.............................

Date caterpillars first noticed:
Description.............................

Date chrysalis first seen:
Description.............................

Date first adult seen emerging:

GUIDE: The eggs should take between one and four weeks to hatch; the caterpillars may feed for up to six weeks, and the adults emerge from the chrysalis in 10 to 20 days.

A butterfly year

See also **Butterfly watching** on page 72

The butterfly life cycle is easy to observe and one of the best places to follow the stages from egg to adult is at a clump of stinging nettles. This is a favourite food plant for the caterpillars of several species including the comma shown here. If you can't find the eggs or caterpillars of this species, don't worry, the stages are the same for all butterflies.

The comma butterfly has two generations in a year. It spends the winter in hibernation and emerges on a warm day in early spring to mate and lay its eggs. On hatching, the caterpillars feed up rapidly, form pupae and produce fresh adults by mid-summer. These quickly mate and lay more eggs which result in a new generation of adult commas on the wing in late summer. As winter approaches these will find sheltered places to hibernate.

Some other butterflies produce only one generation in a year. They pass the winter as eggs, or hibernate as caterpillars, chrysalises (pupae) or adults. A few butterflies will migrate south to warmer countries.

7 WARMING UP

During this period the butterfly basks in the sun, warming up its body in readiness for flight (see page 49). The males usually emerge from their chrysalises before the females. This makes it more likely that the females will be mated as they emerge. The sexes recognize each other by colour, pattern and by scents which both sexes give off. The adult butterfly does not grow any more once it has expanded its wings and flown.

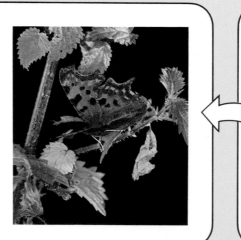

6 EXPANDING WINGS

This is a critical time for the new butterfly. It has to find a place where it can hang downward and expand its wings without them touching anything that would interfere with their growth. Very often the old chrysalis skin is a good place to hang, as here. If you watch carefully you can see the wings expanding. This normally takes about 20 minutes but the butterfly then rests for an hour to ensure they are dry before it attempts its first flight.

3 NEW SKINS FOR OLD

Once fully grown the caterpillar stops feeding and looks for a suitable place to pupate. It anchors itself from a silk pad and then hangs, head down, while a new skin forms underneath the old one. The old skin splits and the soft skin of the chrysalis is revealed. Wriggling movements free the old skin and reattach the chrysalis to the silk pad. You can often find the old skin crumpled up at the base of the chrysalis.

4 TIME OF CHANGE

The skin of the chrysalis hardens and it hangs motionless. It is said to be in the resting stage but great changes are going on inside as the tissues are rearranged to form the butterfly.

5 EMERGING TO FACE THE WORLD

The chrysalis skin is transparent and if you can see some parts of the butterfly through it the insect is fully formed and about to emerge. Watch closely and you may be lucky enough to see the skin split and the butterfly force its way out. Don't expect the new butterfly to be bright and gleaming. It is at first wrinkled and bedraggled because its wings are soft and folded up.

Under the twig pile

See also **Bees and flowers** on page 96 and **Wasps and wasp look-alikes** on page 150

All ants are social insects and live in colonies where a queen lays the eggs and the workers do all the chores. The wood ant is the largest ant species in Europe. It builds huge nests in dry woodlands, especially under pine trees.

The workers gather an enormous pile of twigs and pine needles which forms a roof over the underground nest. The nest lasts for many years and several queens may live there at the same time. In the summer the nest is a hive of industry. As many as 1,000,000 workers tend the eggs and grubs or set out from the nest in search of food.

Tracks and trails

The best time to watch wood ants is on a warm day when streams of workers scurry in and out of the nest. Those returning home will be carrying pieces of twig or leaf to add to the pile, or small animals which will be eaten by the residents. The ants travel on regular tracks which can be followed over the woodland floor for 50 metres or more.

TEST YOUR ANTS' NAVIGATION

Some kinds of ants follow scent trails laid by their companions and they get lost if the trail is wiped out. Wood ants do not use scent and, if you scrape away the soil on a path, the ants still stream across the gap. They are navigating by the sun. Scoop up some ants on a piece of paper (wearing gloves for protection) and put them down somewhere else; they will run in the same direction.

Foraging for food

The paths gradually peter out as the ants spread out to look for food. They seize and overpower small animals and carry them back to the nest. A single wood ant can carry a small insect but several are needed to manage caterpillars which are their favourite prey.

By clearing the woodland of caterpillars and other harmful insects, wood ants perform a useful service for foresters. However, they actually encourage one pest, the aphid, which they 'farm' (see page 146).

Ready for battle

If a wood ants' nest is disturbed, the inhabitants come rushing out to repel the invasion. The ants curl their abdomens forwards and squirt formic acid into the air. If the ants can seize the aggressor they bite to allow the formic acid to get into the wound.

▲ A wood ants' nest of pine needles and twigs. Do not stand too close – the ants can nip and squirt formic acid at you!

▶ Winged male and female wood ants are tended by workers as they prepare to fly from a twig above the nest. Ants fly on only a few occasions in summer, usually when the weather is thundery.

▼ As they move across the woodland floor, perhaps carrying prey such as this small tortoiseshell butterfly, the rustling sound of wood ants can be quite loud.

Heathland and heather

Heaths and moors mean rather different things to different people, but they are essentially the same sort of open countryside with very few trees. The main plants are usually heather with coarse grass or bracken. Heaths are usually found in low-lying country and moors in hill country. Botanists, however, often call all heather country heathland. Heathland can be very bleak and cheerless in bad weather but it becomes very beautiful in late summer when large stretches are covered with the purple flowers of heather. Heaths and moors are also the homes of many kinds of interesting, and often rare, animals and plants.

Tree invaders

Heathlands were once forested but now the only trees or bushes you will see are scattered junipers, pines, birches and shrubby gorse. The heath is an artificial kind of countryside created when people

▼ In late summer the heathland looks its best with heather in flower, dew glistening on the dark gorse bushes and young birch trees turning yellow.

A LOOK BENEATH THE SURFACE

If you can find a place where a sandpit or a road cutting has revealed a slice of the soil under a heath, you will see that it has a definite pattern. On the surface, there is a crust of litter – dead leaves and twigs. Below this there is a layer of humus (rotting plants) which is dark brown or black. Underneath is pale grey sand or clay, from which all the organic plant material has been washed out by the rain. In poorly drained areas, the half-rotten humus accumulates as a thick layer of black peat.

There are few, if any, earthworms in heathland to mix the humus with the sand or clay, and this is why it forms a separate layer on the surface. As it rots, it produces acids which are washed down through the soil, extracting iron salts as they go and depositing them as dark-brown, hard bands of 'iron pan'.

cut down the forests. Heather originally lived in woodland glades and on mountain sides but it spread as the land was opened up for farming. In hilly country sheep farming became common as the trees were cut down for charcoal. However, when sheep, or other grazing animals, are taken away trees start to grow again. To conserve heathland nature reserves the invading birches and pines have to be cleared away.

The heathland plants

Heather is a dwarf shrub with a woody stem and it is related to rhododendrons and azaleas. There are several species. The most abundant is the common heather or ling. Its small, stiff leaves grow in four close-set rows and it has pale purple flowers. Bell heather, sometimes called heath, grows on dry heaths. Its leaves grow in groups around the stem and the plant has red-purple, bell-shaped flowers. Wetter places have crossed-leaved heath with leaves set in groups of four forming a cross, and clusters of pink flowers at the tip of the stem.

Look across a heath and you will see the change between plants of dry and wet ground. The plants on the top of a slope will be quite different from those at the bottom. On the drier parts the heather is joined by gorse, tormentil and bilberry, or blueberry. In wetter places there is sundew (see page 116), club-moss, bog asphodel and common cottongrass.

▶ Heathlands blaze with purple when heather and bell heather are in flower. Other plants on this heath are mat-grass, common gorse (not flowering now) and bracken.

The life and death of a heather plant

A heather plant lives for 30 years or more. The young plant is pyramid shaped and looks like a tiny Christmas tree. As it grows, it sends out side branches which straggle along the ground, and the plant gradually becomes a dome rather than a pyramid. The main shoots continue to grow and develop small side shoots which carry the leaves.

These last for only two or three years. Then they fall off and add to the litter accumulating on the ground. The flowers grow at the tip of the stem and fall off when they have seeded to leave a length of bare stem.

The 'dome' of the heather plant eventually reaches about half a metre in height and it then begins to collapse. The stems fall outwards and lie along the ground, leaving a bald patch in the centre. Eventually the plant dies and is replaced by the young heathers.

In practice, the heather plant does not always get the chance to grow unchecked. Deer, rabbits, sheep and grouse feed on its fresh growth, nipping off the tops of the young plants but leaving the side branches to grow and form a short, spongy mat.

Fresh shoots from the flames

In some places the growth of the heather is deliberately controlled by burning. Patches of the heath are burned when they start to get old and woody, so that new, fresh growth is produced for animals to eat.

▶ Dwarf gorse flowers with the heather, bringing colour to bleak places. Common gorse buds reappear as the dwarf gorse fades, so that some gorse is in flower at any time of the year.

▶ ▼ Male emperor moths fly fast over the heather on sunny days in May. The females fly and lay their eggs on the heather only at night.

▼ In the early morning the sand lizard climbs on top of the heather to bask. Females and non-courting males are speckled brown and well camouflaged. In early summer, the mating season, males turn green on flanks and belly.

At home on heathland

It often looks as if there is very little animal life on a heath or moor when compared with woods and fields. There are, however, some birds that prefer open country and some interesting insects and other invertebrates to be found.

A wealth of insects

Lowland heaths are the home of butterflies such as the grayling, silver-studded blue and small heath. The emperor and fox moths can be found there, too. Crickets and dragonflies (see pages 112 and 122) are common, but bees, wasps and ants (see pages 96, 150 and 106) are perhaps the most entertaining insects living there.

In clearings between the heather plants, along paths for instance, mining bees and digger wasps make their nests. These are solitary insects which do not have large nests full of busy workers like those of the honeybee. Mining bees burrow into sandy soil, leaving little 'volcanoes' around the entrance. They stock the nest with nectar and pollen, often from heather flowers.

Digger wasps are hunters and provision their nest burrows with small animals that they paralyse with their stings. When hunting, the digger wasp zig-zags over the ground until it spots what it thinks may be a suitable victim. Its eyesight is not good enough to be certain so the wasp hovers a few centimetres down-wind to smell the prey. If satisfied, it pounces.

▲ A cock stonechat perched on a bramble near his nest. To make it easier for the tiny nestlings to swallow it, he has removed the grasshopper's spiky hind legs.

◄ This digger wasp has just landed on the sand near its burrow entrance, carrying beneath its body a paralysed weevil with which to provision its nest. The weevil's snout is held securely in the wasp's jaws.

► The fast-running green tiger beetle has excellent eyesight and powerful jaws for capturing insect prey. No other kind of beetle will seem to notice you but the tiger beetle will fly off if you get close.

The digger wasp must know the exact position of its nest so that it can find its way back with its victims. When it leaves the nest, it flies around the entrance in increasing circles so that it can memorize landmarks before it flies off.

Heather plants attract heather beetles which feed on the leaves and sometimes occur in plagues which strip the heather bare. More useful are the round-bodied dor beetles which make neat burrows surrounded by piles of excavated sand. Dor beetles provision the burrows with the dung of sheep or rabbits.

Frogs and toads, lizards and snakes
Heaths are good places to find amphibians and reptiles. Common toads and frogs (see page 16) are still common on unpolluted, undrained moors. Adders (see page 80) are often so plentiful on dry heaths that warning notices are displayed. Heathland animals are well adapted to their environment and find it very difficult to survive elsewhere. As the habitat disappears so do the animals. The smooth snake, for instance, lives in many kinds of open country throughout Europe, but the British population lives only on sandy heathlands. Similarly, sand lizards and natterjack toads are becoming rare in north-west Europe as their sandy-soiled homes diminish.

On the wing
Some of the heathland birds have already been described (see page 36). The Dartford warbler specializes in open-country living. The dry heaths of south-ern England form the northern end of its range. Any encroachment by trees is liable to drive out the open-country species. In the Brecklands of eastern England, for example, the numbers of stone curlews decreased when the heaths were covered with conifer plantations. The birds have been obliged to nest in the broad firebreaks running between the trees.

Meadow pipits are abundant on heaths and moors and so are cuckoos. Cuckoos lay their eggs in the nests of smaller birds, and pipits are among their favourite hosts.

Larger mammals
Small mammals are not very common on heaths and moors but you will see large mammals, such as wild ponies and red deer. The ponies are descendants of domesticated animals. They are not really wild but their owners allow them to roam the moors to graze. Red deer are forest animals that were forced to become moorland animals when the trees were cut down.

BEWARE OF FIRE!
Heather catches fire very easily when it is dry. Be very careful with matches or picnic fires, especially if there has been no rain for some time. Fires are often banned in nature reserves and parks.

On the hop

You might think any fairly long-legged, greenish or brownish insect that jumps out of your way as you walk through the undergrowth is a grasshopper, but it may be any one of three kinds of insect. True grasshoppers or short-horned grasshoppers are distinguished by their short antennae. Bush crickets have thread-like antennae that are longer than the insect's body, and longer, more slender jumping legs. The true crickets are not green; they have rounded rather than elongated heads and their tarsi, or 'feet', have three segments instead of four, as in bush crickets (see page 138). Grasshoppers are busy

▲ The large marsh grasshopper is the biggest and most spectacular of our grasshoppers. It lives in very wet bogs where cottongrass and sphagnum moss grow. His song is a ticking sound.

◄ Two males and a female heath grasshopper on heather. When several males are together their songs are short; one male on his own sings a longer song.

► The male rufous grasshopper on a harebell displays his clubbed antennae while he sings. He gives a little chirp, wags his head and swings his antennae round in a loop.

by day, whereas bush crickets and crickets are more often active at night.

Songs of love

Grasshoppers sing or stridulate, as it is called, by rubbing the hind legs against the forewings. With a little care, you can get near enough to a grasshopper to see the hind legs moving up and down rather like a violinist's bow. Inside the thigh of each hind leg there is a row of tiny pegs which is drawn along the edge of the forewing to set it in vibration.

As with most birds, it is usually the male grasshoppers that sing and their song attracts the females. Once the female has approached, however, a quieter courtship version is produced, and some females join in with a similar song.

The lesser marsh grasshopper of low-lying damp grasslands and dunes sings with a series of two to six soft chirps repeated every couple of seconds. Both males and females are attracted by the song so groups of grasshoppers gather together, and the song changes to the more complicated courtship type made up of longer chirps. The male rufous grasshopper of limestone country goes further and signals to the female by waving his antennae and swinging

them in a loop, as well as jerking his hind legs.

Grasshoppers lay their eggs in a pod on or below the surface of the soil. Some species lay their eggs among grass, others prefer bare ground.

MAKE A CHIRPING CHART

Each species of grasshopper, bush cricket and cricket has its own tune and you can give them names like 'zeeps' or 'fitter-fitters' based on the sound they make. You can study grasshoppers, like birds, by listening to their songs. The species living in one place can be identified and their numbers estimated. Each species also has a song period – the time of year when its song will be heard – and you can draw up a chart to record your observations like those for birds and butterflies (see pages 31 and 73). Most species start to sing in early June; earlier in the year, most grasshoppers you find will be immature nymphs with undeveloped wings.

Plants that eat animals

The idea of plants eating animals seems to belong to the pages of science fiction stories or, at least, to travellers' tales of tropical jungles, but carnivorous plants do exist and live close to home.

Most plants make their food for themselves by photosynthesis (see page 9). They use sunlight as energy to convert carbon dioxide and water into carbohydrates. Other nutrients, such as nitrogen and nitrates, are absorbed from the soil. Most animals get their food by eating plants or other animals. But some plants living on very poor soils need to get some of their food from elsewhere and one way is to catch and digest small animals.

No one knows for certain how many plants are able to eat animals. There are, however, three kinds of well-known insect-eating plants in Europe: the butterworts, bladderworts and sundews. These plants are specialists which can survive in places where the soil or water is often acidic. Unfortunately, insect-eating plants are becoming rare because their homes are being drained and the soil improved. They could survive in the improved conditions but other plants move in and crowd out the insect-eaters.

A sticky end

The three species of butterwort live in bogs, moors,

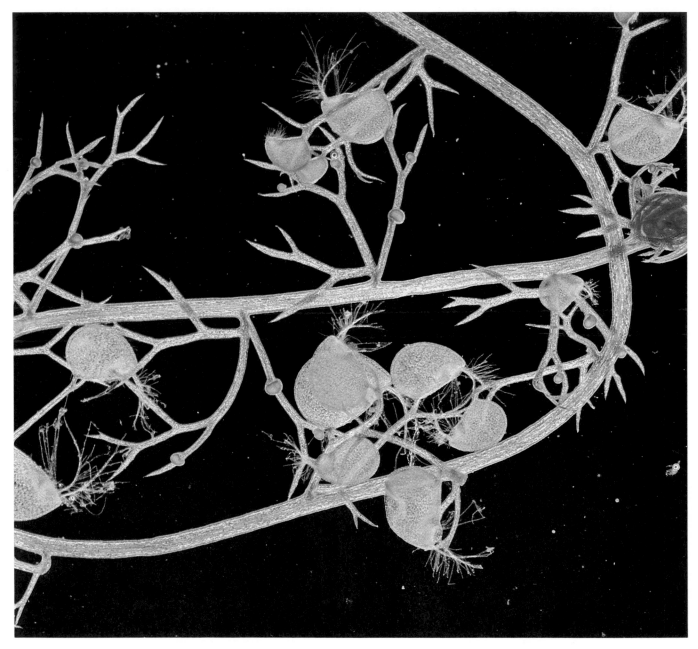

fens and wet heaths. They grow best along the sides of ditches and on damp patches where there is no tall vegetation to crowd them out. Through most of the summer, until the end of July, butterworts are easy to find because they have a single lilac or violet coloured flower, not very different from a real violet, growing on a 6-centimetre stem. The leaves are yellowish green and lie flat against the ground.

The inner surfaces of butterwort leaves glisten in the sun with a secretion which lures and traps insects. These sticky droplets are on tiny stalks which cling to anything that touches them. As an insect struggles to escape, its legs get caught by more droplets which are drawn out in tough strands, until the insect is securely trapped. The usual victims are tiny flies and beetles. Occasionally butterflies are caught if they have been flying low over the ground and are too weak to pull themselves free. Butterworts also digest pollen grains and leaves that land on them.

When the prey has been caught, the butterwort leaf starts to curl up at the edges to cover the insect and to secrete digestive juices over it. These break down the proteins in the victim's body to make a sort of soup on the surface of the leaf. This is absorbed and passed to the rest of the plant.

Underwater trapdoors

Bladderworts are waterplants that live in deep ponds and ditches. The plants float in the water and have no roots. The leaves are fine, branching fronds that spread out in the water but they clump together when the plants are pulled out. From June to August, yellow flowers grow above the water on tall stalks.

Among the feathery leaves there are many small, green, round or egg-shaped swellings, each about 5 millimetres long, which look as if they could be fruits. These are gas-filled bladders, from which the plant gets its name. The bladders are the traps with which the plant catches its prey.

Each bladder has several bristles at one end which act as triggers to open a watertight trapdoor when they are touched. Special glands extract water from the bladder and its walls collapse slightly, like a plastic bottle when the air is sucked out. If a water flea or mosquito larva touches a trigger, the trapdoor flies open and, as the walls spring out, water rushes into the bladder carrying the animal in with it.

▼Three tiny insects have become trapped by the sticky glue on the butterwort leaf whose edges are curling over to cover them.

◄The bladderwort does not have roots and nourishes itself through its leaves and bladders. It rarely sets seed. In winter buds sink to the bottom of the pond and produce young shoots in spring. Here you can see the bladders and feathery leaves.

►This mosquito larva triggered the bladder trapdoor and was drawn in as it rapidly filled with water. There is no escape.

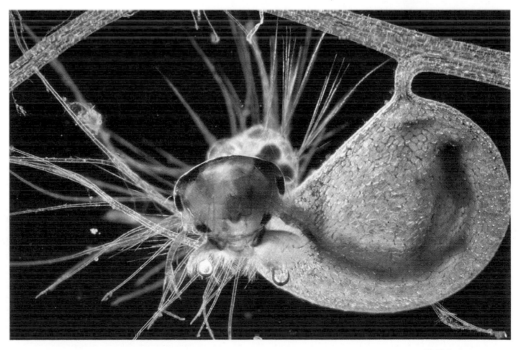

Leaves of death

Sundews live among the mosses and on bare patches of peat in bogs and heaths. There are three kinds: great and round-leaved sundews and the oblong-leaved sundew with tapering, spoon-shaped leaves. The three species often grow in the same place.

The upper surfaces of the sundew's leaves have stiff hairs, each with a drop of sticky liquid on the tip which glistens in the sun, giving the plant its name. Insects are attracted to the secretions and become trapped. As they struggle, they are caught more securely by neighbouring hairs which bend over to glue them down.

Plants do not usually have senses nor are they often capable of rapid movements, but the sundew tastes its victims and electrical messages, like the impulses in an animal's nerves, trigger the bending of surrounding hairs. Several hours later, the whole leaf starts to bend over and roll up to cover the insect. This slow movement is controlled by the spread of a special substance through the leaf from the hairs. It is a chemical messenger like the hormones in an animal.

TEST THE SUNDEW'S TASTE
Drop a piece of cheese on one leaf and a tiny glass bead or metal fragment on another. The plant will react to the cheese but not to the inedible glass or metal.

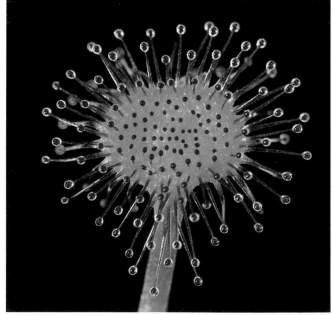

▲ Here an unfortunate lacewing fly has blundered into a sundew leaf and become caught by the sticky hairs. The hairs have bent over and the leaf curled to enclose the lacewing. The insect will be slowly digested and its juices absorbed by the plant. Digestion complete, the leaf will uncurl and the dry husk of the lacewing will blow away.

◄ The sundew leaf is covered with red hairs, each with a knob at its tip coated with a sticky fluid which glistens in the sun like dew; hence the plant's name.

◄◄ This picture shows two of the knob-tipped hairs of a sundew leaf, and the dew-like fluid, greatly magnified.

► The round-leaved sundew is a common plant of damp or boggy places on heaths. Although tiny, its rosettes of bright leaves make it quite easy to find. Each leaf is a sticky trap for unwary insects.

Plants without flowers

When the countryside abounds with trees and grasses and flowering herbs, there are some plants that are easily overlooked and forgotten. These are the ferns, mosses and liverworts. Damp places such as the rocks around a waterfall and bogs are the best places to find them but, where there is plenty of rain, walls (see page 46) and trees become covered with mosses and scattered liverworts and ferns. Mosses prefer the damp, shady crevices in walls and rocks, or the gaps between paving stones. They and the liverworts are often the first plants to grow on bare rock.

A double life

These flowerless plants lead a double life in which two stages alternate. Look under the leaves of bracken or other ferns and you will see rows of small capsules. Each capsule contains large numbers of spores which are eventually blown away by the wind. If a spore settles in just the right kind of cool, damp place it sprouts and grows into a prothallus – a flat green plant only a few millimetres long. It bears male and female organs on its underside and, from the egg which it produces, the familiar fern with its fronds grows and eventually scatters more spores.

Fronds of ferns

Bracken can live in drier conditions than most ferns and it grows in woods and on heaths. Once a prothallus has taken root a mass of fronds grows over the ground. The fronds are linked by underground stems and the dense leaves block the light and prevent other plants from growing. Farm animals do not eat bracken and it can become a serious weed in fields. Other ferns usually grow in small clumps. Wall-rue and maidenhair spleenwort grow on shady walls, while polypody grows on the branches of trees in damp woods.

Mosses

In contrast to the ferns, the plants of mosses and liverworts represent the sexual stage with the male and female organs. The clumps of mosses that grow on walls and roofs are made up of individuals with a single stem and a cluster of leaves. The spore-

▼ *Lunularia* is a liverwort common in damp spots in gardens and greenhouses. It is actually from the Mediterranean region.

▼ *Blasia* is found along the banks of streams and on wet ground. It reproduces from buds growing in cups on the surface of its fronds.

▼ In this large, common liverwort, the male (*centre*) and female (*left and right*) organs are carried on stalks. *Marchantia* may also develop buds in wide cups.

bearing stage (equivalent to the fern plant) is a simple stem with a capsule containing the spores; it looks rather like a lamp post.

Moss plants are not waterproof and they easily dry up, but a clump of them works like a sponge to hold water, and they soak up water vapour from the air.

Bogmoss, or *Sphagnum*, is the main plant in bogs. Bogs are areas of waterlogged ground in which, over hundreds of years, the decayed remains of *Sphagnum* have built up into peat. Pull out a single stem of *Sphagnum* and you will see that the tip is green but the other end is dead and withered. While one end of the plant grows the other is decaying.

The lowly liverworts

Liverworts are only found in damp places. Some kinds are flat and ribbon shaped, and they look like seaweeds. You might easily mistake other kinds for mosses. One common liverwort grows little orange 'umbrellas' which carry the sex organs, while another has small cups on its surface (see opposite page). Buds, called gemmae, grow in the cups and are washed out by rain. If they come to rest in a suitable spot they grow into new liverworts.

▲ On tall bracken unfurling at a woodland edge a wolf spider guards her nursery web, with newly hatched spiderlings clustered inside. Dew, condensed beneath the tent, glistens in the sun.

◀ Hair moss is found on damp heaths and is our tallest moss. This is a female plant with high stems carrying spore-bearing capsules. The tiny toadlet treading its way through the 'forest' has recently left its nursery pond nearby.

▶ *Sphagnum* or bogmoss is the most important plant in a bog. It can hold 20 times its own weight of water, but this clump has almost died out during a drought. Note the round-leaved sundews growing on it.

Plants of pond, lake and stream

See also **Flowers of grasslands** on page 38 and **Wild flowers by the sea** on page 94

Fresh water would have few animals living in it if there were no aquatic plants. The plants give the animals food and shelter, and they help to supply oxygen to the water. Waterplants are descended from land-dwelling relatives and they have had to make some changes in their structure and habits to survive in a watery environment.

The easy life

In some ways, life in water is easier than life on land. Because they are surrounded by water, plants do not face the danger of drying up (unless the pond or stream dries up). They do not need a waterproof covering or cuticle to prevent them from wilting, and they do not need large roots to take up water. Many waterplants have weak roots and they can survive even if they are uprooted and left to float. A few are never rooted, such as bladderwort (see page 114) and floating duckweed. A water-lily leaf lies on the water's surface and has a cuticle on its upperside.

Water buoys up the plant so the stems and leaves do not have to be rigid. If you lift the plant out of the water it will flop. On the other hand, plants growing in fast-flowing streams need to be not only flexible but also tough, so that they are not ripped by the force of the water.

How do waterplants breathe?

Submerged plants get oxygen for breathing and carbon dioxide for photosynthesis from the water. There are always enough dissolved gases in a large lake or flowing stream unless it is heavily polluted. A pond, however, may run short of oxygen in hot weather when the animals are very active and the plants are growing rapidly. Animal and plant life may then die, but the animals that breathe at the surface and the plants that stand out of the water, called emergents, are safe. Air can enter an emergent plant and travel down the stem. Cut a water-lily stem in half and you will see large tubes running down to supply the roots with air.

Water-borne seeds

Most waterplants have flowers on a stem that lifts them clear of the water. Some are specially adapted to use water to carry the pollen, as other plants use the wind (see page 13). Canadian pondweed flowers scatter their pollen on the water's surface and it is blown along by the wind. Male flowers are very rare, however, and the plant spreads by the stems continually growing and snapping in two. Hornwort has underwater flowers. The stamens break off and float to the surface where they release their pollen. The grains sink and, with luck, touch the stigma of a female flower.

◄The white water-lily lives anchored to the bottom in lakes and ponds. Its waxy flowers close up at night. This opportunist sparrow is busy collecting newly emerged damselflies while their wings are still soft and they cannot fly away.

►Plants can grow in profusion on the fertile banks of a clear stream. Here, you can see alder bushes, nettles galore, yellow flag leaves and the purple loosestrife in flower.

▼Water violet has tufts of feathery leaves underwater, but in May and June it sends up delicate lilac flowers on tall stems above the surface. Water mint needs only its roots in the water. Its dark purple leaves smell of tom-cat but its flowers are more sweetly scented.

Water is a great help for dispersing seeds. The fruits of the yellow water-lily are shaped like flasks and smell alcoholic when ripe. These 'brandy-bottles' float for some time before shedding their seeds and they are blown by the wind or are carried by the current.

AN INSTANT DUCKWEED CARPET
For some plants, such as the Canadian pond-weed, flowering and making seed is a rare event. They normally spread by budding and splitting. Duckweed consists of a flat, oval frond, 2 millimetres across, with a single rootlet. It grows on still water and one frond can very quickly grow into a carpet covering the whole surface. Duckweed produces buds that split off and grow into new fronds. In hot weather when the pond is drying out, tiny yellow flowers appear on the edges of the fronds.

Dragons and damsels

Dragonflies and damselflies belong to the same group of insects, but the damselflies are smaller and more delicately built. Both pairs of wings on a damselfly are of equal size, whereas dragonflies have broader rear wings. At rest, damselflies fold their wings over their backs while dragonflies rest with the wings spread.

Dragonflies are expert fliers and hunt smaller insects on the wing. They can reach speeds of more than 30 kph and they are extremely manoeuvrable; they can hover and even fly backwards! Their wings beat at around 20 times every second, which is slow for an insect. As a large dragonfly flies past you can hear its wings clattering.

Hawkers and darters

Dragonflies and damselflies are found mainly near ponds, slow-flowing streams and marshes, but you are quite likely to see them in gardens, along the edges of woods and in open country. Some dragonflies, known as hawkers, patrol to and fro along a regular beat, but others, the darters, rest on a favourite perch and fly out to catch their prey.

If the dragonfly is flying high and is silhouetted against the sky, you can see it chasing flies and other insects. All dragonflies and damselflies hunt by sight and have huge eyes.

THE DRAGONFLY'S EYE

Insects' eyes are very different from ours. Instead of a single eyeball with one lens that focuses light on to a sensitive retina, the insect eye is made up of many units called facets. Each facet has its own lens and retina and an image is made by combining the view of all the facets. The more facets there are, the more detailed is the picture. A dragonfly's eye may have as many as 30,000 facets and can detect insect prey 10 metres away.

Flying in tandem

Dragonflies and damselflies mate in a way that is unlike that of any other insect. Before mating, the male curls his long abdomen forward and transfers sperm from the sex organs at the tip to a special organ at the front of the abdomen. Then he seizes the female by her head or thorax with a pair of claspers at the tip of his tail. The female now curls her abdomen forward to pick up the sperm from the male's body. When this is complete the pair stay united and fly in tandem.

▲Dragonfly nymphs are large-eyed, keen-sighted hunters. You can tell from the wing buds of these two nymphs that they are nearly ready to emerge from the pond and change into adults.

▼When ready to emerge a nymph sits, head out of water, waiting for dark. After nightfall it climbs up a stem and holds on tight. Its thorax splits, the dragonfly's head appears, then the whole insect arches out. After a rest it reaches up, pulls free and holds on while pumping up its soft, crumpled wings. It is helpless and a conspicuous bright green colour but by sunrise it will be dry, hard and ready for flight.

If you see dragonflies flying together in this way, try to follow them and see where they lay their eggs. Some species remain in tandem during egg-laying. They fly low so that the female can dip the tip of her abdomen into the water and wash off the eggs, which will sink to the bottom. Alternatively, she may land and insert the eggs into the stems of waterplants or sand at the edge of the water.

The 'masked' raider
The nymph which hatches out of the egg is as ferocious as its parents. It has large eyes and lies in wait until it sees a water insect, tadpole or small fish swim by. Darting forwards, it seizes its prey with the

▲ A pair of red damselflies in tandem, with the male in front. He is resting with wings folded while she is laying her eggs underwater on a pondweed stem.

'mask'. This is an enlarged lower lip which, at rest, lies folded under the head and is shot out on a hinge to grab its victims.

After moulting its skin between eight and fifteen times, the nymph is ready to turn into an adult. It leaves the water and climbs up a plant stem, where its skin splits open and the adult climbs out. Until its wings have expanded and its skin has hardened, the dragonfly is helpless, but fortunately emergence usually takes place under the cover of darkness.

Flies and true flies

See also **A bite in the air** on page 128
and **Wasps and wasp look-alikes** on page 150

The true flies are a group of insects to which the housefly (see page 194) and mosquito (see page 128) belong. Unlike insects they have only one pair of wings. The true flies also include the hoverflies (see page 100), craneflies or daddy-long-legs and the many kinds of midges and gnats. Most of these insects eat liquid food such as the nectar of flowers and the juices in rotting material, but mosquitoes and some midges and gnats drink blood.

Sawflies and caddis flies

Sawflies (see page 142) are relatives of the bees and wasps, but they lack the 'wasp waist'. They are named after the female's saw-edged ovipositor. She uses it to cut holes in leaves and stems in which to place her eggs. The larvae feed on the plant tissues and some species form galls (see page 136). Several sawflies are pests in the garden.

LANDING ON THE CEILING
Look at a dead housefly with a magnifying glass and you will see, behind each wing, a short stalk ending in a knob. This is called a haltere and it is all that remains of the rear pair of wings. All true flies have halteres. When the insect flies, the halteres beat up and down at the same rate as the wings to help the fly stay on course. If the insect flies slightly off balance, the base of each haltere is twisted. Sense organs relay this information to the insect's brain so that the fly can adjust its direction. Using their halteres, houseflies can turn to land on the ceiling.

▲ This common gnat belongs to the mosquito family, but it does not suck blood and is quite harmless. Its phantom, or ghost, larva is as transparent as glass; you can see its internal organs through its skin. It hangs horizontally in the water, lying in wait for water fleas and other tiny aquatic prey.

▲▼ Mayflies are easily identified by their three very long 'tails'; even their aquatic larvae have three 'tails'. Sometimes vast numbers of mayflies emerge from the river and dance over the water on fine summer evenings.

▼ Like mayflies, stoneflies are found near water. Their nymphs creep about among stones on the bed of a fast-flowing stream. An adult stonefly may live for two weeks, the mayfly for only two days.

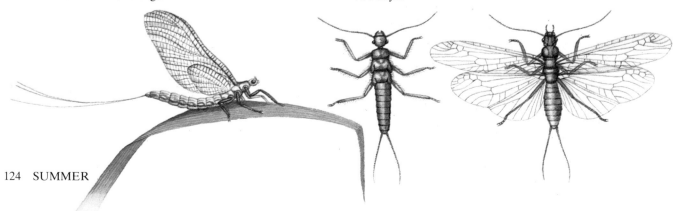

Caddis flies are best known from their larvae which live in cases of pebbles or tiny twigs on the beds of ponds and streams (see page 14). Adult caddis flies emerge at night and they are often attracted to lighted windows. You can recognize them by their long antennae and by their wings which are covered with fine hairs and held over the back like a roof.

Mayflies and stoneflies

Mayfly nymphs also live in water. A mayfly nymph has two rows of gills on its abdomen and three whip-like 'tails'. It beats its gills to create a current of water. The adults also have tails and short antennae. The wings are folded vertically and the rear pair are small or may even be absent. Mayfly adults are not only seen in May. Once in a while large numbers emerge and the males 'dance' over the water, bobbing up and down to attract the females. The adults live for no more than a few days.

A stonefly nymph is very like a mayfly nymph but

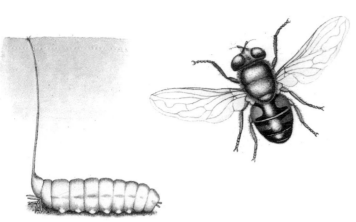

▲The dronefly looks like a stingless (drone) honeybee. Its larva lives in stagnant water or liquid mud and is called a rat-tailed maggot because its telescopic breathing tube looks like a very long tail.

◀The alderfly sits among waterside vegetation, or flies rather weakly on warm sunny days. Its larva might be mistaken for a water beetle larva, as it crawls about on the mud preying on caddis larvae and mayfly nymphs. It seems to have two fringes of extra legs on the abdomen, but these are its gills.

▲The aquatic larva of the caddisfly makes itself a mobile home of sand grains or bits of plants bound together with silk. Like a snail's shell, the case protects the soft body of the larva, which retires inside if threatened. The adults fly around lakes and ponds, some species by day, some at night.

▶The 'daddy-long-legs' cranefly hides by day in damp meadows and flies at night. The female lays hundreds of small black eggs in the earth. From these hatch 'leatherjacket' larvae which feed on plant roots.

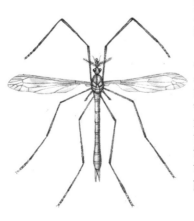

it has only two 'tails' and no gills. Stonefly nymphs are found mostly in streams. The adults, which have long antennae but may or may not have tails, live among the stones and plants at the water's edge.

Alderflies and snakeflies

Alderflies and snakeflies are similar to mayflies but they have long antennae, no tails and they fold their wings into 'roofs' at rest. Alderflies lay their eggs near water. They hatch into nymphs which crawl into the water. Snakefly nymphs live under the bark of trees. The front part of the thorax is elongated so that it looks as if the insect has a very long neck (see page 153).

'Beaked' bugs

The true bugs form a large group of insects widely different in appearance but with several features in common. All bugs have a hollow 'beak', like the needle of a doctor's syringe, and live on liquid food. Some bugs have no wings but most have two pairs. Bugs of one large group have two pairs of similar, transparent wings that form a 'roof' when they are folded. A second group has hard, shiny bases on the forewings which cover both sets of wings when they are folded. You could easily mistake these bugs for beetles.

Sapsuckers and bedbugs
Most bugs feed on the sap of plants. They thrust their sharp, piercing beaks into leaves or stems and the sap is forced up the tube under its own pressure. A few bugs are carnivores as well as sapsuckers. The forest bug, which is found mainly on oak trees, attacks caterpillars in addition to sucking the juices from leaves. Assassin bugs are carnivores which catch other insects and even spiders. Prey is seized in the front pair of legs and sucked dry with the stout 'beak'.

Pondskaters and waterboatmen are well-known pond-dwelling bugs (see page 15), while whiteflies, scale insects and aphids (see page 146) are bugs well known to fruit growers and gardeners. Scale insects hide under a 'cover' made up of previously shed skins glued together by a waxy secretion. The bed-bug, now rare, hides in crevices and comes out at night to suck the blood of humans and animals.

Shieldbugs are large shield-shaped bugs that live on the leaves of various trees. One is called the parent bug because it is one of the few insects to care for its young. The female lays her eggs on the under-side of a birch leaf in June. She remains with them until they have hatched and the young are strong enough to follow her to the seeds on which they feed.

▼Shieldbugs mating tail-to-tail on the flowers of green alkanet. You can tell these are bugs and not beetles because only the bases of the forewings are hard.

THE 'CUCKOO-SPIT' BUG
Leafhoppers and froghoppers are small bugs which leap like grasshoppers when they are disturbed. The common froghopper is the well-known 'cuckoo-spit' insect. The young nymph fastens its 'beak' into the tender stem of a plant and begins to feed on the sap. As the excess fluid is passed out of its body, the froghopper blows air through it to make a foam – the 'spit' – that surrounds and protects it (see also page 39).

▲The waterboatman swims
upside down underwater so it
can grab from beneath any
insect that falls onto the
surface. It rows itself along
with oar-shaped hind legs.

◄Disguised as a dead leaf,
the water scorpion lurks
among waterplants. What
looks like a sting in its tail is a
snorkel tube for taking in air
from above the surface.

►The horned tree-hopper is
a kind of bug that lives among
the leaves of trees and feeds
by sucking sap. Here it is on
an oak leaf beside a small gall.

A bite in the air

Mosquitoes are the most dangerous animals in the world because they carry such serious diseases as malaria and yellow fever. In northern Europe, malaria has died out (although it still occurs around the Mediterranean) and mosquitoes are only a problem here because of their irritating bites.

Only the female mosquito bites. She is armed with a long, tubular proboscis, which you can see if you examine a mosquito resting on a wall or window.

The proboscis pierces the skin and injects a fluid to stop the blood clotting so that it can be sucked up. The fluid also contains a poison that causes pain, inflammation and swelling. Male mosquitoes feed on nectar but the females need blood to help the eggs develop in their bodies.

SPOT YOUR MOSQUITO
Watch out for two kinds of mosquito: the culicines, which rest with their bodies parallel with their perch; and the anophelines, which are malaria carriers and rest with their bodies tilted head down. Both kinds lay their eggs on the surface of water; culicines glue theirs' together in rafts while those of anophelines float singly.

The larvae of mosquitoes are the almost transparent creatures that hang upside down at the surface of the water in ponds, water butts and puddles, and wriggle violently into the depths when disturbed.

◄A floating raft of mosquito eggs with the delicate transparent larvae hatching through underwater trapdoors.

◄▼Two comma-shaped mosquito pupae with several larvae and two old larval skins. The pupae hang at the surface, taking in air through what look like ears, while the larvae, upside down, breathe through their 'tails'.

▼A female mosquito emerges into the air from her underwater pupa skin: a dangerous operation when any puff of breeze could blow her over.

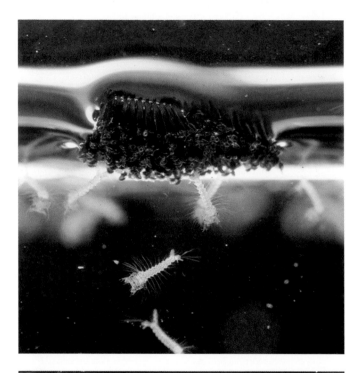

Disappearing ducks

See also **Birds on the water**
on page 20

After all the excitement of courtship in the spring, the ducks disappear from view to sit on their eggs, and reappear one month later with their ducklings. A female mallard followed closely by a string of fluffy chicks is one of the prettiest sights on a pond or stream.

When mallard drakes are freed from their parental duties, they flock together and gather on the bank to rest and preen. Unless you have been keeping a watch on the mallards, it sometimes looks as if all the drakes have disappeared and there are only females to be seen. This is because the drakes have moulted and lost the bright colours they wore for courting. They are now in their eclipse plumage and they look like the females. The glossy green head, white collar, rich brown chest, grey body and the two curled tail feathers have all gone and are replaced by a rather uniform brown plumage. You can still spot a drake in eclipse plumage from its yellower bill and less mottled plumage than that of the duck.

Flightless for a month

The eclipse lasts for two months, starting between early June and August. During this period, all the flight feathers – the long feathers which make up the main area of the wing – are moulted at the same time and the mallards are flightless for a month. The females moult later, when their families are growing up, but their plumage hardly seems to change.

▼Ducks or drakes? During the summer moult it is often very tricky to tell mallard females from their eclipse mates and both from their grown-up ducklings.

FEEDING THE BIRDS

If you feed the ducks regularly they will soon become tame and learn to come at feeding time. Canada geese, which live on many park lakes and gravel pits, mute swans and coots join the throng of ducks, and there is competition for the food. The larger geese and swans may bully the ducks and you will see that one or two ducks bully the others.

Tails from the river bank

Otters are now scarce because rivers have become polluted and their banks have been cleared of vegetation. They now live almost entirely in remote places where they are not disturbed. Even where otters are still common, you will be lucky to see one, but you are quite likely to find signs of their presence.

Otters are solitary animals and each one patrols a stretch of river or lake which is its hunting ground. It informs other otters of its presence by leaving piles of droppings marked with a scent from special glands under its tail. These droppings are called spraints and, surprisingly, they have a pleasant smell. The otter leaves its spraints in conspicuous places. To help find them, imagine you are swimming in a river looking out for good otter landmarks. Large boulders are obvious places, and the foundations of bridges are always worth checking.

The spraints are nearly always crammed with tiny fish bones that reveal the otter's diet. It feeds mainly on eels and other slow-moving fishes because trout and salmon are difficult to catch. The otter is well adapted for life in water but it is not such a good swimmer and diver as a seal, for example. Its dives usually last for less than a minute and it closes its nostrils and ears while underwater, using its eyes and whiskers to find prey.

While the otter has become rare, its place as an aquatic hunter has been taken on many rivers and streams by the smaller mink. The European mink of France, Scandinavia and eastern Europe has also become rare but American mink have escaped from farms where they are bred for their fur and they now live wild in many places.

Plops and splashes

The water vole is the commonest of the waterside mammals. There are few stretches of unpolluted, slow-flowing rivers and streams which do not have

◄An otter's food is rich and it does not need to spend much time feeding, so it uses time and energy in playing to practise hunting skills and keep itself fit.

►A water shrew swimming underwater looks like an animated bubble because of the air trapped in its fur. Notice the fringe of hairs on its toes which convert paws into paddles.

their water voles. The easiest way to find these little mammals is to look for the entrances to their burrows. They are neat, round holes in the bank. Some are below normal water level and are very conspicuous when the river is low. Those above water level may be surrounded by 'lawns' where the voles have been eating the grass. Like otters, water voles also deposit piles of droppings as scent markers on stones or other conspicuous places.

The first sign that a water vole is in residence is often a loud 'plop', which shows that it has heard you and dived for safety. You are unlikely to see it now because it will come up undercover, but you may see a line of bubbles marking its progress underwater. Water voles have weak eyesight so they will not notice if you approach cautiously and quietly. They come out to feed for about half-an-hour every three or four hours so you only need a little luck to spot one.

Water voles swim to cross the river or to cut across a curve but they feed on land. When they feed

▲ You can creep quite close to the short-sighted water vole if you move with great stealth. Its round face and small ears hidden by fur distinguish it from a rat.

among tall waterside vegetation, you may hear the sound of munching or see a stem waving violently as it is cut and dragged down to be eaten.

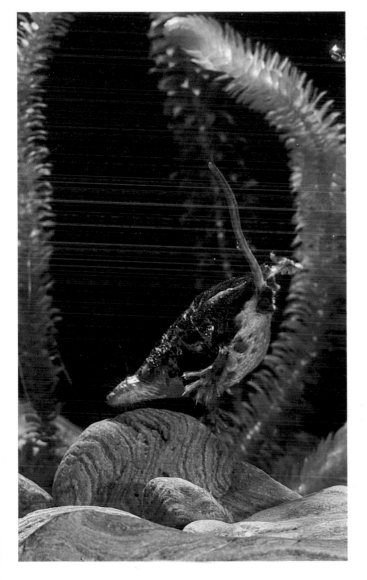

IT IS A VOLE OR A RAT?
Water voles can be confused with common or brown rats which often make their homes in river banks and also swim well. Brown rats are about the same size as the water vole which, like other voles (see page 168), has a short, slender tail, small ears almost hidden in fur and a round, chubby face. Rats, on the other hand, have large ears, a pointed muzzle and a longer tail.

The silvery squeaker
The water shrew is the smallest of the waterside mammals and it is less easy to find than the water vole. Watercress beds are good places for water shrews but they often live some distance from water. They give themselves away by high-pitched squeaks and by swimming in open water. The fur is water repellant and traps air so that the shrew floats very high in the water. When it dives, the air in its coat makes it look silvery. The tail and hind legs are fringed with stiff hairs to help the shrew swim and steer. The water shrew finds food on land or in the water. It feeds on insects, crustaceans, snails, small fishes and amphibians.

Autumn: mornings of mist and dew

Autumn can start with warm, fine weather. With the longer nights, however, the temperature falls so that there is often mist and dew by the morning. Mist and dew form when water vapour condenses out of the air as it cools. When the sun rises in the morning, the mist and dew disappear as the water evaporates again.

The first frosts may occur at this time and by October there may be snow on high ground, and cold spells may alternate with warmer weather. After the autumn equinox on 23rd September, the nights are longer than the days. As the days get shorter and the sun sinks lower in the sky, it has less chance to warm the earth. Fouler weather, with long spells of rain and wind, sets in during October and worsens in November as winter approaches.

Autumn is the season of glowing colours. Many fungi are at their best now; their often brilliant colours and strange shapes add interest to shaded places. It is also the season of harvest. It is the time for the harvest festival and, although some plants are still flowering, most are ripening their various fruits and nuts ready for the hedgerow harvest. They form an important source of food for many animals. Some of these, such as the dormouse, feed on the easy pickings, and grow a thick layer of fat before going into hibernation; others, such as the squirrels and jays, hide the food for use later.

The plants are also preparing for the winter to come. Many of the trees and shrubs lose their leaves but before they fall, the green woods and hedgerows are transformed into a kaleidoscope of reds, yellows and russets. The annuals die off completely leaving only their seeds to survive the winter and sprout in the next spring. Biennials, which last for two years, and perennials, which live for several years, store food in their stems or roots. They die back, often leaving withered stalks and a rosette of leaves which are ready to grow when the days begin to lengthen again.

Among the animals, insects and birds undergo the greatest changes in autumn. As the weather grows cooler, insects are seen less often. Some flies, butterflies, bees and wasps are on the wing as late as October, but the masses of insects which filled the air at the height of summer have disappeared. Many birds rely on insects as food, and they migrate southwards in the autumn when food here becomes hard to find. Other birds arrive from colder countries in the north, and the ripe berries of autumn become a favourite food. Some birds start to sing again after having maintained a period of quiet since the breeding season finished.

Wings across the ocean

See also **Visitors for the winter** on page 208

In autumn, as the weather gets cooler and the days grow shorter, many birds leave their summer haunts and fly southwards. We scarcely notice them going but, one day, we realize that there are no longer any swifts, swallows or martins overhead.

Escape to the sun

Many birds escape the harsh winter weather by flying to warmer countries. Birds such as flycatchers, wheatears, warblers and the cuckoo eat insects and it is hard for them to find enough to live on in the cold northern winter. They therefore fly thousands of kilometres each autumn and face perils such as storms and headwinds on their journey.

Most of these migrant birds travel by night, when we cannot see them, and they are able to feed during the day. But swallows, martins and swifts feed on the wing and migrate by day, catching flying insects as they go. During autumn you may see flocks of small birds along the shore preparing to cross the sea. Sometimes in spring when the migrants return you can watch them flying in from the sea, or see them resting on their arrival.

Travellers' fare

To reach their journey's end birds may have to travel long distances across seas and deserts so they must carry enough 'fuel' for the journey. Many small birds leave southern Europe and fly across the Mediterranean and then the Sahara desert, a distance of nearly 2,000 kilometres. They will have very little chance of feeding on the way. Before they set out, the birds eat

HAZARDS ALONG THE WAY

A journey of migration is full of danger. If the weather is bad, the birds may get held up and starve. Some are blown out to sea and drown. Others are shot or trapped for food. If there is drought in Africa many more perish before they start the long journey back. Yet migration is worth while because the journey gives the birds a better chance of surviving than staying behind for the winter.

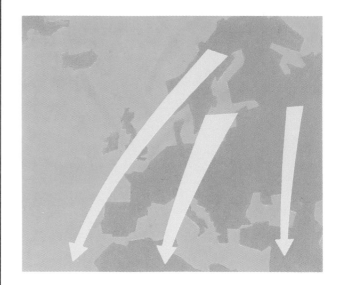

Migrating birds usually try to avoid long sea crossings, so they become funnelled across the narrow parts of the Mediterranean or they detour around the eastern end.

LOOK FOR THE RING!

To find out more about birds' journeys, ornithologists mark individuals by attaching a very light metal ring to the bird's leg. If you find a dead bird look to see if it has a ring. If it has, note the ring number and send it, with details of where, when and how the bird was found, to the address which is also stamped on the ring. To catch birds for ringing or to note previously ringed birds, ornithologists use special kinds of traps or nets. These are used on islands and at places on the coast regularly visited by birds on migration.

◄ A young swift, just out of its nest, clings to the house wall briefly before take-off. Swifts are the first to depart at the end of July, followed by sand martins at the end of August, then swallows and finally house martins.

▲The nightingale heads for Africa and stays mainly north of the equator. It avoids the dense rain forests and finds plenty to eat in the open woodland.

▶▲Some chiffchaffs stay in Europe until October and they can be occasionally heard singing at this time.

▲The turtle dove is the only one of our pigeons and doves that migrates. It spends the winter in tropical Africa.

▲Young redstarts leave the country first followed by the adult females and then the males.

▲Waders, such as this little-ringed plover, are champion migrants. They can fly long distances without stopping.

◀Arctic terns fly all the way to the Antarctic where they find plenty of seafood among the ice floes.

▶Adult cuckoos leave before their offspring. These know instinctively where to fly.

heartily and store the extra food as fat. A small bird, such as a warbler, doubles its weight before migration; this amount of fat is enough to keep it flying for more than 60 hours. At a speed of 40 or 50 kilometres an hour, this little bird should be able to cover 2,500 to 3,000 kilometres provided it is not slowed or blown off-course by the wind.

Short shuttle

Some birds may only migrate short distances. Or part of the population may migrate while the rest stay in the same place all the year. These species are called partial migrants. Reed buntings, for instance, fly south within the British Isles to find warmer weather, and some song thrushes migrate to southern Europe. Because some birds stay behind, while others of the same species that spend the summer farther north join them, it seems to us that these birds do not migrate (see page 208).

◀Swallows (and a house martin) on electric cables are a sure sign that autumn is approaching and summer visitors will soon depart.

Plants with knobs on

See also **Life in an oak tree**
on page 68

The leaves and stems of many plants are often covered with small lumps called galls. The galls occur where the plant grows abnormally as a result of the activity of insects, or sometimes of fungi, eelworms or mites (see page 163). Many of the commoner galls are caused by different species of gall wasps which look like small winged ants. Others are caused by beetles, aphids, midges and moths. One of the most spectacular galls looks like a bird's nest attached to the branches of a birch tree. These 'witches' brooms' are masses of twigs which have grown this way because of the presence of a particular kind of mite.

Marble galls

Oak trees have more kinds of galls caused by insects than have other plants. Among them are marble galls which are perfectly spherical and grow among leaves on the tips of twigs. They are green when fresh but turn brown in September. A marble gall is formed where a tiny gall wasp has laid its eggs. The larva grows inside the gall and feeds on it. Eventually it changes into an adult gall wasp and bores its way out, leaving a small tell-tale hole. Sometimes there are many holes in the marble gall. These are made by insect parasites which grow from eggs laid inside the body of the gall wasp larva.

Spangle galls

Another gall wasp makes the oak tree produce circular spangle galls like flat buttons on the underside of

AN APPLE YOU CAN'T EAT

The oak apple which grows on oak twigs is caused by another gall wasp. Ripe oak apples look like small, rosy-coloured apples which turn brownish yellow. The female gall wasps are wingless. They walk down the trunk of the oak and burrow into the soil where they lay their eggs on the tree's roots. Here another kind of gall grows. The wingless females which emerge in winter climb back up the trunk and lay eggs which cause a new crop of oak apples.

the leaves. The galls fall off the leaves in autumn but the larvae inside continue to grow. Wingless female gall wasps emerge in April and climb up the tree. They lay their eggs in the fresh leaves and catkins where currant galls develop in May and June. From these emerge the gall wasps which will lay eggs to cause spangle galls again.

How are they formed?

No one knows exactly how galls are formed. Somehow the larvae of the gall insects, or other gall formers, make the plant tissues grow into swellings. For the larvae of gall insects these swellings provide food and shelter.

◄These are nail galls on a fallen beech leaf. They look like stubby, furry nails driven through the leaf from below. They are caused by mites that pierce the leaf with sharp mouthparts and suck up the sap. The mites' saliva makes the leaf grow in a mad burst to produce these 'nails'. Mites also cause various pimples on other sorts of leaves. Some mites make leaves curl.

►Robin's pin-cushions look like bunches of red moss stuck onto wild rose twigs. They are galls made by the robin's pin-cushion gall wasp. The female lays her eggs inside leaf buds, causing the leaves to develop into bundles of 'moss'. Here a male great green bush cricket creeps up behind a female as she munches a gall.

Singing bush crickets

See also **A butterfly year** on page 104
and **On the hop** on page 112

Bush crickets are easily confused with grasshoppers. Bush crickets, however, have long whip-like antennae (see page 137) and for this reason they are sometimes called long-horned grasshoppers. You can easily recognize the female by her stout, blade-like egg-laying organ called an ovipositor. It looks like a weapon such as a sting but it is harmless. The jaws of bush crickets are powerful and the great green bush cricket, which is 4.5 centimetres long, can give your finger quite a nip if you handle it carelessly.

Songs by day and by night

The oak bush cricket is nocturnal, and spends the day hiding under oak leaves. The great green bush cricket, however, is active and stridulates by day as well as by night from the thick vegetation of hedgerows and bramble thickets. Try watching bush crickets during the early evening. They stridulate most then and if you catch them in the light of a torch you can see the rapid vibration of the wings.

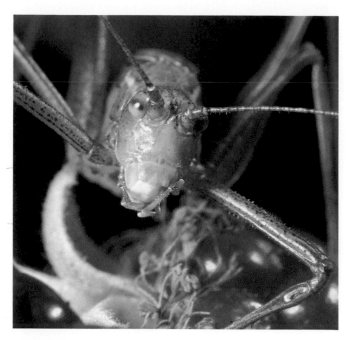

▲ Bush crickets have their 'ears' on their front legs just below the 'knee'. You can see one clearly in this close-up of a speckled bush cricket on unripe blackberries. The 'ears' of a grasshopper are on its abdomen.

◄ The dark bush-cricket seen here on woody nightshade berries and flowers is a male. His wings are small flaps for chirping only. Females have no wings at all and a long, curved ovipositor.

► A bush cricket does not pass through a pupal stage as does a butterfly but, as it grows, it sheds its skin and each time it emerges it looks more like the adult insect. This is a speckled bush cricket nymph near its moulted skin.

You should be able to find adult bush crickets in late summer and autumn. Oak bush crickets are still active in November. Bush crickets lay their eggs in the soil, in stems and in crevices in bark. The eggs hatch in the following spring and the young bush crickets mature during the summer.

WINGS THAT SING

Grasshoppers sing, or stridulate, by rubbing their hind-legs against their wings (see page 112). Crickets rub the forewings together; one wing has a row of knobs which rubs against a special structure on the other wing thus producing a chirping sound. The oak bush cricket can produce only a very feeble sound by rubbing its wings together, and it also drums on a leaf with one hind-leg while the wings are held vertically. The sound this makes is also fairly faint and can be heard by us only within a few metres.

Two ways to grow up

There are two basic ways in which an insect larva grows into an adult. Butterflies, moths, flies, beetles, bees, wasps and ants do it in three stages. The larva, also called a caterpillar or grub, is a sausage-shaped eating machine (see page 78) with small legs. When it is fully grown it turns into a hard-skinned pupa. Within the pupal skin, the body of the insect breaks down and builds up again into an adult.

The other group of insects, which includes grasshoppers and bush crickets, bugs, dragonflies and damselflies, and mayflies, does not go through the pupa stage. The larva, usually called a nymph, is at first merely a squat, wingless version of the adult. But each time it sheds its skin, or moults, the nymph grows and begins to look more like the adult. The most obvious difference between nymph and adult is the size of the wings. Adults have full-sized wings and most are able to fly; the exceptions are the adults of some bush crickets and grasshoppers which remain flightless. Dragonfly and damselfly nymphs may not look much like the adults, but imagine them with wings and more slender abdomens, and you will see the resemblance.

Home in the hedgerow

See also **The inside story of a wood** on page 26
and **The hawthorn year** on page 142

In spring a hedge is a mass of flowers; in summer it is thick with green foliage; and in autumn it bears a heavy crop of hips, haws, sloes, hazelnuts and acorns.

The hedgerow habitat

A thick hedge is like a long slice of woodland, with trees, shrubs and a field layer of herbs (see page 26). You will find the same plants and animals as those that live on the edges of woods. There are often grassy verges and ditches alongside the hedge and these will support plants and animals of open country and water. The shape of the hedge makes it easy to study because you can walk along it and peer in to look for the smaller inhabitants.

A tangle of plants

Most hedges have been planted. The main plant in a man-made hedge is usually hawthorn, but there are hedges of ash, holly, elm, hazel, yew and other trees and shrubs. As well as the main plant, others become established naturally. There may be blackthorn or sloe, elder, wayfaring-tree and wild privet, while roses, brambles, hops, honeysuckle, bryony and bindweed (once called hedge bells) and travellers'-joy, or old-man's-beard, climb over the hedge. Around the base of the hedge there is likely to be a mass of dead-nettles, cow parsley, hogweed, hedge mustard, hedge woundwort and stitchwort. In spring, dog-violets, primroses, ground-ivy and lesser celandines comes into flower.

HEDGEROW LIFE

A hedgerow in autumn is well stocked with food for birds and small mammals: haws (**1**), sloes (**2**), elderberries (**3**) and blackberries (**4**). Old-man's-beard (**5**) and hop vines (**6**) provide dense cover. A wood pigeon (**7**) flies into a pollarded ash (**8**) to sample the fruit while a dunnock (**9**) beneath the hedge searches for insects, oblivious to the weasel (**10**). At the field edge a field vole (**11**) is in clover (**12**). The ditch is full of

The animal residents

The leaves, flowers and fruit of the hedgerow provide food for many animals. For instance, among the insects, caterpillars of tortoiseshell and peacock butterflies feed on stinging nettles; hedge mustard and cuckooflower are food plants of the orange tip butterfly and bramble flowers attract gatekeeper and ringlet butterflies. The rough ground at the base of the hedge is very important for nesting bumblebees, and wasps nest in old mouseholes. In autumn especially, a hedge is an excellent place to find spiders (see page 160) and bush crickets (see page 138).

Two kinds of mammals make nests in hedges. Harvest mice weave balls of grass in the hedge bottom (see page 168) and dormice make domed nests of honeysuckle bark in dense undergrowth.

Larger mammals, such as rabbits, deer, foxes and badgers regularly pass through particular gaps in the hedge. Their paths show up well in autumn. You can find their footprints as well as hairs which have become caught on thorns and barbed wire.

> **SPOT THE NEST**
> The autumn is a good time for finding birds' nests in the hedgerow. The occupants should have flown and the nests are easier to spot when the leaves have fallen.

▼Elm trees used to be a common sight along hedgerows but, now that Dutch elm disease has taken its toll of them, stumps are often all that remain. The red hips of dog roses are valuable food for mice and voles during the long months of winter.

reeds (**13**). Teasel (**14**) is still in flower; its seeds will attract goldfinches (see page 204) which twitter gaily among the swaying teasel heads.

1 HOME AMONG THE THORNS

Many kinds of insect live in hawthorn. For instance, the large hawthorn sawfly (see page 124) feeds on the pollen and nectar of hawthorn flowers, and lays its eggs in the leaves. The larvae, which eat the leaves, look like yellow-green caterpillars dusted with white powder. They pupate in papery cocoons that can be found cemented onto twigs in autumn. In May the adult eats its way out.

2 THE MAY FLOWERS

Hawthorn flowers open in May, and they are sometimes called May blossom. Hedges and thickets become covered with white or pale pink flowers. The flowers attract many kinds of insects, especially flies such as the hoverfly, and beetles such as flower beetles, weevils and longhorn beetles. The insects feed on the nectar and pollen and pollinate the flowers as they fly from one to another. The flowers are also eaten by bullfinches and woodpigeons.

HAWTHORN WATCHING

A hawthorn hedge provides plenty to see all the year round. Record the following events in the hawthorn year and compare the dates with those for other hedgerow plants such as blackthorn:

Date leaves sprout from buds ....

Caterpillars/insects feeding on leaves ....

Date blossom appears ....

Insects visiting flowers ....

Date haws ripen ....

Birds feeding on haws ....

Date leaves fall ....

Date hedge trimmed and how.......................................

The hawthorn year

Hawthorn is a small tree, up to 5 metres in height, which often grows in woods and on uncultivated ground. It may grow in dense thickets because its sharp thorns prevent animals from eating it and because if it is damaged, it grows again very quickly. The thickets give shelter to young trees of other species, such as oak and ash, which eventually outgrow the hawthorn. The most important place for hawthorns, however, is in hedges, and hedges are very important for wildlife (see page 140).

Hawthorn, which means 'hedgethorn', is much used for making hedges because it grows rapidly (another of its names is 'quickset') and because it grows very densely when repeatedly pruned. Many hundreds of kilometres of hawthorn hedge were planted in the eighteenth century when farming finally changed from the old open-field system, in which each villager cultivated several strips of ground on large communal fields, to an enclosed system, in which farmers planted hedges to make smaller rectangular fields.

6 LAYING A HEDGE

In winter, the bare outline of a hawthorn hedge shows how it has been laid. A hedge is laid by trimming off most of the side branches, partly cutting the main stems at the base and folding them over. Different methods of laying are used in different places, but stakes are often planted at intervals along the hedge and long hazel wands woven through the top for extra strength. Hedges are laid every 15 to 30 years but they should be trimmed every year or so.

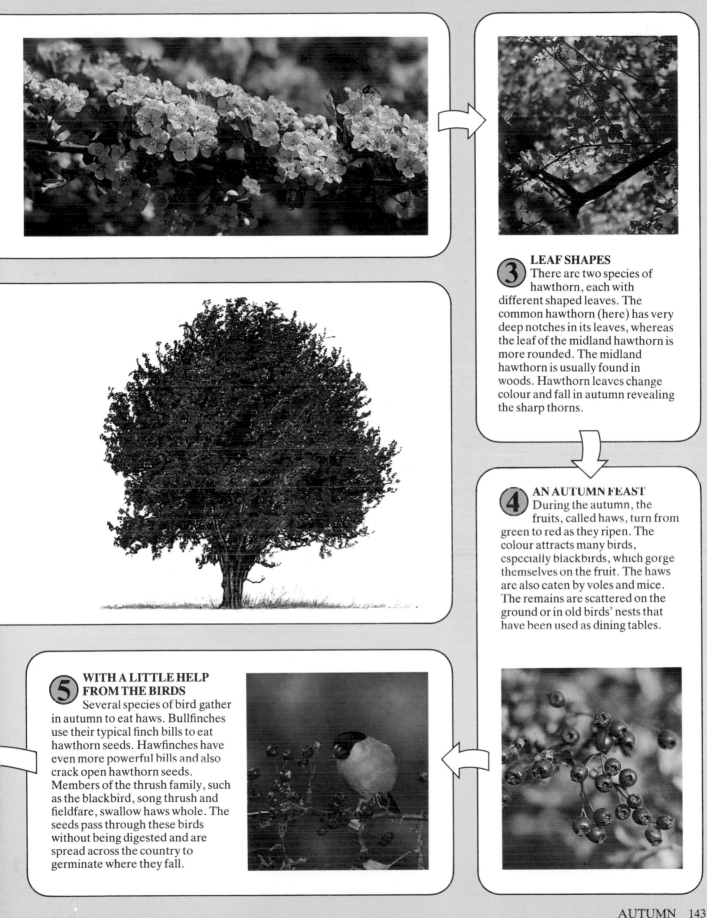

3 LEAF SHAPES

There are two species of hawthorn, each with different shaped leaves. The common hawthorn (here) has very deep notches in its leaves, whereas the leaf of the midland hawthorn is more rounded. The midland hawthorn is usually found in woods. Hawthorn leaves change colour and fall in autumn revealing the sharp thorns.

4 AN AUTUMN FEAST

During the autumn, the fruits, called haws, turn from green to red as they ripen. The colour attracts many birds, especially blackbirds, which gorge themselves on the fruit. The haws are also eaten by voles and mice. The remains are scattered on the ground or in old birds' nests that have been used as dining tables.

5 WITH A LITTLE HELP FROM THE BIRDS

Several species of bird gather in autumn to eat haws. Bullfinches use their typical finch bills to eat hawthorn seeds. Hawfinches have even more powerful bills and also crack open hawthorn seeds. Members of the thrush family, such as the blackbird, song thrush and fieldfare, swallow haws whole. The seeds pass through these birds without being digested and are spread across the country to germinate where they fall.

Leaves and leaf litter

See also **The inside story of a wood** on page 26
and **Dead but not lifeless** on page 70

Trees are divided into two main kinds. The evergreens always have leaves, even though they shed and regrow them throughout the year (see page 202). Deciduous trees shed all their leaves each autumn and grow new ones in spring. Most conifers have needle-shaped leaves and, apart from the larches, are evergreen. Broadleaved trees, such as oak or beech, are usually deciduous, although rhododendrons, holly and box are evergreen.

Leaves and water

A tree takes in water from the soil through its roots. Eventually the water reaches the tree's leaves where it evaporates from their surface. If the roots cannot get enough water, the leaves wilt and die. In hot countries, trees lose their leaves in the dry season but trees also shed their leaves if they are unable to continue photosynthesis in the weak winter sunlight. Without its leaves a tree's body processes almost stop, until the warmer weather of spring arrives.

How a tree sheds its leaves

The first sign of leaf fall is a change of colour from green to reds and browns as photosynthesis (see page 9) stops and the chlorophyll breaks down. Gradually, the leaf tissues decay and their materials are carried back into the stem. In this way, the tree saves energy and leaf material.

At the same time, the leaf stalk gets ready to break off at its base. A plate of corky tissue forms across the stalk. Except for bundles of tubes in the centre of the stalk, which continue to carry water and food substances, the leaf is sealed off. Eventually the tubes are plugged, too, but they continue to hold the

▼Woodlice feed on dead plant material and are valuable decomposers of autumn leaves. This is the pill woodlouse which rolls itself up into a ball when threatened.

▼The earthworm is a prime decomposer. Particularly in autumn it plugs the mouth of its burrow with leaves. It not only composts the leaves but mixes and aerates the soil.

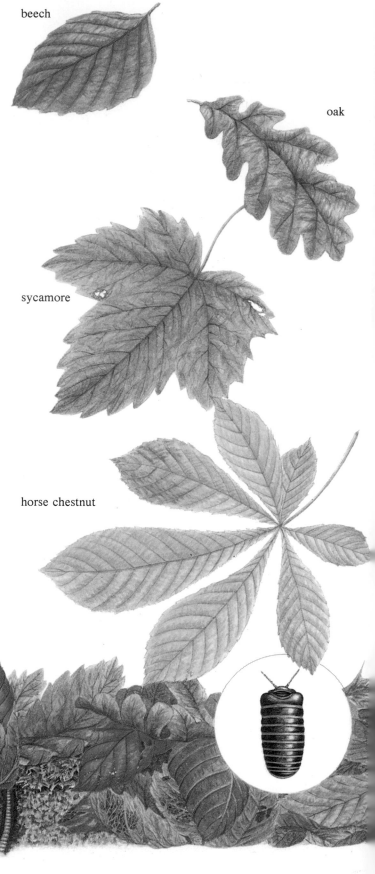

beech

oak

sycamore

horse chestnut

LOOK AMONG THE LITTER

As well as earthworms, all sorts of small animals live among the dead leaves on a woodland floor. Often, they are the same kinds that you find living under fallen logs or beneath the bark of dead trees (see pages 70 and 196).

Scratch about in the leaf litter with a stick and you will find that it is a busy place. You will disturb woodlice, millipedes, slugs, snails, moth caterpillars, the larvae of flies, and mites as well as the spiders, centipedes and beetles which hunt them. You will also find large numbers of tiny springtails as well as species of minute insects. The mites and insects are so small that you will need a magnifying glass to see them properly – a ×10 lens will do very well.

All these animals are called 'decomposers' and, without them, the leaves and dead wood, as well as the bodies of dead animals, would build up year after year into a thick layer and nutrients they contain would not be returned to the soil.

dead leaf in place until frost snaps them or the wind blows the leaf away. The layer of cork seals the wound left where the leaf broke off, and shows as a scar on the twig.

The story of a leaf

In autumn the falling leaves collect as a carpet of leaf litter. These leaves provide shelter and nest lining for many animals.

Even after it has fallen, a leaf still contains valuable reserves of food which can be returned to the soil and absorbed by the tree through its roots. The leaf litter slowly rots through the action of rain and the growth of fungi and bacteria. First, half-decayed 'leaf mould' is formed, then it becomes humus, a rich layer of topsoil.

Leaf decay is slow under conifers or beech trees where the trees' thick foliage cuts down the light, and a deep layer of litter gathers under them. Decay is especially slow where the ground is waterlogged or acid, as it is on heaths and moors (see page 108). Here peat forms from half-decayed plants.

◀▼The shiny black pill millipede, like the grey pill woodlouse, rolls up when attacked.

▼The rove or 'cocktail' beetle adopts a tail-up posture when attacked.

▼The harvestman has a small globular body and very long legs. It preys on other small invertebrates among low vegetation or leaf litter, and is common in autumn.

▼Bristletails are wingless, insects, mostly very small that live in damp places such as the soil, leaf litter and rotting wood. The two-pronged bristletail is very common.

▼Millipedes are harmless animals that feed on dead plant material and are valuable in woodland because they help break down fallen leaves and twigs.

Amazing aphids

Aphids are true bugs (see page 126). Using their sharp mouthparts, they feed by sucking sap from the stems and leaves of plants. Aphids are not popular with farmers and gardeners because they spread diseases among crops.

Take a good look at aphids through a hand lens as they gather in dense masses on plants. The common species include the cabbage aphid, which forms large mealy grey patches on cabbage leaves, the greenfly, which attacks roses, and the black bean aphid, which is a common pest of beans and sugar beet. The woolly aphid lives on apple trees and hides under a coating of fluffy wax.

Mothers but no fathers

During the summer the black bean aphid feeds on the sap of broad, runner and field beans as well as on sugar beet and various wild plants. Then the aphids move to the spindle tree or to garden plants such as syringa or viburnum.

The spindle is a small tree, often hardly more than a bush, which grows in woods and hedges. Once the aphids have settled on a spindle they lay eggs which will hatch in the following spring. In southern Europe the adults survive the winter but in Britain and northern Europe they die.

When the nymphs have hatched they start to feed on the rising sap. After several moults they eventu-ally turn into wingless adults. They are all female. Still more surprisingly, they start to give birth to live young (not eggs) even though they have not been fertilized by males. Several generations are born in this way, and then, in May or June, aphids with wings are born. They fly away from the spindles to the summer food plants where more generations of wingless females are born.

Plagues on the wind

From time to time during the summer more winged females appear. They travel to colonize new feeding grounds. An aphid is not a strong flier but, once airborne, it may be swept up by the wind and carried many kilometres.

WATCH A LIVE BIRTH
Take a hand lens and examine a group of aphids very closely. You should see adult females giving birth to live young. Without needing to be fertilized, a single aphid can land on a plant and soon produce a flourishing colony.

▼ Some species of aphid produce special females in the autumn, like this spiky dark brown creature sucking the sap of a maple twig. She has lived through the winter and is giving birth to many small green offspring.

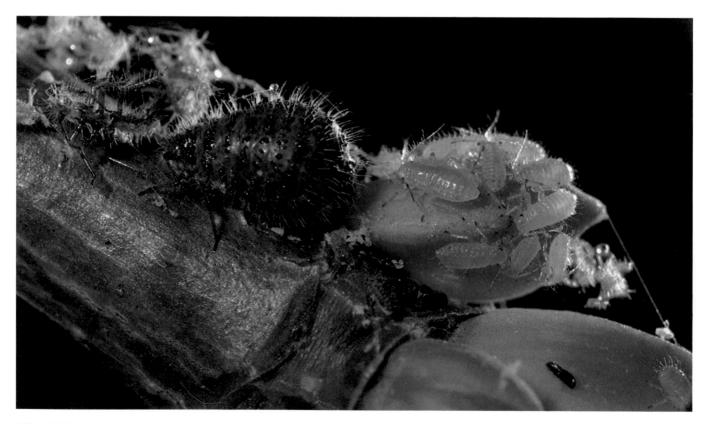

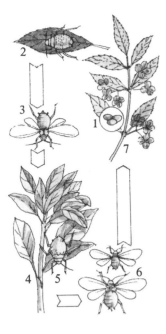

▲Follow the life cycle of the black bean aphid from autumn eggs on spindle (**1**) through wingless (**2**) and winged (**3**) generations. Wingless females (**5**) are produced on bean plants (**4**) until both winged males and females (**6**) appear. These fly to the spindle (**7**) when the cycle starts again.

▲The spiky sausage-shaped creature on the oak twig is a hoverfly larva eating a brown aphid. The small oval shiny objects are fertilized aphid eggs from which wingless females will hatch in the spring.

When the days grow shorter at the beginning of autumn, females give birth to winged offspring, males as well as females. These fly to the spindles where the females give birth to wingless females which are fertilized by the males and then lay the eggs which hatch in the following spring.

Food for others
By the end of the year the descendants of a single aphid would number millions if they all survived, but very many are eaten by other animals or are killed by bad weather. Birds, such as tits, peck aphids off leaves and flycatchers catch them in the air. Scores of winged aphids are caught in spiders' webs. Adult and larval ladybirds and lacewings, and the larvae of hoverflies attack aphids.

The honeydew bug
Plant sap is very rich in sugar but poor in proteins and other food substances. An aphid must therefore eat a lot of sap to get a proper diet. Aphids are able to extract and digest the substances they need from sap and pass out the sugars as a fluid called honeydew. If you look closely, you can see droplets of honeydew forming at the rear end of an aphid and being flicked off by a hind leg. The leaves of lime and birch trees can become sticky and shiny with honeydew. In late summer, the leaves may turn black with a fungus which grows on the sweet sticky secretion.

Aphids and ants
Honeydew attracts insects and especially ants. Wood ants (see page 106) and some garden ants collect large quantities. The aphid allows the ant to stroke it with its antennae, coaxing it to produce a drop of honeydew.

Why do aphids put up with the attention they get from ants? The ants protect the aphids by driving away their enemies but the main advantage to the aphids is that their honeydew is removed. A coating of honeydew slows a plant's growth and may cause it to wilt, and this would reduce the amount of sap available for the aphids. There are other reasons. Predatory hoverflies lay more eggs on leaves which are sticky with honeydew than on any other leaves and the honeydew also encourages moulds which can infect the aphids.

The useful ivy

See also **Green leaves of winter**
on page 202

Ivy is a very valuable plant for animals because of the food and shelter it provides. It is an evergreen, which means that it keeps its tough, shiny leaves through the winter to make storm-proof hideaways for many creatures. It flowers in autumn, supplying nectar and pollen at a time when other flowers have faded.

Can ivy strangle a tree?
When an ivy plant starts to grow it creeps over the ground and in some beechwoods it makes a carpet of shiny green leaves. When the ivy meets a tree, it starts to grow up the trunk. The stem of the ivy clings firmly with tiny roots which are cemented to the tree. It looks as if the ivy is growing into the bark and either drawing nourishment, as mistletoe does (see page 203), or strangling the tree. In fact, the ivy uses the tree only for support, as it does a wall. The ivy's roots may compete with a tree's roots for nutrients in the soil or, if the ivy clambers all over its support, it may cut out the light and smother the tree. In prac-

tice, neither usually causes much harm. Even on buildings ivy rarely causes damage, except when it grows under tiles or slates and forces them out of place.

Autumn feasts and winter hideaways
The yellowish-green flowers of ivy open in October. We hardly notice them, but insects find the flowers very attractive. On fine autumn days they are visited by wasps and hoverflies, while late tortoiseshell and red admiral butterflies feed there when there is little else but rotting fruit to attract them. The holly blue butterfly deserts the holly trees where it has spent the summer and lays its eggs on ivy. Its last batch of caterpillars can feed on the buds and berries and then they pupate on the ivy leaves. Ivy is also a

▼Ivy uses trees, such as this wild cherry, for support and does not generally damage its host. The dense mass of leaves, the small green flowers, and the berries which ripen in spring, all provide food and shelter for many animals.

▼By October when ivy comes into bloom, there are few other plants still in flower. This late-flying red admiral is using its proboscis to suck up the energy-giving nectar.

favourite place for brimstone butterflies to hibernate. These insects are almost impossible to find because they choose a place high up the tree and their colour and shape merge with the ivy leaves.

If you search very hard among ivy branches you may be lucky enough to find the caterpillar of the swallow-tailed moth. The pale yellow adult moth is on the wing along hedgerows and woodland edges in July and it lays its eggs on ivy leaves, and other plants.

Spring larder and summer cover
The insects that feed on ivy attract birds that feed on insects. Other birds come later to feed on the ripening berries. Wood pigeons and blackbirds are particularly fond of this fruit. The network of stems fixed to tree or wall and the mass of short branches with their thick foliage provide a good foundation for nests of robins and wrens, and good perches for many roosting birds. Pipistrelle bats also roost in the ivy cover. Night-flying insects, such as the herald moth which visits the flowers, attract long-eared bats. These flying mammals hover close to the foliage to snap up insects.

HOW DOES IT GROW?

Ivy can live for over 100 years and grow a thick trunk. Sometimes the original supporting tree dies and rots away leaving the ivy still standing on its own solid stems. Ivy leaves occur in two quite different shapes. When it is creeping along the ground or up a tree, the leaves are broad and have three to five lobes. As it grows upwards, the plant sends out short, horizontal branches which bear the flowers and berries. These branches have oval or pointed leaves without lobes.

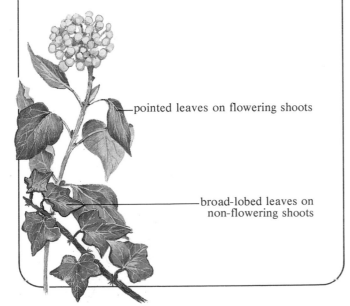

pointed leaves on flowering shoots

broad-lobed leaves on non-flowering shoots

▲Drone flies, whose larvae are called rat-tailed maggots (see page 125), feed on the nectar and pollen of various flowers, but here one is sucking up moisture from between the flowers of ivy.

AUTUMN 149

Wasps and wasp look-alikes

See also **Bees and flowers** on page 96 and **Under the twig pile** on page 106

The life story of wasps is very similar to that of honeybees (see page 96). The nest is the home of a queen, who spends her time laying eggs, and of thousands of her workers, offspring that gather food and tend the eggs and larvae. At the end of the summer, young queens and drones, or males, are reared in special cells and they leave the nest to mate.

Unlike honeybees, however, wasps do not survive the winter. They all die, except for the young queens that hibernate in hollow trees or garden sheds.

The two most abundant wasps are the common wasp and the German wasp. They usually build their nests underground, but they may also suspend them from rafters in the roofs of houses. The tree wasp and Norwegian wasp build their nests in trees, hanging them from branches. The hornet is a large orange and brown wasp which nests in hollow trees.

Nests of paper

Wasps cannot manufacture wax as honeybees do and they build their nests from 'paper'. They scrape fence posts and other dead wood with their strong jaws, making a loud rasping sound. The wood shavings are mixed with saliva to make a pulp which is worked into shape and applied to the nest like putty. The nest is made up of several storeys of six-sided cells in which the eggs are laid and the larvae are reared. Each storey is separated from its neighbours by slender pillars, so that the openings of the cells can be reached. The nest is covered with a skin of paper which has an attractive scalloped pattern of curved bands. Each band is made by a single worker wasp applying one load of paper. A full-sized nest may be about the size of a football or even larger. It is very fragile but may be home for 20,000 wasps.

Building the new home

The queen wasp must start building the nest by herself when she comes out of hibernation in spring.

> ### DON'T BE AFRAID!
> You need not worry about being stung while you are watching wasps. They are not so fierce as people often think. They are too busy collecting food and carrying out their duties in the nest to show any interest in us. They are only likely to sting when they are provoked; for instance if you try to brush one away and it gets trapped, or if the nest is disturbed.

She looks for a crack in the ground or an old mouse burrow and digs out a chamber, using her jaws to loosen the soil and carry it away. The foundation of the nest is a pad of wasp paper glued to a solid root in the ceiling of the nest hole, or to a rafter or branch. From this pad, the queen constructs a curved canopy with a stalk hanging from the centre. The stalk supports a lemon-shaped bag with an entrance at the bottom. This bag contains the cells where she lays her first eggs.

The worker wasps emerge from the cells three or four weeks after the eggs are laid. They take over the running of the nest and make it bigger.

Helpful and not harmful

Wasps make no honey; they are hunters and feed their larvae on insects. People who do not like wasps

WASP-WATCHING

To find a wasps' nest look for a steady stream of wasps flying in and out of a hole in the ground, a hollow tree or a building.

If you find a new nest in spring when it is still small, you can block up its entrance at night when the queen and her few workers are at home, and transfer it to a glass tank. Sew the 'stalk' of the nest with a needle and thread to make a loop, and hang the nest from a hook screwed into the wooden lid that fits over the tank. Provide a glass exit tunnel and you will be able to watch the workers coming and going. When the young queens and drones have flown and the workers are all dead, open up the nest and see how it was built.

3

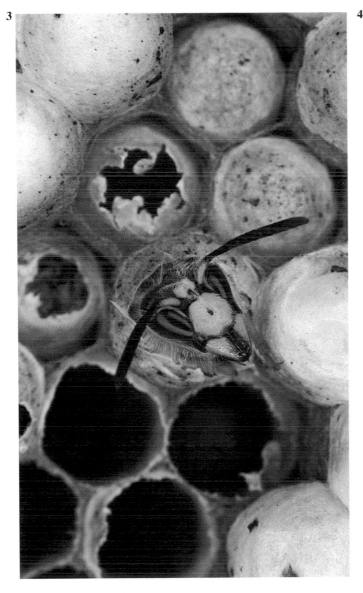

4

If you could see inside a wasps' nest towards the end of the season you might still find a few new-laid eggs. The old queen goes on laying throughout the summer. She has laid this egg (**1**) in a cell in which several generations of workers have already been reared. Full-grown larvae seal themselves into their cells by weaving a silk cap (**2**). Inside, they turn into delicate ivory-coloured pupae. When they emerge as adult wasps, they chew the cell caps away and pull themselves free (**3**). At the end of the summer young queens and drones are produced in special large cells. Here a queen and drone explore the outside of the nest (**4**) before flying away. They do not stay together, so that the drone will probably mate with a queen from another nest. After mating, the queens go into hibernation to survive the winter whereas the drones die of cold.

and destroy any nests in their gardens should remember that wasps can be useful to us. With so many mouths to feed, the workers must kill large numbers of insects, many of which are harmful, such as bluebottles. *Continued on page 152*

▲ A ripe apple is being hollowed out by worker wasps after a blackbird had first pecked a hole in the skin. A greenbottle fly is also sucking up apple juice.

The sweet things in life
Wasps feed their larvae on insects, but adult wasps eat sweet things. They take sugary saliva from the larvae and visit flowers for nectar but, as they lack the tubular tongues of bees, they cannot reach deep into a flower. They can be a nuisance when they raid the kitchen or picnic place for jam.

'Leave me alone' stripes
Some animals frighten us as soon as we see them.

Everyone leaves wasps alone; we immediately recognize the black and yellow stripes and know we will be stung if we annoy the insects. The stripes are a warning that wasps are dangerous. Other, harmless, insects copy the wasps' stripes to fool insect-eating birds into thinking that they, too, can be dangerous (see page 100).

The giant wood wasp or greater horntail has a 5 centimetre wingspan and is often mistaken for an outsize wasp or hornet. It has broad black and yellow stripes and seems to be armed with an enormous sting. However, although it can give you quite a nip with its jaws, the long 'sting' is the harmless ovipositor tube through which the eggs are laid.

Horntails live in conifer woods and they lay their eggs in the trunks and branches of trees that are either diseased or have been cut down. The female lands on the bark and bores her ovipositor deep into the wood and lays an egg.

The egg eventually hatches into a white grub which eats its way through the timber for two or three years. It is helped by a fungus that grows from spores its mother injected into the wood with each egg. The fungus weakens the wood so that it is easier for the grub to chew.

Ichneumon flies are also sometimes mistaken for wasps. They, too, look rather wasp-like and the ovipositor seems like a long sting. They are delicately built insects and they use their long ovipositors to lay their eggs in other insects. Although the ovipositor is as fine as a hair, it can bore through wood to lay eggs in the grubs of a horntail.

▲ The giant wood wasp or horntail is a frightening beast, as she zooms about like a huge wasp apparently ready to sting. But the female's 'sting' is really her ovipositor, with which she lays her eggs in the wood of a dead or dying conifer.

◄ The snake-fly appears to have a long neck and a long needle-like sting. But like that of the wood wasp, her 'sting' is for egg-laying. Here a female has curved her ovipositor round and is delicately feeling for a tiny crack in the bark.

Claiming a patch in autumn

See also **Claiming a space** on page 28
and **Finding a mate** on page 30

For most animals the breeding season starts in spring. In autumn, however, after the families have been reared and the adult birds have moulted, there is sometimes a return to springtime behaviour. Birds, that have been quiet all summer burst into song, sing for a few minutes, and fall silent again.

Autumn songsters

Many small birds abandon their territories after nesting and gather into flocks that roam the countryside (see page 205). They keep on the move so that they can find enough food in the cold weather. A few birds, however, such as robins and wrens, start to sing seriously in the autumn and they continue through the winter. They sing to show that they own their territory which, if they can keep other birds out, will give them their own private food supply. The robin is unusual because the hen bird owns her own territory in the autumn and defends it by singing, until it is time to join the male in spring.

Winter feeding grounds

By holding territories in autumn and through the winter, birds become familiar with the ground and learn the best places to find food. They can also begin courting and nesting as soon as possible in spring. If there is likely to be enough food to rear a family very early in spring, breeding may start towards the end of the previous autumn or in the winter.

Buzzards pair for life. They advertise their territory by soaring in circles high overhead with their wings stiffly outstretched. The pair may circle together and they call with ringing, far-carrying mewing cries. They chase away trespassing buzzards, which are often young birds that have left their parents and are wandering across country in search of somewhere to set up their own territories.

Buzzards lay their eggs early in the year when there are dead lambs and other carrion to feed on. The young buzzards can then take advantage of abundant prey later in the year.

You will hear the tawny owl hooting in the autumn because it has to have its own hunting territory where, if it is to survive the winter, it will be familiar with the best perches and flight paths for spotting prey. The young owls have stayed in their parents' territory until they have learned to hunt for themselves. They will be harassed if they try to stop in another owl's territory and they will die if they do not find an unoccupied area to settle in.

In a rut!

If your first visit to moorland is in the autumn, you may be puzzled to hear a bellowing sound like the

▲ Male and female robins both have red breasts and both sing, in autumn as well as in spring. This robin is warbling its quiet sub-song, through closed beak.

mooing of a cow. This is the roaring of a red deer stag challenging his rivals.

In September the herds start to break up and the stags move towards the traditional courtship, or rutting, grounds. Their antlers, which were growing

---

EAT OR BE EATEN

Red grouse, which live on moorland, provide us with a good example of the importance of a proper food supply. They eat heather shoots. The cocks establish territories between August and October and they are joined by hens during the winter. Any grouse unable to make a territory among the heather are pushed into areas where there is less food. They become weakened from lack of food and rarely survive the winter; most are eaten by predators.

▼The red deer rut takes place in autumn. This stag has come from his mud wallow and is patrolling his territory, roaring a challenge to other stags. His hinds rest and graze.

▲The foxes' autumn courtship involves much playful chasing. The dog-fox and the vixen spar with one another with mouths wide open, making cackling, screeching calls. They mate in winter (see page 62).

throughout the summer, are now fully formed. After a summer's feeding on the hills and moors, the stags are in prime condition. The hinds (females) gather too, and the aim of each stag is to claim the territory with the most hinds. This will give him the biggest possible harem but he will have to fight off other stags that are trying to steal the hinds.

Trials of strength
The stag patrols around his harem, roaring, running with neck outstretched, and pawing the ground. Young stags will retreat as soon as he approaches but more mature animals hold their ground. Two stags will walk side by side, 5 to 10 metres apart, and eventually one turns inward to face his opponent. The other turns too; they lower their heads and advance until their antlers are locked together. They push hard against each other and each stag tries to gain advantage by turning so that its opponent is downhill. Eventually, one stag gives in and breaks away, leaving the harem to the victor.

Defending a harem is a strenuous and ceaseless task; the stags have no time to feed, so they lose weight and eventually have to give up. By the end of November the rut has finished and the sexes form their separate herds again.

Hunt the hedgehog

To see hedgehogs you will have to go out at night although they are sometimes active at dusk or dawn. Often a hedgehog can be heard snorting and snuffling as it searches for small animals to eat. If you approach carefully, you can follow it without disturbing it. During the day hedgehogs sleep in a nest of dead leaves and grass, hidden in long grass or undergrowth.

A ball of spines
When the hedgehog is alarmed, it stops and raises its spines, but it does not roll up immediately. Each spine is controlled by small muscles. When the hedgehog is relaxed, the spines lie backwards. When the hedgehog is frightened the needle-sharp spines immediately stand up and point in all directions.

When it rolls up the hedgehog tucks its head and legs under its body and using a special muscle it pulls the loose skin with the spines around itself. With this defence the hedgehog is safe from most of its enemies, although badgers, foxes and crows occasionally kill and devour one.

A prickly nestful
Baby hedgehogs are born in a nest. They have no spines at birth but a sparse coat of white spines soon protrudes through the skin. A second coat of dark spines appears a couple of days later. At 11 days old, the young hedgehogs can roll up but they will not leave the nest until they are three weeks old.

▼Hedgehogs come out mainly at night and shuffle about finding all kinds of invertebrates to eat. This young one has found a large earthworm on the lawn.

Litters of hedgehogs are produced at any time between May and October. Two-thirds of the babies are likely to die before the next spring, especially if they are born in the autumn. They will not survive the winter unless they can put on a large amount of fat. If they survive the first winter, however, hedgehogs can live for seven years or more.

The long sleep
Hibernation (see page 192) starts in October, but some hedgehogs stay awake until December. Each hedgehog makes itself a cosy nest in undergrowth, beneath a tree stump or garden shed. It will probably wake up and move nests at some time during the winter and eventually emerge in April or May.

HELP A HEDGEHOG!
Remember to place some bricks or a sloping plank at the edge of your garden pond. Hedgehogs often fall in and will drown unless they find a way of getting out. In autumn be careful when you are clearing up or burning piles of dead leaves, especially if they have been standing for some time. A hedgehog may be sleeping underneath.

▶A hungry hedgehog may occasionally come out before sunset to forage, grunting and snorting and crunching crispy prey.

▼Nobody knows why an albino hedgehog should suddenly appear in the wild. He is most unusual. He lacks dark pigment in his hair and skin, so looks white with pink skin and pink eyes. (See also back jacket.)

Traps of silk

See also **Eight-legged hunters**
on page 160

The best time to look at spiders' webs is on a foggy or misty morning when the silken threads have trapped beads of moisture. They are a beautiful sight in the morning sun and the number you will see shows how abundant spiders are.

Hammocks and orbs

The hammock web is commonly seen in autumn. It looks like a dense sheet of silk supported by silken scaffolds above and below. The spider lives upside-down underneath the web and waits for an insect to fall on to it. The web is not sticky but the insect's legs get caught up so that the spider can rush across and bite it before it can escape. The similar but much smaller sheet webs that cover lawns and pastures are woven by the related tiny money spiders.

Orb webs are slung vertically rather than horizontally and they have threads of sticky silk to trap prey until the spider can seize it. The biggest orb webs are made by the garden spider. Another kind of spider, called *Zygiella*, makes an orb web with the sticky threads missing from two sectors of the web. You might see the spider in the centre of the web in the early morning but it shelters under a nearby leaf during the day, so that it will not attract the attentions of a hungry bird. Although spiders' silk is very

◀A large female garden spider sits in the hub of her dewy web waiting for the morning sunshine to evaporate the glistening drops strung along its sticky spiral threads.

tough in relation to its thickness, webs are easily destroyed and the spider may have to make a new one every night.

The building of an orb web

The first task is to sling a thread between two supports. If the web is to be placed in the corner of a doorway, the spider can fix one end of the thread and walk around to the other point, paying out silk as it goes. But if the web is slung between unconnected twigs, the spider must spin a thread and let it drift out on the wind until it catches the other twig. Then the spider pulls the thread tight and reinforces it by running along it and laying down more threads.

Next the spider attaches a loose hanging thread and then fixes a third thread between its centre and another anchorage point. When this is pulled tight there is a Y-shaped frame, and the junction in the middle becomes the centre of the web. More threads are added, like the spokes of a wheel, and the spider makes a platform in the centre.

Next the spider lays a thread, working out from the centre in a flat spiral. This is a temporary walkway for the spider to use as it lays a second spiral of sticky silk to form the trap for its prey. The sticky silk is laid from the outside and the first spiral is taken up and eaten as the spider goes. The spider has an oily substance on its feet to stop it getting caught in its own web.

▲Like its relative the garden spider, this small green spider also builds an orb web, but a smaller one. Here a female is being courted by a male, as she hangs in her web on a stinging nettle.

▶We might not notice these hammock webs slung among the heather, were not dew-drops glistening on them. They are particularly obvious on damp, autumnal days.

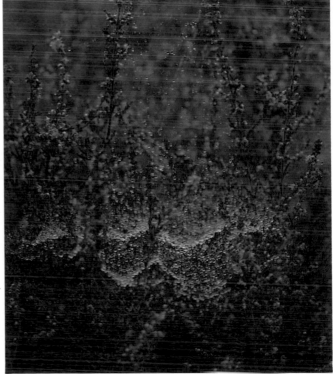

Eight-legged hunters

See also **Traps of silk**
on page 158

Not everybody likes spiders, but they are fascinating animals not least because of the many different ways in which they catch their prey. Spiders are not insects, although their bodies work in several similar ways. They belong to a group of animals called the arachnids, which includes harvestmen or daddy-longlegs (do not confuse them with craneflies), mites (see page 162) and scorpions. Spiders have four pairs of legs, compared with the insects' three pairs. The spider's body has two sections: head and thorax combined, and an abdomen.

A SPIDER'S BITE

All spiders are predators. They kill their prey with poison injected through their jaws. Then they suck out the victim's blood. They never eat solid food. Although no spider living in northern Europe is as dangerous as those living in warm countries, some spiders do bite people. The effects are not serious; at worst they are as bad as a wasp sting. Sometimes there is no more than a prick as the jaws penetrate the skin and there is no irritation or swelling.

Tubes and tripwires

Not all spiders spin orb webs or hammock webs in which to trap their prey. One type of spider lives in the cracks in the mortar of old walls (see page 46). It spins a silk tube in one of these cracks and then lays out 'tripwires' over the bricks. When an insect blunders over a 'tripwire', the spider rushes out and seizes it. Another kind of spider spins a tube along the ground and runs upside down inside it to seize unwary prey walking over it.

Spiders without webs

Several spiders do not use webs. The crab spiders (see page 44) rely on their camouflage so that unsuspecting victims come close enough to be seized. Others chase their prey. The zebra spider lives on sunny walls and fences. Its black and white stripes break up its outline and it is difficult to spot. It stalks its prey, then pounces like a cat. The raft spider can run on the surface of the water. It taps with its front feet on the surface to attract small fishes such as sticklebacks. When a fish investigates, thinking it has spotted a fly struggling in the water, it is seized by the spider and carried to the bank.

Hello, it's only me!

In most species of spider the female is larger than the male. Most of the spiders that you see are females;

◄Before entering a female's web, a courting male garden spider twangs a thread to signal he is a mate not a meal. Now he carefully approaches her, ready to drop off if she grabs at him.

►▲The water spider is the only spider in the world that lives underwater all the time. It traps bubbles of air in a silken diving bell. Near its bell this spider has stored a bluebottle to eat.

►Raft spiders are wolf spiders so they have good eyesight. The male signals to a possible mate by vibrating his front legs. Then he approaches and cautiously touches her.

the males are often so small that they are hard to spot. You may have heard it said that the female spider always eats her mate. This is not true of all species but, because the females are fierce predators, the males have to court them with care. They must make sure that the females realize they are suitors and not possible victims.

When a male spider approaches a female in a web, he signals his identity by plucking the web with his legs. At first, she may not recognize him and attacks, but he escapes by dropping off the web on his silk lifeline. After a while, he will return again, until the female changes her attitude and allows him into her web. Wolf spiders have good eyesight and they court by the male waving his legs at the female so that she will recognize him.

The easiest spider courtship to watch is that of the garden spiders which takes place on their large orb webs. The male usually gets away after mating and may visit the web of another female, but he may lose a leg or two this time. As he left his own web behind when he began courting, the male cannot catch prey. He slowly grows weaker until he is no longer alert and quick enough to avoid a female's jaws. By this time his function has finished and the female benefits from the extra meal to form her eggs.

Safe inside the silk

The garden spider lays 600 to 800 eggs in a cocoon of yellow silk which she fixes underneath a leaf or in some other secluded place. The eggs do not hatch until the following year and the tiny spiderlings immediately spin an irregular mass of silk under which they hide. If you prod the silk, they scatter in all directions, and gather again when the disturbance is over (see page 35). In this way a predator cannot catch them all in one mouthful and may be so confused by all the rushing about that he fails to catch any. After a few days each spiderling goes its own way and spins a small web, about 5 centimetres across. At this stage, males and females are the same size but, a year later, the females start to grow very rapidly and their large, 60 centimetre orb webs seem to appear quite suddenly in the late summer.

Mother and spiderlings

Although they are potentially lethal to their mates, some female spiders are good mothers. They guard the eggs and spiderlings. Wolf spiders even carry their families while they are hunting. A rear pair of legs holds the cocoon to the spider's abdomen and, if you were to remove it using tweezers, the spider would search frantically and pick it up again when you gave it back. After the eggs have hatched, the spiderlings are carried for a few more days. One spider actually feeds her babies, first by dribbling fluid from her mouth for them to pick up, and then by letting them share her prey.

More silk spinners

Spiders are not the only animals to spin silk. Some millipedes lay their eggs in silk bags and weave a protective tent to cover themselves when they moult. The best-known silk shelters, however, are the cocoons which most moths make when they pupate. Spiders' silk is made in special glands called spinnerets on the tip of the abdomen, but caterpillars spin silk from glands around the mouth.

Cocoons and tents of silk
When a moth caterpillar is about to pupate, it spins a pad of silk on which it clings. Then it weaves the cocoon around itself in a continuous thread, sweeping its head from side to side. The silkworm caterpillar makes a three-layered cocoon. Some moths, such as the oak eggar, have hardened cocoons which are difficult for birds to open. The puss moth, among others, sticks pieces of wood in the silk for camouflage and to make a really tough home.

Before pupation, some moth and butterfly caterpillars live inside silk tents for protection. An entire brood of the young caterpillars of the small tortoiseshell or peacock butterfly lives in a silk tent among stinging nettles. The tents of small ermine moth and lackey moth caterpillars are even more conspicuous. They can be found on hedges and in fruit trees.

Insect 'fishers'
Some caddis larvae use silken nets to catch food. They live under large stones or on plants in fast-flowing streams. They weave a net with the open end facing upstream to trap tiny animals in the current.

▼ Each gorse spider mite is tiny, but when thousands infest a gorse bush they smother it with webs until it seems to be covered with a tent of clear polythene.

The mighty mites
The silk tents that smother the twigs and leaves of fruit trees, gorse bushes and other plants are not the work of spiders or caterpillars but of spider mites. The tents are shelters for the eggs and adults. Most people have never seen a mite and would not recognize one if they did. Yet mites are extremely important animals. Some cause disease, but others help in the natural process of decay in the soil.

> ### HOW TO MEET A MITE
> Mites are very abundant; there can be hundreds of thousands in a square metre of soil. Many are too small to be seen with the naked eye. To see a mite you will need a magnifying lens and you must know where to look. You may never see the mite that lives in the nose of the grey seal, but it is easy to find water mites swimming in clear ponds. A compost heap is another good place for finding mites.

Like their cousins the spiders, mites have four pairs of legs although, in some species, the rear two pairs are very small. The body is round or oval and is not divided into two parts like a spider's. Mites lay their eggs in crevices, where they hatch in spring. The larvae have only three pairs of legs and they moult several times before becoming adult.

Harmless mites
Most mites are harmless and feed on decaying leaves and fungi. They are natural composters and help to break down dead plant tissues into food to nourish new plants. They are especially important in conifer woods where there are no earthworms because the soil is too acid. Other mites are carnivores that kill and eat small animals, including other mites, living on the surface of the soil. The carnivores are active, fast-moving animals. Even without a lens you should be able to see tiny red-bodied velvet mites running over paths and tree trunks.

Dangerous mites
A few mite species are harmful to larger animals. One kind lives on bats, another infects the breathing tubes of honeybees and suffocates them. 'Red fowl mite' sucks the blood of chickens; mange in dogs and canker in cats' ears are caused by mites. The harvest mite or bracken bug attacks any warm-blooded animal, including humans. If you visit the countryside in late summer or autumn, the bites of harvest mites may make you itch badly.

Spider mites are among several kinds that attack plants. The red spider mite is now a serious pest of

▲ This bright red water mite is the size of a large pinhead and bumbles conspicuously among pond algae.

▼ Parasitic mites scurry on a dor-beetle's underside. They pierce the chinks in its armour and suck its blood.

orchards. It was not a problem until its natural predators were killed by the DDT sprays used to destroy other pests. Without enemies, the red spider mite increased in numbers until it became destructive. Other mites cause 'big bud' in which unopened buds swell but fail to open. Yet others cause galls, such as the witches' broom (see page 136).

Hitching a ride

Although they are tiny wingless animals, some mites can cover long distances by hitching lifts on larger animals. The mite which causes 'big bud' in black-currants waves its legs in the air until it can grip a passing insect. Bumblebees and dor-beetles often carry a cluster of mites. Queen bumblebees are sometimes so heavily loaded they can hardly take off. Nevertheless, the mites do not seem to do any harm. They ride on the queens until the bees have built their nests, when they drop off to feed on scraps. But the mites on dor-beetles are not just hitch-hikers, they are parasites. One beetle was found to have 488 mites hanging on.

Mildew, moulds and mushrooms

Fungi are plants but they cannot make their own food by photosynthesis (see page 9) because they lack the green chemical, chlorophyll. They get their nourishment from dead organic matter or from living plants and animals. Some of the familiar toadstools feed on humus in the soil, while others grow on dead trees. Mildews and moulds grow on stale loaves and damp clothes; rusts and bracket fungi attack living plants. A few are especially useful: certain moulds colour cheeses such as stilton and Danish blue; yeast is a fungus which feeds on sugar, making alcohol in the process; the drug penicillin is produced by the fungus *Penicillium*.

The main part of a fungus is a mass of fine threads called hyphae. Hyphae grow through the soil, old logs, plants or animals and take in nourishment from them.

Plants with no seeds

Fungi reproduce by spores instead of seeds. The hyphae gather in a thick mass which pushes through the surface of the soil or host organisms to form the part of the fungus which we normally see. This is called the fruiting body. The fruiting body of mushrooms and toadstools consists of a stalk and a cap. The spores form in the gills or in tiny tubes on the underside of the cap. The underside of mushrooms and toadstools with tubes looks spongy.

Puffballs and fairy rings

Ripe puffballs are no more than bags of spores. If you prod one it puffs out a cloud of spores which are carried away by the wind. In nature, the spores may be blown out when the puffball is hit by large drops of water dripping from a tree overhead.

A fairy ring is caused by a mass of hyphae in the soil which is growing slowly outwards. The bright green, long grass which marks a fairy ring results from the hyphae releasing fertilizing nutrients into the soil.

▲The beefsteak fungus grows on living or dead oaks or sweet chestnuts. It resembles raw meat and even 'bleeds' when cut. Despite its name and pleasant smell, it is not at all good to eat.

BEWARE THE POISONOUS MUSHROOM!
Don't eat any fungus unless you know exactly what kind it is. If you pick fungi make sure you wash your hands afterwards.

▲Fairy ring toadstools are common on lawns and close-grazed pasture. On very still days, white spores coat the grass beneath the caps.

▼The honey fungus is a very serious pest because it causes a killer rot in all kinds of trees. You can find large tufts of it growing on dead stumps and at the base of living trees.

▼Grey bonnets grow on old wood such as this sweet chestnut stump. Though most common in autumn, they may pop up at any time.

▲There are many different kinds of *Boletus* which grow on heaths and in woods in late summer and autumn. This is an edible fungus, with a shiny brown bun-like cap.

MAKE A SPORE PRINT
Place a ripe mushroom or toadstool cap on a sheet of clean white paper or glass for a day. Carefully lift the cap and there will be a 'print' of its shape made by the spores.

▲Bracket fungi grow in many shapes and sizes on a variety of trees. This yellow one is on the trunk of a yew. Tree slugs have been eating it in the night, as their slime trails show.

Spreading the seed

See also **Flowers, pollen and insects** on page 40

Plants cannot move from place to place so that, if they are to spread, they must be able to disperse their seeds. They make use of wind, water and animals to spread them.

Blowing in the wind
To be carried by the wind seeds must either be very small, like the powdery seeds of foxgloves, or have some kind of 'wing' to help them keep airborne. Seeds usually stay in the dried fruit until they are shaken out by the breezes. This prevents them from just falling to the ground under the plant in still air. The harebell's fruit has small holes like a pepperpot and the cowslip has a single large hole like a salt cellar. If you tap the stem of these plants you will see the seeds being tossed out.

The winged seeds of the sycamore are known as keys. They grow in pairs, but split from the stem singly and spin in the air like the rotor of a helicopter. The wing slows the seed's fall so that it is blown well away from the tree. Field maple has keys like the sycamore's, and ash and lime have seeds with twisted wings. The elm produces masses of seeds, each one surrounded by a round papery wing.

Some plant seeds have a plume or parachute. Willow, willowherb, dandelions, thistles and groundsel sometimes fill the air with their feathery seeds. The parachute of the dandelion closes up in

▲ The seeds of horse chestnut are called conkers. Voles, mice and squirrels eat them but only when tastier foods are scarce.

wet weather and opens in dry weather so that it only takes off in the best conditions.

With a little help from their friends
Plants with seeds set in fleshy fruit and nuts rely on animals for transport. The fruits are edible and often brightly coloured to attract the animal. The seeds of hawthorn, for example, survive being eaten by birds (see page 143). The flesh is digested and the seed is more likely to germinate after the bird's stomach juices have acted on it. Other seeds may survive because the animal drops them, or stores them and then forgets them.

Animals also disperse seeds which have hitched a ride on them. Cleavers, agrimony, burdock and bur-marigold seeds are equipped with tiny hooks and cling to animals' fur and to our clothes.

▲ The winged seeds or 'keys' of sycamore hang on the tree until blown off by a strong wind. Then, spinning like propellers, they are carried long distances. The green insect is a female oak bush cricket.

> **DISPERSAL BY BOOT!**
> Small seeds are carried in mud sticking to animals and motor vehicles. Pineapple mayweed (pinch and smell it!) is an example of a common roadside plant that has been spread by vehicles. Scrape the mud off your boots and mix it with some potting compost. See what plants grow.

▲ A crossbill's worked cones have this twisted, shredded appearance.

▲ The nuthatch wedges a hazelnut before hammering a hole in the shell.

▲ The great spotted woodpecker also wedges an acorn or nut into a crack. Its bill leaves characteristic marks.

CRACK THE CLUES

Tree seeds are packages of concentrated food which many animals depend on during autumn and winter. Some trees rely on the seed-eaters to disperse their seeds. Though most seeds will be shredded, a few will remain whole, buried or dropped and not retrieved, to germinate next spring. The seeds of many broadleaved trees have hard shells; those of most conifers are in tough cones. Animals have to work hard to extract them, and different species have different techniques for doing so. Broken nut shells and worked cones provide clues to the identity of the seed-eaters.

▲ Prickly sweet chestnuts could be a problem for a grey squirrel to open but the ripe fruits usually split when they fall.

◀ A pine cone stripped by a red or grey squirrel has a characteristic tuft of ungnawed scales at its tip.

▶ A squirrel gnaws a little hole in the top of the hazelnut, inserts its lower incisors and deftly splits the shell.

▲ A nut shell gnawed by a dormouse has a very regular round hole with an almost smooth edge.

▲ A wood mouse digs its lower incisors into the hole, scratching the shell with its upper incisors.

▲ Mice and voles may pick hawthorn fruits from the tree, or they may find the seeds scattered far from the tree by birds.

▼ Gnawed fragments of nut shells or cones show where a squirrel has sat up on a stump to feed.

Animals small and furry

See also **Tails from the river bank**
on page 130

When we disturb a small animal, it usually rushes to safety so fast that we do not get a chance to see it properly. We often say, 'There's a mouse!' but it may not be a mouse; it could be a vole or a shrew.

House mice and harvest mice
You can recognize a mouse by its large, round ears, large beady eyes and fairly pointed nose. House mice make their presence known even if they do not show themselves (see page 195). They are sometimes confused with wood mice and yellow-necked mice which also come into houses. The yellow-necked mouse has a yellow-brown stripe between its front legs. The wood mouse has little or no yellow.

The wood mouse is also called the long-tailed field mouse. It is not only found in woods but also lives in gardens, hedgerows and sometimes in open country or on cliffs. It is the commonest mouse in most parts of Europe. The wood mouse spends the day in a nest and comes out at night, especially around dawn and dusk. The nest is sometimes made in a hole in a tree but usually a wood mouse digs an underground burrow which has a nest chamber, underground stores of food and several entrances. The entrances may be blocked with leaves or pebbles. Wood mice also store nuts and berries in old birds' nests and hollow trees. If you find a hoard of nuts, it will belong to a wood mouse rather than to a squirrel, which buries its nuts singly.

The harvest mouse is the smallest mouse and it has a blunter nose and smaller ears than the others. It lives on waste ground and in reedbeds as well as in corn fields. It is an agile climber, wrapping its tail around plant stems for extra support. To find harvest mice, look for their nests of woven grass fixed 30 centimetres above the ground in dense vegetation.

Voles, the predator's favourite
Voles are rodents with blunt noses, small ears and eyes and short tails. Voles live above ground level and burrow less frequently than mice. The nest is constructed underground or under a log or plank. They make pathways through coarse grass and they are active by day as well as by night.

The field vole or short-tailed vole lives wherever there is thick grass. In some years field voles are so common that you can see them running ahead of you as you walk through the grass. These voles are a favourite prey of owls, hawks, foxes and other predators whose numbers also increase when the voles are plentiful.

Secretive shrews
The shrews are insectivores, the groups of mammals to which hedgehogs and moles also belong. Whereas

the mice and voles are rodents and eat mainly plants, insectivores eat insects and other small animals. Shrews have long noses which are more pointed than those of mice. The fur is short and dense. With a body length of 55 millimetres and a thick tail about 40 millimetres long, the pygmy shrew is one of the world's smallest mammals.

Shrews live on the ground among grass and dead leaves. You can often hear their very high-pitched squeaks sounding rather like bird calls, coming from ground level. Shrews are very difficult to find because they keep well hidden in the vegetation. Their tunnels are smaller and more oval in shape than those of voles.

Shrews are extremely active. They spend a couple of hours at a time running about in search of food. Every now and then, they stop and sleep for a few minutes, then run on again. Shrews do not live long and never survive more than one winter. They are eaten by owls, but although foxes and cats kill shrews, they rarely eat them because they have an unpleasant taste.

▲ A yellow-necked mouse carrying a hazel nut to its nest passes seedheads of old-man's-beard and wild rose hips.

▼ A common shrew foraging for invertebrates among the fallen leaves and marble galls beneath an oak tree.

► A bank vole pauses to wash a hind foot. It has been eating an acorn on this old *Boletus* dining table.

Hunters of the air

There are three main kinds of birds of prey: owls which hunt mainly at night, and hawks and falcons which almost always hunt by day. They all have hooked beaks and sharp talons for killing their prey. The hawks, including the buzzard, golden eagle and the harriers, have wings with rounded tips. Falcons, such as the kestrel, peregrine and hobby have pointed wings. Many birds of prey became very rare because they were shot or trapped or because they were poisoned from eating food treated with pesticides. Unfortunately they still suffer in this way although they are legally protected. Nowadays, some of the rare species are increasing in numbers.

Eyes for the night

You may see short-eared owls on the wing during the day, and little owls and barn owls in the evening when it is still quite light, but the night is the main hunting time for owls. Owls' eyes are very good at gathering light because the pupils open very wide in the dark. An owl needs its night vision to see its way when it is flying among trees, but it also uses its exceptional hearing to enable it to find and catch its prey. It can detect and pinpoint the faint rustlings of a mouse among dead leaves and then pounces unerringly. The mouse has little hope of being warned of the attack because the owl's fluffy feathers, especially those on the edges of its wings, muffle the sound of its flight.

PLUNGE DIVER
The osprey specializes in catching fish. It dives headlong, then throws its feet forward to catch a fish just below the surface. Sometimes it almost submerges.

Windhovering and surprise attacks

The kestrel is the most common of the daytime birds of prey. You can easily recognize it from its habit of hovering while it searches the ground beneath for small animals. Many kestrels hunt along the sides of main roads and motorways.

Sparrowhawks have a different hunting method. They hurtle along hedges and through woods and catch small birds unawares.

▲ The tawny owl has huge eyes set in the front of its head to make full use of dim light and judge distances accurately. It can fly through the woods at night without blundering into branches.

▲ The sparrowhawk's eyes are day-bird eyes, set more to the side but also able to look forward to focus close-up. In good light it has almost unbelievably keen vision.

tawny owl pellet
(rough and lumpy)

kestrel pellet (no bones)

PULL APART A PELLET

Birds of prey eat small animals whole and get rid of the indigestible parts by coughing up pellets of bones, wrapped up in fur or feathers. You can find these pellets under the birds' favourite roosts. The easiest way to take apart a pellet is to soak it in a jar of water for several hours. Pour the remains into a shallow dish and pick out the interesting bits. You will find the skulls of mammals and birds and the wing cases of beetles.

▲ Hovering enables a kestrel to hunt for prey in open grassland. Kestrels also keep watch on the ground below from perches in trees or from posts.

▲ The buzzard is a hawk. It uses its broad wings to soar in rising currents of air.

▼ A barn owl can hunt in pitch darkness by listening for noises made by its prey.

▶ The peregrine is a falcon that catches birds in flight by diving on them at great speed.

Where fresh water meets salty

See also **Life on the shore** on page 84 and **Wildflowers by the sea** on page 94

In an estuary fresh water from the river mixes with the salty sea water to become brackish. At low tide, fresh water flows into the sea but, as the tide turns, salt water is forced up the estuary. At any point along the estuary, the amount of salt in the water changes as the tides rise and fall. Fresh water is lighter than sea water and floats at the top so that, if the river is large, fresh water will flow well out into the sea to make it less salty as it mixes.

A richness of life

Few animals can survive in both fresh and salty water. Therefore, in the same way that animals and plants live in zones down the seashore (see page 84), there are zones along the estuary. Most of the animals are sea creatures which can tolerate brackish water. Barnacles and shellfish such as cockles, close their shells when the tide falls and they become surrounded by brackish water, and open them again when the salt water returns. Mussels can survive in fresh water. Shore crabs use their efficient kidney system to bale out any extra fresh water which soaks into the body. Although only a few species of animals live in estuaries, they may be present in huge numbers. There can be 2,000 cockles in a square metre of mud. They and other animals live on the rich organic mud brought down by the river and they attract flocks of birds and shoals of fishes.

▼The sea aster grows on coastal saltmarshes and cliffs. Like its garden relative, the michaelmas daisy, it flowers when the days are shortening.

▲When you see distant shelduck feeding out on the estuary mud, they look black and white. Listen for the drakes' whistling calls, sounding like wingbeats, when flocks fly overhead.

▲This little creature is called an opossum shrimp because it carries its babies in a pouch like a mother opossum. It is also called a chameleon shrimp because it can change its colour to match its background. Here it matches pink seaweed.

▲ Glasswort growing on an estuary mudbank. High spring tides cover this mud, but at neaps it may dry out and crack. A shore crab shell has been left by the tide.

Life on the mud

If the mud in the river water is not swept out to sea it gathers around the estuary as mudbanks. These banks may shift and grow or be washed away by the changing flow of the river, but in sheltered places the mud builds up above the high tide and plants can become established and saltmarshes form (see page 94). At the lower edge of the bank, where the mud is covered every day by the tide, green seaweeds flourish and a grass called eelgrass or seawrack forms large 'lawns'. Brent geese, which overwinter along the coast, graze on the eelgrass beds.

The snail called *Hydrobia* is another very abundant animal on the mud and it is a favourite food of the shelduck. At low tide it lives under the mud and it comes to the surface when the water returns. It then blows bubbles to make a raft and floats to the top of the mudbank on the rising tide. As the estuary empties again, the snail crawls down the mud, feeding as it goes.

▼ The lower spire shell *Hydrobia* lives in vast numbers on the mud and on the green seaweeds called laver. Rock pipits, waders and shelducks, eat *Hydrobia*.

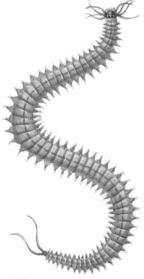

◀ Golden samphire is another saltmarsh plant that flowers later in the year. Its tough fleshy water-storing, mud-shedding leaves are characteristic of plants that grow in salty places.

▲ The common ragworm lives in the mud of estuaries feeding on any live or dead animals it can manage. You can identify it by the red line down its back.

> ## WATCH THE TIDE!
> When you are exploring an estuary, it is easy to get caught by the tide as it races across the mud flats. Make sure you check the times of the tides before you cross a mud bank or saltmarsh, and that you know the way back.

Seals at sea

Seals are mammals that eat mainly fish, as well as some shrimps, shellfish and other sea creatures. They find their prey chiefly by sight, but in murky water they may use their whiskers to feel for food. Scientists think that they may also use sonar, rather like bats (see page 52) and dolphins. Seals can dive for half an hour or so, but most dives only last for a few minutes. They eat small fishes underwater but they bring large ones to the surface and hold them in the foreflippers while they bite off chunks.

Where do they go?
Outside the breeding season, the seals spend most of their time at sea. No one knows where they go or how they spend their time, although young grey seals born in British islands have been found as far away as Iceland and Norway.

During the summer especially, grey and common seals like to bask on rocks at low tide. In some places

▶ Two grey seal cows, that have just come ashore to suckle their pups, threaten each other fiercely because each fears the other is going to bite its pup.

IS IT A GREY OR A COMMON SEAL?
All you usually see of a seal as it floats in the water is its head. It is not easy to tell whether it is a grey seal or a common seal. The grey seal's head is rather like the head of a horse with the muzzle level with the top of the head; whereas the common seal's head is shaped more like that of a dog. It is more rounded and the muzzle is lower than the top of the head. This difference is not so obvious with young grey seals but, if you can get near enough to see clearly, you will see that the nostrils of a grey seal are nearly parallel slits and those of a common seal are set in a V.

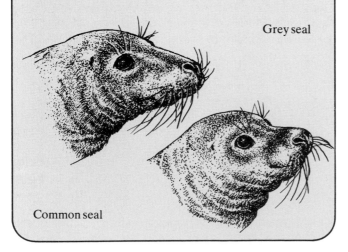

Grey seal

Common seal

▼A grey seal cow rolls over so that her whitecoat pup can suck comfortably. When it has fed she will leave it asleep on the beach while she goes back into the sea.

scores of seals gather as the tide goes out. The seals make themselves comfortable and sleep until the tide returns. They do not seem to like getting their fur wet when they are basking. As the waves break over the rock the seals try to avoid them, but eventually they have to slide into the water and swim away. Seals also rest and even sleep in the water. They float vertically with only their heads showing and sometimes disappear altogether. This position is called 'bottling'.

Fattening up on mother's milk

Like the red (see page 154) and fallow deer, grey or Atlantic seals mate in the autumn. While deer give birth in the following summer, however, grey seals produce pups one year later the next autumn. The pups are born only a few days before the mother mates again.

Grey seals gather to breed on islands or in sea caves, where they will not be disturbed. When the pup is born it has a white fluffy coat and it is very thin and weak. Almost immediately it has a drink of its mother's milk. The milk is very rich and at the end of three weeks, the pup is so fat it has difficulty moving. Its mother, who has now mated, abandons it and goes to sea. The pup sheds its white coat to reveal the adult coat underneath; it is now ready to go to sea and fend for itself.

Pups ready to swim

The early life of a common seal is rather different from that of a grey seal. Common seals prefer to live in sheltered bays and among groups of small islands. They breed in summer. They give birth to their pups at low tide on sandbanks and rocks. The newborn pups already have their adult coats and they are much more lively than grey seal pups. This is essential because they have to swim when the tide comes up a few hours later.

Beachcombing

See also **Life on the shore** on page 84

Originally, someone who earned a living by 'combing' the seashore was called a beachcomber. Today, a modern beachcomber just walks along the beach looking for anything interesting. The storms of autumn and winter throw plenty of objects on to the seashore. The waves pluck animals from the sea bed, and bring in driftwood as well as rubbish such as plastic bottles and rusty cans. It is easy to find items of interest among all the rubbish because everything, including loads of dead seaweed, is cast up in a narrow strip along the high-tide mark.

▲ Autumn is often the season of gale-force winds and storms at sea. When huge breakers pound the shore they wash out animals normally hidden in the sand (see page 86).

▲ Waves roll chunks of rock up and down and along the beach, wearing them into smooth rounded pebbles. These are mostly granite. Quartz and quartzite pebbles are often colourful.

Mermaids' purses and shells

Lumps of sticky tar, which are the remains of oil spilled or emptied from ships, are all too common on the beach but there are also the remains of animals that live in deeper water and which you are unlikely to see alive. 'Mermaids' purses', which are the egg cases of rays, dogfish and related fishes, are a common find, as are various shells and skeletons.

Razorshells and the shells of cockles and tellins are often abundant but you may also find the fragile shells or 'tests' of sea urchins as well as the shells of clams, gapers and slipper limpets. Gapers' shells 'gape' at one end when they are shut. The slipper limpet has a ledge on the inside of its shell so, when it is held upside down, it looks like a slipper or shoe.

The piddock is a shellfish that bores into rock by scraping away with its saw-edged shells. You may find a live piddock in soft limestone, chalk or sand-stone. A relative is the shipworm which burrows into pier piles and driftwood. Find a piece of wood with small round holes in it and break it open. You will see that the holes open into wide tunnels. The shipworm may still be inside. It has a long soft body with two small shells which the animal uses as a drill to bore through the wood.

Revealing the past

If the shore runs beneath a cliff made of soft rock or clay where rockfalls and landslides are caused by the pounding of the waves, you might be lucky enough to find fossils which have been washed out.

Fossil shells, such as the flat coils of ammonites, and the relatives of modern two-shelled molluscs, are easy to find. A fossil may be revealed when a stone has split open but the nicest fossils may be found lying in the sand.

▼Oarweed is one of several sorts of very large tough brown seaweeds which flourish below the low tide. They grow attached to rocks by tangles of thick root-like 'holdfasts'.

▼A 'mermaid's purse' is the egg case of a dogfish or ray. Usually the baby fish has already hatched out before the case is thrown up on the beach.

▲The prickly bodies or tests (see page 86) of sea urchins are found washed up on sandy shores after storms.

▲Fossil ammonites are the beautifully preserved remains of extinct animals of the octopus family.

▲The sea mouse is a worm, though with its iridescent 'fur' it hardly looks like one. It normally lies beneath the sand near low tide.

▲Bleached white cuttle 'bone' is the familiar skeleton of the cuttlefish, a swimming octopus relative that hunts for shrimps.

▲The large empty egg masses of the common whelk are found along the strand line.

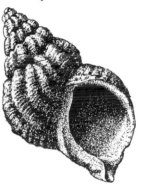

▲Empty whelk shells may be taken over by hermit crabs. Whelks are carnivorous snails.

LEAVE IT ALONE!
Lumps of tar are not the only objects on the beach which should be left alone. Tar is messy but old mines and gun shells are dangerous. They may explode if handled, so leave anything suspicious alone and inform the police.

Winter: the year's end

There seems little to tempt us out of doors during winter. On dull days you might not expect to see anything very interesting, and few of us would venture out for a country ramble in a storm. On a bright day, however, especially after snow has fallen, it is different. This is a time to look for things that go unnoticed at other times of the year when there is so much activity. Animals are easier to spot against a white background, and their tracks in the snow give away their presence.

In winter, it is a good idea to try to think of how animals manage to survive during the harsh weather and food shortages. Some escape the cold by hibernating or migrating. Others grow thick coats, store food, or change their feeding habits.

Birdwatching is a profitable pastime in winter. If you have a bird-table in your garden, you will be able to enjoy the antics of the birds visiting it. You should also be able to see flocks of many different kinds of birds in fields, on lakes and reservoirs, or along the seashore. They often include species which live farther north in the summer, and a storm can bring some unusual visitors.

Make sure that you do not disturb animals in winter; remember that they face many hardships. This is as important now as it was during the breeding season.

Like midsummer's day, midwinter's day, 21st December, occurs near the start of the season. This is the shortest day of the year, when the sun rises at its latest and sets at its earliest. As you travel northwards, midwinter's day becomes even shorter until, at the Arctic Circle, the sun does not rise at all and the night is 24 hours long.

During the winter months climatic depressions sweep eastwards across the Atlantic. These are masses of air at low pressure and they are shown on weather maps by lines of equal pressure called isobars. Depressions bring high winds and rain and they often follow one another every other day so that the bad weather is almost continuous. The closer together the isobars the stronger is the wind.

At other times, the country is covered with a mass of high-pressure air. The weather then is calm and bright but it is often very cold, especially when the winds come from the east. These cold spells are more likely to occur in late winter and this is the time when frost and snow are most common.

By February, however, the days are lengthening and the sun is getting stronger, so there are times when the weather is almost spring-like. The first flowers and bursts of bird song show that the new wildlife year is about to start.

Coping with the cold

See also **Life under the ice** on page 182
and **Winter coats** on page 190

A spell of cold weather is a very dangerous time for animals. Despite their furry coats or layers of feathers, they find it hard to keep warm. To stop themselves from freezing, they have to use up their reserves of fat to generate warmth (see page 190). Food is hard to find in cold weather so that animals cannot always replace the fat they have used up. If the weather is wet as well as cold, animals find it even more difficult to survive because damp fur or feathers are not so good at keeping in the body heat.

Despite the hardships of winter, animals do find clever ways to keep warm. Squirrels and badgers stay in their snug nests rather than waste valuable energy looking for food, while deer try to find a dense thicket to rest in, away from the chill winds. You will often see birds sheltering from the worst of the weather in trees and bushes.

A glistening killer

Food is so much more difficult to get if everything is covered with frost and ice. Waterbirds suffer very badly when ponds, lakes and streams are frozen over. Kingfishers suffer disastrously if they are prevented from fishing. After the two severe winters which struck Britain and Europe in 1962 and 1963, the number of herons in England was halved. Land birds suffer, too, if their food supplies are hidden by frost and snow. A hard frost freezes the surface of the soil so that lapwings, rooks and blackbirds cannot reach worms and insect grubs. These little ani-

▼Fog is the condensation of water vapour into tiny droplets that float in the air. Freezing fog makes rime ice. Water droplets below freezing point become ice when they touch solid objects, and 'frost feathers' grow on every leaf and twig, as on these brambles.

mals burrow deeper to avoid the frost themselves. This makes it still harder for the hungry birds to find them.

The hardest frost is at ground level because cold air sinks. Animals feeding in trees and hedges may be unaffected, but hoar frost, rime ice or freezing rain smother the vegetation and birds then cannot get at the buds or at insects hiding in crevices.

A snowy quilt

A covering of snow can have the same effect as frost and ice but, if it is not too thick and has not drifted in the wind, it may not be too bad for the animals to cope with. Birds can still reach the undersides of evergreen foliage and they can also feed on the bare ground beneath trees and undergrowth.

Some animals may even find the snow helpful. Air is a good insulator and it can be trapped between snowflakes so that a blanket of snow may keep in the warmth in the same way as an eiderdown or a quilted

◄A pond or lake freezing over means hard times for waterbirds, such as this coot walking on the ice. Birds cannot reach food beneath the ice, where plants and animals survive as long as the water does not freeze to the bottom.

▲Hoar frost is frozen dew. Moisture in the air froze on this fallen oak leaf, vapour either at once becoming solid, or forming liquid which was then converted into crystals.

▼When rain is below freezing point it solidifies as soon as it lands. These icicles were made when freezing rain fell on oak twigs. They have grown bent as the twigs became weighted down.

jacket. Then, when the temperature of the air drops many degrees below freezing point, the ground beneath the snow stays less cold. The plants and small ground animals are therefore relatively warm and they also escape the extra chilling effect of the wind.

LIFE BENEATH THE SNOW
On fine days, the warmth of the sun penetrates the snow and warms the ground. The layer of snow next to the ground melts and a space is formed. Push your hand through the snow crust and you can feel it. Voles and mice can live here. they feed on the grass and other low plants which are not frozen, and they are safe from kestrels and owls. Rabbits and deer dig through the snow to feed on the soft vegetation.

Life under the ice

The special properties of water mean that a pond or river is a good place in which to spend the winter. Unless the weather is so cold for so long that the water freezes solid, it will be comparatively warm. Water also warms and cools more slowly than air does (which is why a hot-water bottle stays warm throughout the night), so that water animals do not suffer the sudden changes in temperature that land animals do.

Most animals survive beneath the ice because the water stays above freezing point. Fishes, waterfleas and many kinds of insect carry on their activities but, because they are cold, they are rather sluggish. Otters and mink eat more fishes in the winter because they are easier to catch.

Common frogs hibernate either on land or in water. They often go back to the same streams and ponds winter after winter although these may not always be the ponds that they spawn in. Sometimes they lie on the bottom of the pond and, if the water is clear, you should be able to see them; at other times they burrow into the mud. The cold water makes their bodies work so slowly that the small amount of oxygen they need for survival can be absorbed through their skins. They thus do not have to come up to breathe air. When they are cold, fishes also need very little oxygen, and they can survive in the mud at the bottom of a pond even when the water is almost frozen solid.

An icy grave

Once water has turned into ice, its temperature can drop below freezing point. If animals become trapped in ice, their bodies will then freeze solid. Fishes,

▼In autumn, the water flea *Eurycerus* produces about a dozen special cold-resistant winter eggs which she carries in her brood pouch. When she moults or dies, the pouch with eggs sinks to the bottom of the pond for the winter. The eggs hatch into females in the spring.

▼Dero is a small freshwater worm that lives in a tube in the mud. It has red blood, which makes its body look pink. Here a *Dero* crawls on stonewort, a slender plant that encrusts itself with minerals extracted from the water.

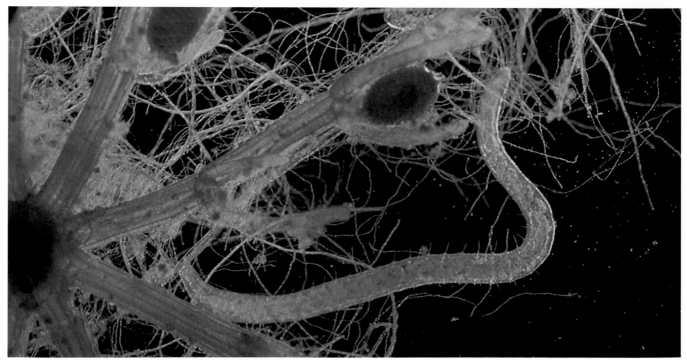

for example, cannot survive if they become frozen in, nor can other animals such as freshwater mussels and snails. They must live in deep water which will not freeze solid. Some mayfly larvae crawl deeper when the shallow water at the edge of the stream or pond freezes. A few animals can withstand freezing. Certain worms, caddisfly larvae and snails burrow into the mud and still survive when it freezes solid. The snails make a trapdoor to close the entrance of the shell, while the other animals curl up inside cocoons. They are protected from freezing by 'antifreeze' in their blood like hibernating land animals (see page 193). The advantage of living in a 'deep freeze' is that they cannot be found by hungry predators.

DON'T BREAK THE ICE!
It is fun to jump on the ice of a shallow pond to see if you can smash it, but this will harm the animals sheltering underneath. The shock of your weight hitting the ice is carried through the water and hits the animals almost as if you had stamped on them. Fishes and hibernating frogs can be concussed or killed in this way. If you want to open a frozen pond so that birds can drink, melt the ice with a kettle of boiling water.

Never venture out on to the ice of a large expanse of deep water which could suddenly collapse under you.

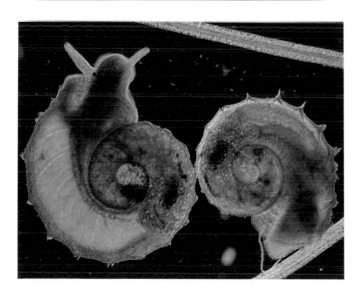

▲ Young ramshorn snails hatch from a flat jelly capsule stuck on an underwater leaf. Like the worm *Dero* their blood also contains the red pigment that absorbs oxygen, which means they are well fitted for life in stagnant water. When their pond freezes they become inactive in the mud at the bottom.

HOW ICE FORMS
Water is a unique liquid. It does not behave like other liquids when it is cooled. Normally, when a liquid, such as petrol, paraffin or even molten fat, cools, it shrinks and becomes denser. Colder layers of these liquids then sink. If the temperature stays low enough, this process continues until all the liquid freezes. You can see this happening when hot fat is left to cool in a frying pan.

When water cools, cooler layers sink to the bottom (1) until the temperature reaches 4 degrees centigrade (2). Then a remarkable thing happens. The circulation of the water stops and the cold layer stays at the top until ice forms (3). This is because, below 4 degrees centigrade, water actually expands instead of continuing to shrink and it becomes less dense and thus floats on denser water. If it were not for this property of water, ponds and puddles would quickly freeze solid in winter. When a pond is about to freeze over, the water at the surface forms a thin, almost transparent 'skin' of ice. If the cold weather continues, water freezes underneath and the ice gets thicker. The deeper water remains at 4 degrees centigrade, so that it is 'warmer in than out', and animals can survive in water when the temperature of the air is far below freezing. The layer of ice insulates the water below from the cold air above so that the water cools more slowly.

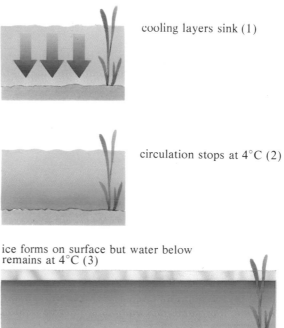

cooling layers sink (1)

circulation stops at 4°C (2)

ice forms on surface but water below remains at 4°C (3)

Fishes in fresh water

See also **Finding a mate**
on page 30

Ponds and streams seem to be virtually lifeless during the winter but if you look into clear water you may see tightly packed shoals of small fishes swimming slowly or resting on the bottom. The body temperature of fishes is about the same as that of the water and, in cold winter water, their body processes are working very slowly. This means that they do not need much energy to survive and fishes do not usually feed during the winter.

It's safer in a shoal
The shoal that you are looking at will probably be gudgeon, sticklebacks or the young of a species of the carp family, such as dace, carp or bream. Banding together in a dense shoal is a defence against predators such as kingfishers and pike which get confused by the mass of fishes. If it is on its own, a little fish can be chased until it is tired and easily caught. If it is in a shoal, the predator cannot concentrate on chasing it. This is also one of the reasons why birds gather in flocks.

Fish-eye view
Although the winter shoals of fish are sluggish, they will dart away as soon as they are disturbed. Fishes have good eyesight. Each eye has a broad field of vision so that a fish can see all around it. Enemies have difficulty catching it unawares. The pike is a hunting fish and it has 'sighting grooves' along its long snout so that it can see forwards to aim at prey.

▼The brown trout spawns in winter. When the eggs are due to hatch the dark eyes of the fry show through. Newly hatched fry wriggle further down into the gravel away from the light.

▲Three small tench with a baby pike. When the water temperature drops in winter, the fishes hibernate.

Listening with the lateral line
As well as ears, fishes have a special vibration-sensitive organ called the lateral line. This is a line of tiny holes along the side of the fish, like a row of stitches. The holes connect with a tube running under the skin and lined with organs sensitive to pressure. These record the pattern of vibrations in the water. The fish can then detect any approaching danger or an obstacle and if it is a predator itself, it can locate prey. A blind goldfish, for instance, does not bump into the sides of an aquarium, because the vibrations set up by its own movements are reflected from the glass and detected by the lateral line.

Salmon and trout
Salmon and trout are particularly active during the winter. Both species like clean water and are less common than they once were because of pollution in streams and rivers. Salmon, especially, have disappeared from many rivers but trout can still be seen in streams and lakes. They have been introduced to some waters for angling and can often be seen in clear water.

Trout living in lakes or large rivers move into the shallower water of feeder streams during the autumn to be ready to spawn in early winter.

The female looks for a patch of gravel which is kept clear of mud and silt by the current. Then she starts to dig her nest, called a redd. She turns on her side and makes vigorous swimming movements, which lift the gravel so that it is carried away by the

▲ The crucian carp is the hardiest freshwater fish. It can hibernate buried in the mud, surviving the freezing of the water.

current. When the redd is finished a male joins her and fertilizes the eggs as they are laid.

The eggs sink into the gravel where they will be safe while they develop. The time taken for the eggs to hatch depends on the water temperature. The hatchlings, called alevins, carry a yolk sac as large as themselves to nourish them until they can feed. They are then called fry or fingerlings and each lives in its own small territory. Enormous numbers of young fishes die and only two or three out of every 100 hatched survive to their first birthday.

Parr, smolts and grilse

Young salmon, called parr, live a life similar to that of trout until, at two or three years old when they become silvery and are known as smolts, they swim down river and out to sea. The smolts travel to the cold waters off Greenland where they grow rapidly and return a year later.

The salmon, now known as grilse, find their way back to the stream where they were hatched by following the scent of the water. The urge to swim upstream is very powerful and the salmon leap as high as 3 metres over waterfalls and through the salmon ladders – series of weirs – specially provided to enable them to get round hydroelectric power stations and mills. It is well worth visiting a salmon ladder to see them leaping. They normally make their strenuous journey upstream at the same time each year. When the salmon reach the spot where they were born, they spawn between November and

February and some small streams become packed with fishes. The salmon do not feed while they are in fresh water and most die after spawning. A few manage the journey back to the sea where they start to feed again.

NO LITTER PLEASE!

Anglers keep still and quiet in order not to frighten away the fishes and they often have good views of other animals which get used to their presence. Unfortunately, some of these animals can be harmed by careless anglers.

It is easy to lose fishing tackle when the hook is caught in a tree, a sunken log or a water-lily stem. When the line breaks, the hook part of the nylon cast and often some lead weights are left behind and become a serious danger for birds. The nylon gets wound around their legs so that they become crippled and may lose the leg altogether.

Many swans die from poisoning by lead weights on the bank or in the water. They swallow grit to help digest their food and take in the lead weights at the same time.

You can help wildlife by making sure you take all your tackle away, or pick up any that you find lying around.

▼ By day, stone loaches hide among pebbles or leaves. In summer they feed at night, on insect larvae and worms; but during the winter they stop feeding.

1 THREATENING BEHAVIOUR

The aggressive display of the mute swan is a magnificent sight. Its wings are arched, the neck is fluffed out and arched back, and it swims by thrusting with both feet at the same time. Male swans use this display when they are defending their territories and both sexes use it in defence of the nest and cygnets. You can see it throughout the entire year. The aggressive display is fierce enough to drive away most people.

2 NEST AND EGGS

In spring, the eggs are incubated by the female mute swan, while the male stands guard or swims nearby. He sometimes takes over from her when she goes to feed but if not, she leaves the eggs covered with nest material so that they stay warm and hidden.

The nest is a large pile of reeds, rushes and other plants. It is usually built on a bank or in a reedbed, always near water and may often be by quite a small pond or stream. The same nest is sometimes used year after year.

SWAN WATCH

Observe a pair of swans in residence on a nearby pond or lake, and record their activities. Here are a few suggestions for points to note:

How do they divide up their day?

What do they eat throughout the year?

How long do they spend eating, resting and preening?

Date nest built ....

Date eggs laid ....

Date cygnets hatch ....

How many cygnets....................

How does plumage change?

Date of young bird's first flight ...

Date family split up..................

The mute swan's year

See also **Birds on the water** on page 20

Weighing around 11 kilograms, the mute swan is one of the heaviest flying birds in the world. It is a powerful flier, but it is not very agile. The swan takes off by running over the water, or sometimes the land, to gain momentum. It touches down by using its wings as airbrakes and then skidding on outstretched feet.

Mute means silent, but mute swans do make some sounds. The cygnets call softly to keep in touch and loudly when lost, while their mother quietly burbles back to them. The adults snort and hiss loudly when they greet each other and to threaten rivals or intruders. But the most likely sound you will hear is the throbbing noise of their wings as they fly, a sound which carries over quite a considerable distance.

Bewick's and whooper swans breed in the Arctic and fly south for the winter. Their necks are straight and their bills yellow, whereas the mute swan has a curved neck and an orange-red bill with a black knob at the base.

7 FLOCKS OF FAMILIES

Young swans which do not breed sometimes spend the summer together. They are chased away by the resident male if they enter his territory. He swims after them with his wings arched and they retreat with their wings held flat. Large flocks of up to 100 swans are more common in winter and they include family parties. Part of the flock may rest on the bank of the lake where they regularly spend the winter. Families stay together and prevent other swans from coming too close.

6 TOGETHERNESS

Mute swans mate for life and the pair stays together throughout the winter. These two birds have just bathed briskly in the icy water and they are preening to rearrange and oil the feathers. The male is standing to dry his wings by beating them vigorously.

British swans rarely move far from their breeding places, but during severe winters they may be joined by more birds from the continental mainland of Europe. Cold weather, when the ponds and lakes ice over, is a difficult time for swans and other waterbirds.

3 LEAVING HOME

The cygnets leave the nest with their parents when they are one or two days old. They may return to be brooded during the day and night. The cygnets can swim well, but while they are still young they ride on the parent's back and sleep there at night.

From the start, the cygnets feed themselves on plants and on some small water animals. They are also helped by their mother who picks grass for them and puts it on the water for them to eat.

4 FIRST FLIGHTS

The cygnets stay with their parents throughout the summer and start to fly at four to five months. They are usually driven away by their father during the autumn or early winter.

5 GREY TO WHITE

This 10-month-old swan still retains some of its grey plumage. It started to turn white during its first autumn, partly through moulting and partly because the grey edges of the feathers wore away to reveal the white central parts.

A mute swan does not become fully white until its second winter and until then it can be recognized as a young bird. It then starts to look for a mate, but it will not breed until it is three or four years old. Swans may live for 15 years.

Tracks and trails

Looking for animal tracks can be rather frustrating. The footprints may not be very clear and there is often a jumble of prints on top of one another in snow that has lain for some time. The best prints are found in fresh snow and in the very fine mud left in a dried-up puddle or at the edge of a pond or stream. If the ground is at all hard, only the toes or the claws of the animal will make an impression. Even clear mammal footprints can be confusing because, as it moves, the animal usually places its hind foot almost on top of the print left by the forefoot. This is called registering. If you follow the tracks you may find a perfect print where the animal has broken its stride to go over or under an obstacle.

It takes a good deal of practice to be able to identify an animal just from its tracks. It is very

▼Mammals, like children, enjoy a fresh fall of snow and have a great time romping in it. In a while, however, this fox will feel hungry and start hunting. A single line of footprints then tells that he has set off in a purposeful manner away from the churned-up snow.

useful to have with you a reference book with drawings. Skill is needed to 'read' the track and work out whether the animal was walking or running.

Animal detective work

It has been said that you can learn more about a mammal by following its trail than by trying to watch it. Mammals are shy and are usually most active at night, but in winter you can easily follow their trails in the snow during the daytime. The tracks are freshest in the morning, and the best place to look is alongside hedges and walls. Small mammals, such as voles, mice, stoats and weasels, live in places like these, while larger mammals such as foxes, badgers and deer often walk along them or have favourite gaps through which they pass. At other times of the year a good place to look is in the bare sand of coastal dunes or heaths. In summer you should see tracks of snakes, lizards and insects.

The tracks of wading birds show up very well on sandy and muddy beaches. You can also see where they have probed in the mud with their long beaks, and you may find the remains of a cockle or crab which show where they managed to find food.

▼The track of a badger is easy to recognize. It has five toes with long claws and is usually distinct because the animal treads heavily.

►The footprint of a fox shows four toes with neat pointed claws. It is very like the tracks of a small dog, but the fox's foot is longer and more slender.

Well-worn paths

Most mammals, from deer to mice, have regular trails which they follow throughout the year. When you have discovered a track in the snow, you can go back later to look for more signs of the animal. Families of badgers use the same tracks year after year. They lead from the sett to other burrows, feeding places and drinking places. Some tracks mark boundaries between the territories of two families, and the badgers leave dung-filled pits as smelly signs of ownership. The track may be so well worn that you might easily think it is a human footpath until it passes under a fence or a low branch. Where the path leads into a field, look for small conical pits where the badgers have dug out earthworms. They usually catch them on the surface but sometimes a worm escapes and must be dug for.

◀ Perhaps the fox track will cross those of rabbits, or scuffed places where rabbits have dug to find food. Soft snow is no problem for such good diggers, except that it forms snowballs between the toes.

▶ The house sparrow is a small light bird. In fine new snow it leaves characteristic double tracks where it has hopped along.

STORIES IN THE SNOW

Always follow an animal's trail by walking to one side of it. You may be lucky enough to see signs of what the animal has been doing. Rabbits dig in the snow to find leaves to eat or reach up to nibble bark from twigs. Fox trails may lead for long distances. Every now and then there is a strong smell where the fox has left its scent. You may find the signs of where it has made a kill. Walk back and see if you can see where the fox has lain in wait, or has stalked forward and made its final pounce. A fox catches a mouse by leaping up and smacking down on its victim (see page 62). There may be some remains to show what was caught. If the fox is well fed, it buries its prey to eat later, and the place shows up well in the snow.

▲ A pigeon walks with its toes turned in. The jackdaw makes tracks of similar size but with toes straight.

▼ On firm ground the rabbit's hind-foot track clearly shows its four toes. Sometimes a roe track can look very similar.

▼ The tracks of blackbirds in snow may end with wingtip tracks where the bird has taken off.

Winter coats

See also **Coping with the cold**
on page 180

A good layer of fat and a coat of fur or feathers help mammals and birds keep warm. They generate their own heat, unlike reptiles, fishes or amphibians, but they need to be insulated so that the heat is not lost. Like the clothes we wear to keep warm, fur and feathers trap layers of air next to the skin of the animal. Air is a good insulator and it prevents the body from losing heat. Fur and feathers also help to keep out rain and wind.

Two layers are better than one
A mammal's fur is made up of two kinds of hair. The long guard hairs are waterproof and protect the short, soft underfur which traps the air to keep the mammal warm. A sheep's wool is very long under-fur, but in most other mammals the underfur is hidden under the guard hairs.

A bird's coat of feathers, called its plumage, is similar. There is a covering of outer feathers, called contour feathers, which overlap and make a water-proof covering like the mammal's guard hairs. Each feather has a shaft with a flat vane made up of barbs which are hooked together. Under the contour feathers there is a layer of down which keeps the bird warm. The down is either made up of fine separate feathers or of small tufts sprouting from the base of the contour feathers.

A change of coat
Like clothes, fur and feathers become worn. They are replaced regularly by the process called moult-ing, in which the old hairs or feathers are shed and new ones are grown. Just before the moult, mam-mals often look scruffy because their coats are worn, and birds look drab because the colours of their

---

FASHIONS FOR THE YOUNG
Young animals often have special coats. Young deer have spotted coats, which help to camouflage them. Young robins do not have red breasts nor young goldfinches the red, white and black head patches of the adults. These young animals moult and grow adult-coloured coats in the autumn. A her-ring gull, however, takes four years to turn from a mottled brown youngster to a grey and white adult.

▼Northern stoats turn white for the winter, except for the tail tip which always stays black. White stoats are called ermine. In the south, the winter coat stays brown. Midway between north and south, a stoat may be partially white, like this one.

▼The summer coat of the roe deer is bright foxy red, the winter coat grey-brown. This buck is marking his territory with scent from a gland between the antlers.

feathers are faded. After they have moulted they look much smarter and birds have brighter colours.

Most adult animals moult twice a year, although seals and badgers moult only once and some species moult three times. Winter fur and plumage is thicker than the summer coat. You can see this on a horse or a dog. A fox has a single moult each year but it still has thicker fur in the winter. It starts to moult in the late spring. When the tail moults it looks very thin. By autumn the long guard hairs have grown again and the tail is a thick 'brush'; the underfur does not reach its full length until winter. Then it is so thick that it makes the guard hairs stand up to give the fox a fluffy appearance.

Colours for all seasons
Many birds have different coloured sets of feathers for summer and winter. By the time that the breeding season is over, the summer plumage is very worn, and it is replaced by winter plumage. Wading birds, such as knots, dunlins and turnstones, have dull brown or grey plumage when they spend the winter on the seashore, but they moult into bright colours when they migrate northwards to nest in the Arctic. Grey squirrels are among the mammals that change their coats in winter and summer. They are sometimes brown enough in summer to be mistaken for red squirrels, while in winter their ears have white patches and the tail has a broad white fringe.

White for winter
A few mammals and birds turn white in winter. They live in the north, where the winters are colder. The stoat moults very quickly in the autumn and turns white all over, except for the black tip of its tail. In spring it moults back to its summer brown coat.

The mountain hare moults three times a year. It turns white in autumn, then greyish brown in spring. Shortly afterwards, it moults again into another brown coat.

The ptarmigan is a bird which also has three moults. It lives on mountains and turns white in winter. When the snow melts in spring, the hens moult very quickly and become mottled brown, except for the wings and underparts which remain white. They are beautifully camouflaged on the nest. The cock birds moult later in the summer, and both sexes turn greyish brown at the third moult in the late summer.

A coat of white fur or feathers is good camouflage in the winter when the ground is covered with snow, but stoats turn white in some parts of northern Scotland where there is very little snowfall! White fur probably helps the animal to keep warm because the little sunshine there is in winter can warm an animal's body more easily through white than through dark fur.

▲The ptarmigan's winter plumage is pure white for camouflage in the snow. In spring the hen moults to mottled brown to be camouflaged on the nest among the low vegetation.

Sleeping away the winter

One way to escape the worst of the winter cold is to go to sleep and wake up when it is warm again. Several mammals stay in their nests during the coldest weather but they sleep only for a few days at a time. If they stay in their nests for too long, they will starve. Squirrels do not hibernate; they shelter in their nests when it is cold, wet or windy but they must come out to look for food after a few days. Contrary to what was once thought, badgers do not hibernate either. You may find their tracks in the snow around the sett but if the weather continues to be harsh they, too, will spend several days without emerging.

When an animal hibernates properly its body temperature falls. A hedgehog's body temperature drops from 34 degrees centigrade to that of the surrounding air. Its heartbeat slows from 190 to 20 beats per minute and its breathing also slows down. Hedgehogs start to hibernate in October, but they may wake up again and they will not all be safely tucked up until December. Dormice sleep for a longer period; they go into hibernation in September and do not wake again until April.

Fat for life

Before an animal goes into hibernation it has to eat plenty of food and store it as fat. Although its body temperature, heartbeat and breathing are very low so that it uses very little energy to stay alive, it has to survive on its own resources for a long time. A cosy nest will help to keep the animal warm, but if it gets too cold it will automatically wake up and look for a better place to settle. Bats come out occasionally during the winter. They wake up when it gets too cold, in order to look for a warmer place. Greater horseshoe bats prefer a temperature between 5 and 10 degrees centigrade for hibernation.

Animal antifreeze

Warm-blooded animals, such as hedgehogs and bats, can control their body temperatures during hibernation so that they remain above freezing point. If it gets very cold and they freeze, they will die. Many cold-blooded animals, from frogs and toads to insects and snails, can survive temperatures below freezing. Their bodies are still just working and they do not freeze because they contain an 'antifreeze', rather like that in a motorcar radiator. However, when it gets very cold they may eventually die without ever waking.

▲ The dormouse is a true hibernator; it may spend over half the year asleep. In autumn it makes a special nest in which it curls up for the winter, hardly breathing until spring.

◀ Condensed moisture covers this herald moth with dew as it hibernates in a sheltered place among dead leaves. 'Antifreeze' in its body helps it survive the winter.

▶ Ladybirds sometimes cluster to hibernate in very exposed places offering no protection from frost and rain.

Sharing your home

When people first made warm, snug houses to live in, animals were soon attracted to join them. They liked the shelter and the food they could find in houses. Most of these animal 'guests' were unwelcome, but the human occupants found that they were very hard to evict! Some animals, like rats and mice, silverfish and cheese mites, raided the larder to feed on stored food. Others, such as bedbugs and fleas, actually attacked the people themselves, while a third group, such as woodworms and clothes moths, preferred the house and its furnishings. Thankfully, these pests are now much rarer.

Through cracks and plug hole

Some animals still manage to find their way into modern, clean houses. Spiders enter through cracks around doors and windows, or even up the plug holes of sinks and baths. Moths and other insects which fly at night come in through open windows because they are attracted by the light (see page 74). Wasps, bees and flies come in during the day and become a nuisance when they buzz at windows in their efforts to get out again. Ants are occasional invaders.

Flies in the ointment

The big, shiny bluebottles and greenbottles are only temporary visitors to the home. House flies, on the other hand, live indoors all the time.

grooves in the pad. The saliva may carry germs, so this way of feeding will spread disease.

House flies lay their eggs in any rotting rubbish. Each fly lays as many as 900 eggs, in batches of about 150. The eggs hatch, in as little as eight hours, into white, legless maggots. When full grown they pupate and the adult flies emerge from the pupae two weeks after the eggs were laid. In another two weeks, their offspring will appear. In two months, a single female house fly could have 1,000 million descendants! Or she would have if the majority of them were not killed off.

From cricket to cockroach

Centrally heated houses are warm enough for flies to breed in all the year round, and restaurant kitchens, bakeries and boilerhouses are even better for warmth-loving insects. When houses had large kitchen stoves and bread ovens, the continuous heat attracted the house cricket. This was one of the few animals welcomed in the house because of its cheerful chirping.

The house cricket originally came from the deserts of North Africa but modern hygiene has made it rare. Its place has been taken by the cockroach. Most kinds of cockroaches come from warm countries and they live mainly indoors. They are large insects but they have flattened bodies so that they can hide in crevices and, in cool countries, they are

> **KEEP IT COVERED!**
> House flies could increase enormously if they were not kept in check. Good hygiene is essential. Refuse must be kept in dustbins with tight-fitting lids or in plastic bags, and should be collected regularly. Food must be kept in a refrigerator or under cover to prevent flies soiling it.

House flies do not attack humans although their close relative, the stable fly, does bite and sometimes comes indoors in the autumn. House flies are dangerous because they may carry disease. When they fly from rotting food and rubbish they carry germs on their feet and in their mouths which they leave on our food and drink, or on our skin. You can watch a house fly feeding. It walks over its food, tasting it with sense organs in its feet. Then it unfolds its tubular tongue which ends in a flat pad. The fly squirts saliva on to its food which starts to digest it so that the fly can suck up a kind of 'soup' through the

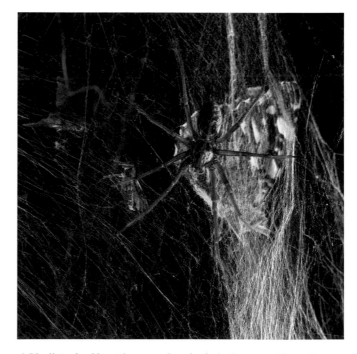

▲ Undisturbed in attic or garden shed, the house spider spins a large sheet web with a tunnel retreat in one corner. This spider's last meal was a red admiral butterfly.

▼ Booklice can turn up anywhere indoors, in books, furniture and stored food. They eat things like book-binding paste and mould on damp plaster. These booklice were in flour.

▲ House sparrows almost always live around buildings. They nest in the roof-space of houses and in winter may roost in their old nests. Here a cock sparrow peeps from behind a roof tile.

not easy to find. They come out at night to feed on anything edible, including paper, woollen clothes and leather, but they scuttle to safety at great speed as soon as a light is turned on.

Bristletails and booklice

The firebrat is another insect that has become less common as the old kitchen stoves have been replaced by modern cookers. However, central heating boilers do provide the heat they require for breeding. The firebrat is a member of the group of wingless insects called bristletails because of their three-pronged tails. Another member is the silverfish which has a covering of shiny scales. It lives in damp bathrooms and kitchens where it eats scraps of food, fungi and wallpaper. Silverfish sometimes attack books, especially old ones with paste in their bindings. Booklice also like old books.

Bad news beetles

When wood is said to be 'worm-eaten', it means that it has been attacked by 'woodworms' which are the larvae of beetles. The rafters and beams of old houses are often damaged by different kinds of woodworm. One of the most unwelcome is the furniture beetle. As its name suggests, this beetle also attacks wooden furniture. Its natural home is in tree trunks and old stumps. The female lays her eggs on wood and the grubs burrow in, using a special yeast to break down the wood before they eat it. Up to three years later, the adult beetle emerges, leaving a small round hole. Apart from ruining the appearance of furniture, large numbers of woodworm can, over the years, eat away furniture and house timbers until they collapse.

The larger deathwatch beetle has a similar life story but the adult beetle spends some time in the wood before it emerges. During this time it taps the wood with its head. This is believed to be a signal to other deathwatch beetles. The sound of the tapping, like a watch ticking at night, when everything is very quiet, led to the idea that it was a warning that someone was going to die.

Bigger housemates

As well as insects and other small animals, the house attracts some larger creatures. House mice, common, or brown, rats and black, or ship, rats have come from warmer countries and like living in houses, although they also live out of doors. They are pests because they steal food or dirty it, and they may carry disease. In winter they are joined by wood mice and yellow-necked mice (see page 168).

The space under the roof may become the temporary home of a squirrel, but house sparrows regularly move in if there are gaps they can get through. Bats may occupy a house either for breeding in the summer or for hibernation in winter.

Bark to cover and protect

See also **Dead but not lifeless** on page 70

Bark is a tree's skin. It grows on the outside of tree trunks and branches and on the stems of smaller shrubs. It is waterproof; it protects the tree from too much heat or cold and from attack by fungi and insects. The inner layers of bark carry food materials from the leaves to the roots. If a complete ring of bark is removed from a tree, it will die. This practice is called 'ringing'.

Corks from oak

Bark grows from a thin layer of tissue on its inside, which contains a corky substance called suberin. New bark is continually being formed to keep pace with the growth of the trunk or stem, and prevent it from splitting. The outer bark tissue dies and is turned into a strong, waterproof, virtually airtight material full of tiny airspaces, rather like foam rubber, that make it a good insulator. The thickness of the corky material varies from species to species, but oak has a thick corky bark. The corks used in bottles come from the cork oak. Sheets of cork are stripped from the trunk of cork oak about every ten years.

▲ Silver birch is one of the most graceful trees, with its silver-white bark particularly conspicuous in winter. Its old bark is shed in papery rings. This trunk has been holed by woodpeckers, and scratched by climbing squirrels.

Only the dead part of the bark is removed, so the tree is not harmed.

> **BARK CLOSE UP**
> As a tree's bark gets thicker, the outside splits and forms the familiar furrows that run up tree trunks. The furrows form a characteristic pattern in different trees which, with the difference in colour, enables trees to be identified even in winter when they have no leaves. Oak and elm have deep furrows, while beech is smooth and black poplar has a network of ridges.

Flaky and spongy

Some trees shed the old bark. Birch bark comes off in papery strips, and plane trees and Scots pines lose their bark in flakes. The wellingtonia, a conifer native to California and named after the Duke of Wellington, has a thick spongy bark which you can punch without hurting your knuckles. This bark protects the tree from fire and it also provides a home for birds. Treecreepers have learned to excavate holes, about 6 centimetres across and 4 centimetres deep, in the soft bark. They roost in them with their feathers fluffed out for warmth. You can find these holes at about eye level; there are usually piles of droppings below them.

If bark were completely airtight, the living tree inside would suffocate. There are tiny breathing holes called lenticels running through the bark. You can see them as pale spots or cracks in the bark itself and as the small splits which run from side to side across a bottle cork. Trees are sometimes killed when the lower part of the trunk is surrounded by floodwater or has earth piled around it. This is because the lenticels become blocked.

The bootlace peril

Bark is very good at protecting the tree but it does not always succeed completely. Some fungi attack living trees. Honey fungus is a yellowish toadstool which grows in clumps on or near trunks and stumps. It spreads, using its long black strings of hyphae (see page 164) called 'bootlaces', which grow under the bark and may even spread from one tree to the next. The hyphae grow into the living tissues between the bark and the wood and kill them.

▶ The bark of a mature Scots pine trunk glows pink in the low winter sun. A bluebottle fly hibernating in a crack has crept out to bask in spite of the cold wind.

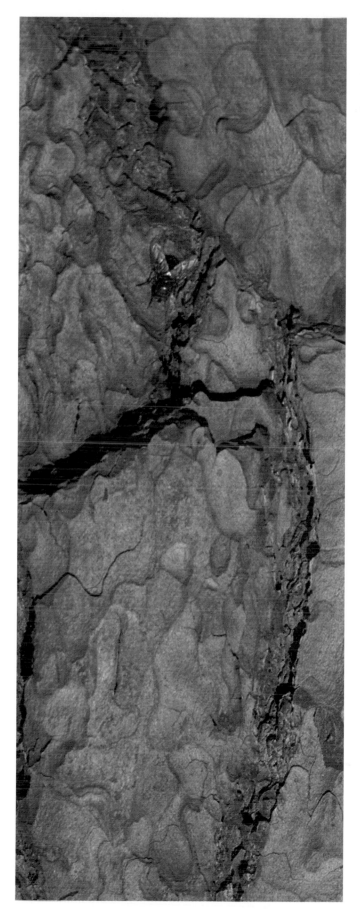

The death of the elm

Honey fungus has not caused so much destruction as Dutch elm disease. Its name arose because Holland was the first place in Europe where the disease was found. Dutch elm disease is caused by a fungus carried by bark beetles that burrow into bark to lay their eggs. The fungus blocks the water-conducting tubes of the sapwood and kills the tree.

If you look closely at a dead or dying elm you will find small, round holes made by the beetles. The bark can be pulled off dead trees in large sheets and then you can see the mining operations of the beetles on the surface of the wood and on the inside of the bark. Tunnels leading away from the entrance holes for several centimetres are made by the adult beetles. The rows of smaller tunnels running out at right angles are made by the grubs.

Life under the bark

Once the bark of a tree has been damaged, many small animals such as woodlice, centipedes and millipedes (see page 71), find homes there. These animals like damp and darkness so they spend the day under the bark and emerge at night. In turn, woodpeckers and other predators come to feed on them.

▲ Oak bark is deeply fissured into furrows with a characteristic pattern that run up and down the trunk. Cracks in the bark shelter many over-wintering invertebrates. The ridges become coated with a green alga, especially on the north-facing side.

Lichens: two plants in one

See also **Life on the wall** on page 46 and **Plants without flowers** on page 118

The first form of life to show itself on bare rock is lichen, a kind of plant that does not need soil. Lichens can even find a hold on the smooth surface of marble gravestones, and there they live by taking food from rainwater washing over the surface of the stone. They can also survive getting dried up.

As lichens take hold and spread, they form a foundation for other plants. When they die, their decaying remains gather in nooks and crannies and, over many years, form a simple soil covering. This encourages larger plants and animals to move in.

Living together

Lichens are unique. They are made of two plants, a fungus and an alga, growing together. The two provide each other with the necessities of life so that each benefits. The alga contains the green pigment chlorophyll and is able to make sugars by photosynthesis (see page 9). It shares these sugars with the fungus. The hyphae (see page 164) of the fungus grow around the algal cells to protect them and prevent them from drying out, but they may also digest some of the alga. The fungus gives the lichen its shape but it cannot live alone whereas the alga can. On the under side of the lichen the hyphae grow out to make tiny roots which absorb moisture and anchor the lichen. The hyphae release acids which dissolve the surface of the rock and enable them to get a better grip. In this way the rock is slowly broken down to dust in which mosses and other plants may gain a foothold.

Ever so slowly

Although lichens can survive in very dry places, they grow best where there is plenty of rain and mist.

▼There are several sorts of orange lichens, and they all look much alike. Some grew on old walls and roofs; this one is on a rock beside the sea.

Masses of lichen grow on tree trunks and branches as well as on rocks.

Lichens grow extremely slowly and some growing on mountains live for well over 1,000 years. During this time they spread over the rock at a rate of about 2 centimetres in 100 years. Some of the flat, seaweed-like lichens grow as rapidly as a centimetre a year! Find out how slowly a lichen grows by looking at the ones growing on gravestones. They cannot be any older than the date carved on the stone.

HOW CLEAN IS THE AIR?

Unfortunately, lichens have disappeared from many places. They take their food directly from rainwater and they are very sensitive to air pollution. Lichens have gone from most cities, especially where there are a lot of factories. As they grow only where the air is clean, they can be used to indicate the level and spread of air pollution.

Two-way split

Lichens reproduce in two ways. Some lichens grow little cups on the upper surface from which fungal spores are released. The spores develop into fungi which must combine with some algal cells before they can grow into lichens. Other lichens grow bundles of fungal hyphae containing algae which break off from the parent lichen and blow away.

▶Three species of map lichens are encrusting this mountain boulder: green, rust-red and grey-black. The lines formed where the plants touch one another look like boundaries on a map.

▼This grey branching lichen is growing on a stem of dead heather. It may also grow on rocks, walls or trees.

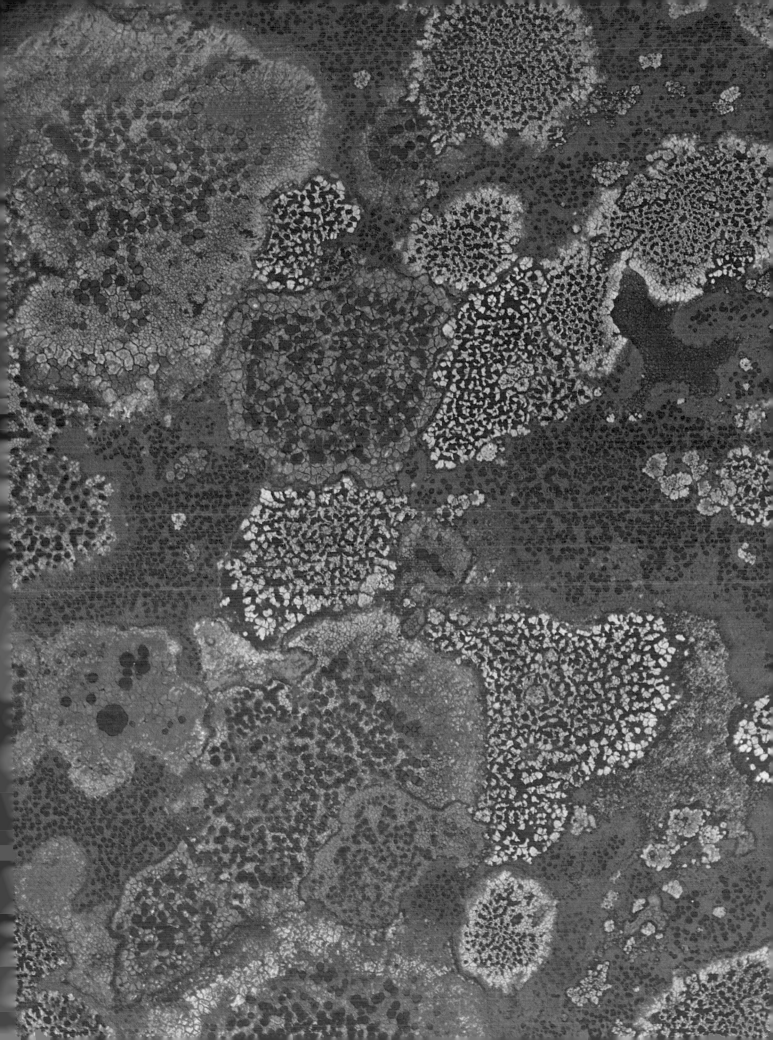

Life underground

Turn over the top layers of the soil and you are certain to find some animals. Most of them will be earthworms, but you will also find centipedes, millipedes and insect grubs. In the winter months these little creatures are not very active and they are probably resting until spring. There are also shiny brown moth pupae and snails' eggs looking like tiny pearls. These animals either shelter in the soil and spend their active life above ground, or they find their food underground. They feed on plant roots or on decaying plant matter, or even on one another. Soil animals are much more abundant in the rich soil of woods and pastures than in the poor soils of moors and heaths.

Pullers and probers

Animals are safe from predators if they burrow deep into the soil, but they can still be caught if they stay near the surface. Blackbirds, for instance, seize earthworms which have pushed their heads above the surface. The bird has to be very quick to catch the worm and it has to pull hard to draw it out because the worm is able to cling to the sides of its burrow. Starlings find leatherjackets, which are the larvae of craneflies, by probing into the soil with their beaks. You can see how efficient and successful starlings are by watching a flock on the lawn and counting how

often they probe into the soil before swallowing something.

The not-so humble worm

Earthworms play a very important part in the life of the soil. They spend their time burrowing through the earth, either by pushing between the grains of soil or by eating their way through it. If you let a worm crawl over your hand you will feel its bristles against your skin. The worm moves forwards by anchoring the rear of its body with these bristles and then pushing its 'nose' into the soil crevices. Then it anchors the front of its body and the rear after it. As we have seen the worm also holds onto its burrow using these hairs. Worm burrows help to drain and

▼Starlings walk quickly and jerkily over the ground constantly probing with their beaks for leatherjackets and other insects. Birds at the back of the flock 'leap frog' over the others to get to the front.

▼The blackbird runs along the ground in short bursts, then pauses to watch. If it notices the tiny movement of a worm's head poking out of the soil, it darts forward and grabs the worm.

▼Earthworms are the mole's chief food, found when they enter its underground tunnels. When worms are plentiful, the mole stores them, first biting the head off so they cannot burrow and escape.

▼The mole sometimes makes its nest in an extra large mound, or sometimes deep underground. The nest itself is made of dead leaves or dry grass. Both holes connect with the mole's tunnel system.

aerate the soil around plant roots and, by eating the soil, the worms help to break up decaying plant material. The remains of their meals are passed out on or near the surface so that nutrients which have been washed downwards by the rain are brought up again. Two species of earthworm deposit the digested soil on the surface as 'worm casts', which we see on lawns from autumn to spring.

Earthworms also help to make new soil by dragging dead leaves into their burrows. They come out of their burrows at night and feel around until they find a leaf and then drag it backwards (see page 144). In turn, earthworms become the food of many animals. A badger, for example, can eat several hundred worms in a night, if it can get them. Badgers look for worms which are partly out of their burrows, grip them with their teeth and haul them out. Worm eaters are most successful at hunting on the warm, still nights that attract the worms to the surface. Foxes, weasels, hedgehogs, shrews and even owls join the badgers on the rich pastures where earthworms are abundant.

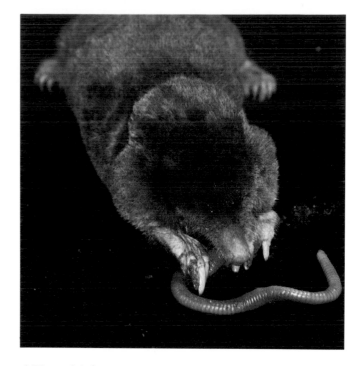

▲ The mole's front paws are shovels for digging; they are useful, too, for cleaning soil off an earthworm as it eats it.

UNDERGROUND RUNNER

The mole is superbly designed for life underground. It constructs a system of runs which it continuously patrols to catch the worms and other animals which have accidentally tunnelled in. When new runs are needed or old ones have to be repaired, the mole digs with its shovel-shaped forepaws and gets rid of the excess soil by pushing it to the surface as molehills. When the earth is frozen, moles cannot make molehills, but they can do so under snow which protects the earth from freezing.

Green leaves of winter

Evergreens are plants which stay in leaf all through the year. They shed their leaves continuously but new ones grow to replace them. When the deciduous trees have lost their leaves in autumn (see page 144) evergreens are easy to find in the woods. The commonest are holly and the many conifer trees, but there are also several shrubs and herbs, such as gorse, juniper, dandelion and daisy. The leaves of many evergreens have a thick waxy layer on their surface which helps them to save water.

Cones and needles

Most evergreen trees are coniferous and reproduce by means of cones instead of by nuts or berries like deciduous trees. Conifers include pines, fir, juniper, yew, spruces and the larches. Unlike those of broad-leaved trees, the leaves of conifers are slender needles. (Larches are unusual because they are deciduous. Their needles change colour and drop in the autumn.)

The cones of a pine grow from the tips of the twigs. The larger female cones are fertilized with pollen blown by the wind from clusters of small male cones. After pollination the cones take two years to ripen. A seed develops on the inside of each of the scales of the cone and it drops out when the scale bends outwards in dry weather. The seed has a small wing so that it can be carried by the wind. It would not be carried so far in wet weather but the cone stays closed when it rains. You can see how cones open if you bring one or two indoors and keep them in a warm place.

Yews and junipers bear, instead of cones, a kind of berry containing a single seed. The juicy flesh of the berries attracts birds which eat them and so help to spread the seeds.

Long-lasting leaves

Holly tolerates dim light and often grows as a shrub under taller trees. The thick wax coating the dark green leaves resists water loss so that holly can retain its leaves in winter. This also makes holly ideal for

---

WHY IS HOLLY PRICKLY?
The prickles on holly leaves probably protect them from being eaten by deer, ponies and other large animals. If you look at a tall holly tree you will see that the leaves near the bottom are very prickly, while many of those near the top, and out of reach of animals, have almost smooth edges. Holly leaves are often eaten by deer, however, and farmers once cut holly branches for cattle and sheep to eat in winter. Perhaps even more would be eaten if there were no prickles!

▲Mistletoe, with its shining white winter berries and evergreen leaves, has been revered as a magical plant since ancient times. Most of its relatives live in the tropics, in the tops of jungle trees.

▲By the time pine cones are ripe, they are no longer at the tips of twigs as the catkins were. By then the tree has put out two more years' growth of needle-bearing shoots.

▲Bright red holly berries are an important food for birds such as wood pigeons, blackbirds and thrushes. They are conspicuous and attractive and so holly trees are often stripped by the birds long before Christmas.

Christmas decorations because the leaves and berries last a long time indoors before withering or dropping. On the tree each leaf lasts for up to four years but if there is a drought or if frost locks up supplies of water, many of the younger leaves fall.

Holly trees are either male or female, and only female trees bear berries. The berries develop from white flowers which blossom in May. The berries ripen in October. They would last until late winter if pigeons and thrushes did not strip them from the trees.

A sticky business

Birds help to spread the holly's seeds by eating the berries (see page 166), but mistletoe is even more dependent on birds. Its flowers appear in early spring and the white berries ripen in the following winter. The berries attract mistle thrushes and other birds although their sticky flesh is difficult to eat. It clings to the birds' beaks and they wipe it off against a twig or branch of a tree, at the same time depositing the seed. The seed eventually sprouts and sends peg-like growths into the wood of the tree, to obtain water and food materials. It also grows slender leaves for its own photosynthesis (see page 9). Bunches of mistletoe are most often found on lime, poplar and apple trees and they are easiest to find in winter, when the leaves of the host trees have fallen.

Birds in winter

See also **Birds at the table**
on page 206

Not everyone realizes how many small birds die during the winter. At the end of summer, when the young birds have left their nests, the bird population is at its highest. But, by spring, bird numbers will have fallen to the same level as in the previous spring, or even lower if it has been a hard winter. Birds can either risk the hazards of a long migration to a warmer country (see page 134) or they can stay at home and face the perils of winter.

The cupboard is bare

In winter the weather is often very cold and food for birds is in short supply. Birds that normally feed on insects, worms and other small animals are the hardest hit because these small creatures also become scarce in winter and may almost disappear in times of ice or snow (see page 180). Birds that eat seeds or fruit are better off, provided that there has been a good crop. Bullfinches, for example, may survive a hard winter if there is a good crop of ash seeds while other species die of starvation.

Keeping on the move

A bird needs plenty of food in winter to help it keep warm. A thick layer of fat insulates its body from the cold air and it needs the energy stored in food to maintain its body temperature. Unfortunately, during the short winter days there is hardly enough time to find food. A bird spends 15 hours roosting in the dark and it has only 9 hours of daylight in which to find enough food to keep it going until the next day. Therefore it cannot afford to be idle during the day.

HOW THEY COPE

There are several ways in which birds can improve their chances of getting enough to eat. Some tits, especially the coal tit, and nuthatches hide energy-rich nuts in places such as bark crevices and remember where they hid them. Jays bury acorns and find them again by looking for the seedlings poking through the soil. Other birds defend territories (see page 154) to give themselves their own familiar feeding ground. Or they become nomads and fly across country in search of new feeding places. A fall of snow sends flocks of lapwings and fieldfares long distances in search of clear ground.

Tits, for example, spend over three-quarters of their time searching for food. To make the most of the day, birds start foraging well before sunrise and continue after sunset.

Sometimes, thick ice or a heavy fall of snow makes it impossible for birds to find food, and they may not even try to do so. Rather than waste energy in a fruitless search, it is better to sit still with feathers fluffed up for extra insulation.

Learning from others

Living in a flock is helpful because birds can keep a close eye on each other. If one finds a source of food, the others start to look in the same place. Tits flock together in this way, and they fly from tree to tree piping shrilly to keep in touch. Long-tailed tits spend the winter as a family and even roost together, gathering in a fluffy ball to keep each other warm.

When birds roost together, individuals may have a better chance of learning from the others where to find food. Starlings, chaffinches and blackbirds roost together and fly out in flocks to feed in the morning. Birds that found a good feeding place on the previous day set out at first light to return to it. They are followed by the birds that did not feed so well, but which noticed the departure of the well-fed birds.

▲ A long-tailed tit rests for a moment in a winter oak. Families of long-tailed tits gang up in winter with other tits and stream from tree to tree in search of insects.

◄ In winter goldfinches feed on seeds. A bird will perch on a swaying teasel deadhead while it extracts and eats the seeds. It is also very fond of seeding thistles and forget-me-nots.

► A little brown bird flying along the rocky beach or perched on a boulder is not a sparrow but a rock pipit. In the short 9-hour days of a hard winter, a rock pipit may spend over 8 hours looking for food.

Birds at the table

▲ Not everyone loves to see a starling on the bird-table: it is noisy, quarrelsome and greedy, eating food intended for robins and blue tits. But a starling's antics are comical and its plumage is gorgeous in close-up.

▼ In hard weather when food is scarce you may be able to attract unusual visitors. Here redwings and a fieldfare, together with a blackbird, are feeding on apples and pears bought for them.

In winter, when food is scarce, birds may become quite tame and will often come into your garden in search of food. If you feed them, the birds will have a better chance of surviving, and you can enjoy watching their antics, especially if you make a simple bird-table.

How to make one
Fix a board, about 30 centimetres square, to a post stuck in the ground. A strip of wood, 2 to 3 centimetres high, around the edges prevents food being blown off. But you must leave a gap so that rain can drain away and old food can be swept off. Alternatively, the board can be hung by string or wire from the branch of a tree, from a clothes-line, or fixed on a wall bracket. A low-level table attracts chaffinches, blackbirds and dunnocks which may be too shy to come to a higher table. Place the table in the open so that cats cannot wait in ambush.

DON'T FORGET!
Birds usually ignore bird-tables in the summer because they have plenty of natural food. Once you have started to feed the birds in winter, you must feed them every day. They will learn to come to your bird-table for food and will waste time waiting if you forget to put it out.

Different food for different birds
You can feed the birds either by throwing crusts of stale bread on the lawn or by providing a wide variety of food in different kinds of dispensers. Fat supplies lots of energy for cold days. Marrow bones,

BIRD-TABLE BEHAVIOUR
When you keep watch at a bird-table you will notice that each kind of bird behaves in a different way. You can often see birds trying to show that they are the boss by threatening other birds and keeping them away from the food. A great tit threatens by spreading its wings and tail while a robin raises its beak to show off the red breast.

◄▼ Robins hold territories in winter (see page 154) and so you may get only one at your table.

▼ The nuthatch will eat fat and pastry from the table.

▼ Like all tits, the great tit is very acrobatic, but it often feeds on the ground. You can tell the male from the female by the broader black line down his front.

► After the blackbird, the blue tit is the most likely visitor to the bird-table. Scores can call at one table in a day.

▲ Coal tits often hide their food. They carry seeds and nuts away and poke them into nooks and crannies.

◄ Peanuts and wheat are a great attraction for the greenfinch.

lumps of suet or other fat can be hung up for the birds to peck at.

Nuts provide good, rich food for birds and plenty of entertainment for onlookers. Peanuts in their shells can be threaded on to a wire, and shelled nuts can be hung up in a net bag. They attract agile tits, nuthatches and greenfinches but sparrows and even woodpeckers soon learn how to cling to the net and peck out pieces of nut.

The birds to see
You can keep a chart to show how frequently different species of birds appear at your table and which foods they prefer. If there are woods nearby, woodpeckers and nuthatches are likely visitors. Moorhens and mallards may wander in from nearby ponds and lakes. Rare visitors may include blackcaps and crossbills (see page 208).

MAKE THEM A PUDDING
Making a bird pudding is a neat way of using up kitchen scraps. Mince or finely chop pieces of meat, cheese rind, stale cake, bread or biscuit, and peanuts. Meanwhile gently melt fat from the frying pan or from pieces of fat trimmed from meat before cooking. Stir the fat into the mixture.

You could pour the pudding into a half coconut shell or some other container before it sets and hang it under the bird-table where only the agile birds can reach it, or you can turn it out on to the bird-table for them all to enjoy.

Visitors for the winter

See also **Wings across the ocean** on page 134
and **Birds in winter** on page 204

You may know that some birds fly away to Africa for the winter and return in the spring, but did you also know that other birds appear in the autumn and spend the winter with us? These birds have nested in the arctic regions of Greenland, northern Europe and Siberia where there is plenty of food during the short summer, and they migrate southwards to avoid the long, cold winter.

Thrushes to stay

The best known of the winter visitors are two kinds of thrushes, the redwing and the fieldfare, which come from Scandinavia. Keep a watch for them from September onwards. They can be mistaken for song or mistle thrushes which live here all the year, but they have distinctive plumage. Flocks of these birds live mostly in the fields and they visit the hedgerows to strip the haws (see page 143).

Waders flock to the shore

Estuaries and shores become the winter home of flocks of waders from August onwards. They leave the Arctic as soon as they have finished nesting and head southwards. Some remain around the coasts of Europe but others continue to Africa. When the tide is low they spread out over the mudflats (see page 172) and beaches to look for shellfish and other animals to eat, and as the tide rises they fly in dense flocks to roost on dry land. Some waders, such as the knot and turnstone, have a dull plumage in winter but a few species change to their bright summer dress before they fly north in the spring. Dunlin and golden and grey plovers have black underparts in summer which become grey in winter.

At this time of the year the coastline is also the haunt of flocks of geese and many kinds of duck. Grebes and divers also leave their freshwater breeding grounds and spend the winter at sea. They are often visible from the shore, but less easy to identify in their winter than in their summer plumage.

Visiting now and then

Some birds only appear irregularly. In some winters they are common, but in other years very few are seen. For instance, there are winters when large numbers of waxwings come into gardens to feed on the berries of rowan, cotoneaster and pyracantha. Waxwings breed in northern Europe and, every few years, there is a shortage of food which forces the birds to fly south. This irregular migration is called an irruption.

Another bird that arrives in Britain in irruptions is the crossbill, but it arrives in summer. It uses its unique crossed beak to get the seeds out of the cones of conifers. Crossbills fly southwards when there is a shortage of cones and they sometimes stay to breed.

▼A large flock of dunlins in winter plumage takes off from a shingle bank. As the birds all wheel and turn together, their grey backs blend with the background, then their white bellies flash in the sun.

FLEEING THE COLD

Some winter visitors arrive from places as far apart as Arctic Canada, Greenland, Scandinavia and Siberia, but others come from just across the North Sea. The time of their arrival depends on the weather.

◄Bewick swans keep together in families. You can recognize the young birds by their grey plumage.

►Barnacle geese nest in the Arctic and the whole population migrates to a few wintering grounds in the British Isles and northwest Europe.

▲Fieldfares arrive in flocks during the autumn and every year more stay to nest in the following spring.

▲In some winters waxwings are very common migrants but in other years they stay in their northern homes.

▲Redwings do not always return to the same place each winter. They may go to another country hundreds of kilometres away.

▲Turnstones are one of the many kinds of wader which live in flocks on estuaries during the winter. Waders are not always easy to distinguish in their winter plumage.

◄When snow buntings fly up they show white on their wings which is not obvious when they are on the ground and their wings are folded. They are most often seen around coasts in winter.

Last flowers of winter

The year ends where it started. A few flowers open and, on fine days, even a few insects may emerge to pollinate them.

All through the year
Throughout the late autumn and early winter, a few plants come into flower long after the main flowering season. A few scattered plants of hogweed appear in a second flowering in the autumn, a few even survive into December. Ivy-leaved toadflax (see page 46) is a regular autumn bloomer and some flowers last into December. Red dead-nettle, dandelion and groundsel are among those that continue flowering throughout the year.

Flowers without petals
Stinking hellebore plants which flower from January and February onwards. They are close relatives of the Christmas rose. Hellebore flowers are made of large sepals instead of petals (see page 41). The petals are tiny and secrete nectar which attracts the first honeybees, bumblebees and droneflies.

Brave new flowers
At the end of winter the earliest of next season's flowers appear. Dog's mercury carpets the floors of old woods, although its green flowers hardly show. The first colt's-foot and primrose flowers appear among the short grass on banks and verges. by the time they are in full flower, it is spring again.

▲Butcher's broom is an evergreen bush growing about knee high. Its prickly 'leaves' are flattened branches. The flowers open in winter; dark green berries follow, ripening to holly-red.

▲ Gorse can be found in flower at almost any time of year; its bright yellow blossoms are particularly welcome in the short, dark days of winter. They have a strong smell of coconut and produce no nectar, but insects visit them for pollen.

◄ Stinking hellebore grows wild in a few woods in chalk and limestone districts, but it is also grown in gardens alongside its sweeter garden relative, the Christmas rose. Both these plants flower in winter.

► Red dead-nettle is an annual weed of cultivation, so you could find it growing in any garden or field. A member of the mint family, it produces pinkish-purple 'snap-dragon' flowers throughout the year.

Glossary of terms

In this book, technical words have been avoided wherever possible but where they are used they are explained at the first mention. If you come across a word later in the book and you have forgotten its meaning, look it up here for a reminder.

abdomen In insects, spiders and mites the last body section; in vertebrates the part of the body containing the digestive organs

alga (plural algae) Algae are simple, usually aquatic, plants. Seaweeds are large marine algae, but many algae are microscopic

amphibian An animal which lives in water and on land; young amphibians breathe through gills and cannot survive out of water

antenna (plural antennae) A jointed 'feeler' found in pairs on the heads of insects and other invertebrates. Usually sensitive to smell as well as touch

anther The top part of the stamen in which pollen is produced

aquatic Living in or on water

bacteria (single bacterium) Microscopic simple organisms found in large numbers in soil, air and in the bodies of animals. They help the decay of dead plants and animals. Some cause diseases

brackish Slightly salty water

brood patch A bare patch of skin on a bird's breast, well supplied with blood vessels. It acts as a hot water bottle for the eggs

bud An undeveloped shoot consisting of a short stem bearing crowded, overlapping, immature leaves

bulb Underground storage organ consisting of a short stem bearing fleshy scales which surround the bud for the following year

calyx The outer ring of the parts of a flower, usually composed of green sepals

camouflage A colour pattern which conceals an animal against its background

canopy The layer of vegetation in a woodland consisting of the upper branches of trees; the tree layer

carbohydrate A compound made of carbon, hydrogen and oxygen. Carbohydrates are made by green plants during photosynthesis. Sugars are carbohydrates

carnivore A flesh eater

carpel Part of the female organs of a flower. Contains the future seed box

catkin A long tassel-like spike of small flowers, each spike consisting of either male or female flowers

chlorophyll The green pigment found in plants, essential for photosynthesis

chrysalis The pupa of a butterfly

cocoon A protective covering for eggs or larvae. The larvae of many insects spin a silky cocoon before they pupate

coppice (copse) A small wood which is cut periodically

corm A short, swollen underground storage stem arising on top of the previous year's growth

corolla The petals of a flower

crustaceans A large group of mainly aquatic animals including water fleas, barnacles, shrimps, crabs and woodlice

cuticle The protective outer skin of insects and plants. It prevents water loss

dabbling Of ducks, feeding by filtering water from the surface through the bill

earth A fox's burrow

eclipse plumage The dull plumage of ducks after moulting at the end of the breeding season

egg-tooth The small horny knob at the tip of the bill used by a baby bird inside the egg to crack the eggshell on hatching. It falls off later

evolution The gradual development of organisms from pre-existing organisms since the beginning of life

fledgling A young bird with a complete set of feathers and able to fly

gait Way of walking

gall Abnormal growth of plant tissue, most often caused by fungi, insects or mites which find food and shelter inside

gill An organ to enable breathing in water as in amphibians and fishes

harem A group of female animals mated by a single male

herb A plant with no woody or persistent stem above the ground. Also, a plant for flavouring food

hibernation Condition of passing the winter in a resting state

honeydew A sugary secretion produced by certain insects such as aphids; also exuded by the leaves of many plants

hormone A chemical which acts as a signal in the body. It is produced in minute amounts in a gland and is transported to another part where it has a large effect

hypha (plural hyphae) A thread-like fungal growth

invertebrate An animal without a backbone. An invertebrate usually has a hard external skin or shell which acts as a skeleton

juvenile Of a bird, after its first true feathers have grown but before its first moult (when it becomes an immature); any young animal

larva (plural larvae) An immature but active stage in development of an animal, very different from the adult (for example, a caterpillar)

leveret A young hare

littoral Growing or living on or near the seashore; the seashore itself

mimicry The resemblance of one animal to another so that a third animal is deceived into confusing them

molluscs A large group of animals, most of which have shells, including snails, slugs, cockles, mussels, oysters, octopuses

neap tide A tide with a small range so that high tide is lower than at other times and low tide is higher. Neap tides occur twice each month

nidicolous Birds which live in the nest for some time after hatching

nidifugous Birds which leave the nest soon after hatching

nymph Early stages of insects, for example dragonflies, in which the young looks like a small, wingless adult.

organism An animal or a plant; any living thing

ovule The structure in plants which develops into a seed after the egg cell within it has been fertilized

parasite An animal which feeds on another animal without killing it or steals its food. Some plants are parasites on other plants

pheromone A chemical given out by one animal which acts as a signal to another of the same species, for example in moths

photosynthesis The process by which green plants, in sunlight, produce carbohydrates from carbon dioxide and water

pipping The first sign that an egg is about to hatch, when the chick makes a hole in the shell using its eggtooth

pollard A tree which has been cut off about 2 metres from the ground

pollen Powder produced by anthers which fertilizes female flowers

pollination The transfer of pollen from the male to the female parts of the flower

predator A hunting animal which eats other animals

preen To clean the feathers and restore them to the correct positions

proboscis A trunk-like process on the head; sucking mouthparts used in feeding by insects

proleg An unjointed leg on the abdomen of some insect larvae (for example caterpillars); not a true leg

Pupa (plural pupae) Stage between larva and adult of many insects. Locomotion and feeding cease in this stage and the body is rebuilt

radula The rasping 'tongue' of molluscs such as slugs and snails

retina The part of the eye which is sensitive to light

rhizome An underground stem

rut The mating period in deer when the males roar

scale A flat, rigid plate. Scales cover the body of a fish and the wings of moths and butterflies

sett A badger's burrow

spawn A mass of eggs laid in water

species A kind, or sort, of animal or plant. The smallest group in the biological classification of organisms. Members of the same species can interbreed; members of different species normally do not

speculum A bright patch on a bird's wing, especially of ducks

spraint Otter droppings

spring tide A tide with a large range so that the high tide is higher and the low tide lower than at other times

stamen Male reproductive organ of a flower consisting of a stalk with the anther at its tip

standard A tree left growing in a coppice

stigma The part of the female organ of a flower which receives the pollen; the end of the style

style The stalk coming from the ovary of a flower which bears the stigma

tadpole A young frog, toad or newt in its aquatic, larval stage

tapetum The pigment layer of the retina which reflects light and makes the eye appear to glow

tendril A specialized twining stem or leaf by which climbing plants support themselves

territory An area defended by an animal, usually during the breeding season

tuber A swollen food-storing part of an underground root or stem

ultrasonic Of sound of a higher frequency than the sound waves we can hear

ultraviolet Beyond the violet end of the visible spectrum, that is, having a wavelength shorter than those of the colours we can see

vertebrate An animal with a backbone. Fishes, amphibians, reptiles, birds and mammals are vertebrates

Further reading

After reading this book you may want to find out more about certain animals and plants or aspects of the natural world. Here are a few carefully selected books which you should find useful and which will be available at your local bookshop or public library.

Books for identification:

Gem Guides published by Collins, London:

Wild Animals by John A. Burton
Birds by Richard Perry
Wild Flowers by Marjorie Blamey and Richard Fitter
Butterflies and Moths by Brian Hargreaves and Michael Chinery
Mushrooms and Toadstools by John Wilkinson and Stefan Buczacki

Observer's Pocket Series published by Frederick Warne, London:

Trees by Herbert L. Edlin
Seashells by Nora F. McMillan
Wild Flowers by Francis Rose
Insects by E. F. Linssen
Larger Moths by R. L. E. Ford
Butterflies by W. J. Stokoe
Caterpillars by David J. Carter
Ferns by W. J. Stokoe
Lichens by K. A. Kershaw and K. L. Alvin
Fungi by W. P. K. Findlay
Wild Animals by Maurice Burton

Oxford 'Book of' series published by Oxford University Press, Oxford:

Invertebrates by David Nichols and John A. L. Cooke
Flowerless Plants by F. H. Brightman and B. E. Nicholson
Insects by John Burton

Field guides published by Collins, London:

A Field Guide to the Insects of Britain and Northern Europe by Michael Chinery and Roger Peterson
Collins Guide to the Freshwater Fishes of Britain and Europe by Bent J. Muus and Preben Dahlstrom
A Field Guide to the Birds of Britain and Europe by Guy Mountfort and P. A. D. Hollom

Others:

A Guide to Freshwater Invertebrate Animals by T. T. Macan, Longman, London

The Fishes of the British Isles and North-west Europe by Alwyne Wheeler, Macmillan, London
The Birdlife of Britain by Peter Hayman and Philip Burton, Mitchell Beazley, London
Mammals of Britain: their tracks, trails and signs by M. J. Laurence and R. W. Brown, Blandford, Poole

Books for general reference:

Severn House Naturalist's Library published by Severn House, London:

Mammal Watching by Michael Clark
Butterfly Watching by Paul Whalley
Pond Watching by Paul Sterry

The Countryside Series published by Collins, London:

Insect Life by Michael Tweedie
Life on the Seashore by John Barrett
Birds by Christopher Perrins
Woodlands by William Condry

Others:

Britain's Green Mantle by A. G. Tansley, George Allen & Unwin, London
A Complete Guide to British Butterflies by Margaret Brooks and Charles Knight, Jonathan Cape, London
AA Book of the Countryside, Drive Publications, London
Freshwater Life by John Clegg, Frederick Warne, London
Discovering Hedgerows by David Streeter and Rosamond Richardson, BBC Publications
Nature's Nightlife by Robert Burton, Blandford, Poole
Ponds: their wildlife and upkeep by Robert Burton, David and Charles, Newton Abbot
Trees and Woodland in the British Landscape by Oliver Rackham, Dent, London

Clubs and societies to join

If you would like to meet more people who share your interest in natural history, and perhaps take part in outdoor events in groups, why not join one of the organizations listed here? Send a self-addressed envelope and you will receive their details.

The Mammal Society, c/o Harvest House, 62 London Road, Reading, Berkshire. Youth membership for the under 18s

Royal Society for the Protection of Birds, The Lodge, Sandy, Bedfordshire. There are local Members' Groups and the Young Ornithologists' Club (for 15 year olds and under)

British Trust for Conservation Volunteers, The Zoological Society of London, Regent's Park, London NW1

County Trusts for Nature Conservation There is a Trust for every county in England and Wales. For details of your Trust, contact The Royal Society for Nature Conservation, The Green, Nettlcham, Lincoln. This society has a junior branch called WATCH, for 8 to 15 year olds

Ulster Trust for Nature Conservation, c/o Dept of Extra-mural Studies, The Queen's University, Belfast

The Scottish Wildlife Trust, 8 Dublin Street, Edinburgh

British Naturalists' Association, 43 Warnford Road, Tilehurst, Reading, Berkshire. Contact your library for the local branch

The Wildlife Youth Service, Marston Court, 98-106 Manor Road, Wallington, Surrey. This is a junior branch of the World Wildlife Fund

The Council for Nature, The Zoological Gardens, Regent's Park, London, NW1. A representative body of more than 450 societies which will supply the address of your local natural history society

Jersey Wildlife Preservation Trust, Trinity, Jersey, Channel Islands. Runs The Dodo Club for the under 17s

The XYZ Club for Exceptional Young Zoologists, The Zoological Gardens, Regent's Park, London NW1

The Young Peoples' Trust for Endangered Species, 19 Quarry Street, Guildford, Surrey

The Wildfowl Trust, Slimbridge, Gloucester. Junior membership for the under 18s

Index

218

HOUSE ACKNOWLEDGEMENTS

Managing Editor Ian Jackson
Art Editor Nigel Partridge
Indexer Jackie Pinhey

Eddison/Sadd Editions acknowledges with grateful thanks assistance received from Neil Curtis, Diana Levinson, Christine Johnston, from Dennis Bosdet and Martin Gibbs of Linden Artists Ltd, and also from Stephanie Mullins of Frederick Warne Publishers Ltd.

The photographs in this book were taken by Jane Burton and Kim Taylor with the exception of page 200 bottom (Dennis Green) and pages 191 bottom and 142 bottom (Robert Burton).

All the photographs have been selected from the photographic library of Bruce Coleman Limited

The artwork was prepared by the following artists:

Sarah De Ath, pages 1, 3, 4-5, 6-7, 71, 91, 140-41, 144-45, 172-73, 188
Jim Channell, pages 73, 83, 183
Tim Hayward, pages 60, 62, 93, 94-5, 118, 147, 149, 200-01, 207
Nick Loates, pages 134-35, 170-71, 187, 209
David More, page 143
Joyce Tuhill, pages 84-5, 87, 167, 170 (pellets), 175, 177
David Webb, pages 17, 97, 124-25

All artists are represented by Linden Artists Limited

SEABIRD SIGHTINGS (page 93) **1** guillemot; **2** oystercatcher; **3** razorbill; **4** gannet; **5** fulmar; **6** puffin

SPECIES	JANUARY	FEBRUARY	MARCH	APRIL	MAY	JUNE	JULY	AUGUST	SEPTEMBER	OCTOBER	NOVEMBER	DECEMBER	✓
BIRDS													
HOUSE MARTIN				SUMMER VISITOR				BREEDING			MIGRATES		
MOORHEN					BREEDING	BREEDING							
NIGHTJAR						BREEDING CHURRING							
NUTHATCH		SONG		BREEDING									
TAWNY OWL		SONG		BREEDING						SONG			
PHEASANT					BREEDING	BREEDING			SHOT				
PUFFIN						BREEDING							
REDWING		WINTER VISITOR	WINTER VISITOR						WINTER VISITOR				
ROBIN	SONG				BREEDING			SONG					
SHAG					BREEDING								
SKYLARK		SONG			BREEDING	BREEDING				SONG			
HOUSE SPARROW		SONG	SONG		BREEDING	BREEDING							
STARLING		SONG		BREEDING				SONG					
STONECHAT				SONG			BREEDING						
SWALLOW				SUMMER VISITOR		BREEDING					MIGRATES		
MUTE SWAN					BREEDING								
SONG THRUSH		SONG			BREEDING	BREEDING					SONG		
BLUE TIT	SONG			BREEDING									
GREAT TIT	SONG	SONG		BREEDING									
TURNSTONE	WINTER VISITOR							WINTER VISITOR					
WOOD PIGEON		SONG			BREEDING								
WAXWING		WINTER VISITOR	WINTER VISITOR							WINTER VISITOR			
WREN	SONG				BREEDING							SONG	
GREAT SPOTTED WOODPECKER			DRUMMING			BREEDING							
MAMMALS													
BADGER		CUBS BORN	CUBS SEEN ABOVE GROUND						COLLECT BEDDING				
PIPISTRELLE AND SEROTINE BATS		HIBERNATES				FEMALES IN LARGE NURSERY ROOSTS					HIBERNATES		
RED DEER					YOUNG BORN				RUT				
ROE DEER					YOUNG BORN		RUT						
DORMOUSE		HIBERNATES					BREEDING		HIBERNATES				
FOX	BARKING		CUBS BORN		CUBS ABOVE GROUND								
BROWN HARE					BREEDING CONTINUOUS	BREEDING						BARKING	
HEDGEHOG	HIBERNATES					BREEDING	BREEDING			HIBERNATES	HIBERNATES		
MOLE					BREEDING	BREEDING							
HARVEST MOUSE					BREEDING CONTINUOUS			BREEDING					
HOUSE MOUSE	INDOORS						BREEDING				INDOORS		
WOOD AND YELLOW NECKED MOUSE				BREEDING									
RABBIT				BREEDING									
BROWN RAT					BREEDING CONTINUOUS								
GREY SEAL										PUP BORN			
WATER AND COMMON SHREWS					BREEDING	BREEDING							
GREY SQUIRREL		BREEDING				BREEDING							
STOAT				LITTER BORN									
BANK AND MEADOW VOLE							BREEDING						
WATER VOLE							BREEDING						
WEASEL							BREEDING						